The Elephant and the Wasp

by John McArdle

To Martin

Best Wishes

John McArdle

Published by JJ Moffs Independent Book Publisher 2018

The author is donating his profits from the sale of The Elephant and the
Wasp to UNICEF.

JJ Moffs Independent Book Publisher Ltd
Grove House Farm, Grovewood Road,
Misterton, Nottinghamshire DN10 4EF

ISBN 978-0-9957881-4-5

Printed and bound in Great Britain by Clays Ltd, St. Ives plc
Typeset and cover design by Anna Richards

FOREWORD

Even as a very young lawyer I was attracted to the cut and thrust of civil litigation, which deals with the many disputes that people find themselves involved in, either by accident or design. As a young man I was unaware of the stress it inflicted upon clients as I rather two dimensionally thought that as it was me doing the fighting, the client would be either relaxed or disconnected from the dispute. As I matured I realised this was not the case and that stress levels increased for people once the lawyers became involved.

In my new found maturity I tried a number of ways of calming the clients' nerves, such as making comparisons with criminal courts where the outcome may be prison if they lost (no surprise that one didn't work!) or examples of more serious disputes where a lot more was at stake (no success there either as people tend to focus on their own problem, not somebody else's). It was when I was acting for someone against a large company that I managed to come up with something that I was to use hundreds of times in the years that followed. When people took on a much bigger opponent such as a bank, a large company, police force or Government office they would see themselves as very small and their opponent as massive and unassailable with endless resources that would eat up their own meagre finances. It was on such a case when I said to my client,

"Yes this is a fight, but it is a fight between an elephant and a wasp. We are the wasp and we will be quick, hard to catch and dangerous. The elephant is huge but slow and remember, we are not trying to kill the elephant, but simply cause it so much aggravation that it will do anything for us to leave it alone and go and irritate another animal." This had an instant effect on the client who seemed much more relaxed and much less intimidated by the prospect of battle with a bigger opponent. As you will see in the pages of this book, I have not only been a wasp for hire, but have needed to deploy the same instincts in my career to both qualify and then practice law in the way I wanted to. The title seemed very apt when I'd finished writing the book.

I started to write this book when I retired to make sure that I remembered a career that I had enjoyed so much. Also being a child of a parent who died prematurely, I have spent a lifetime of curiosity as to what my father's life was like and what he may have thought about mine. My family may have no such interest in my life, but at least they will know where to look if they do.

The book itself is dedicated to my parents John and Mary McArdle and to my English teacher Austin Flynn. My parents' dedication is not just because l loved them, but because they taught me by example to search for the difference between right and wrong and not to allow intelligence or eloquence to disguise it. l am not saying that l always do the right thing, but at least l am always searching for it even when stumbling in the dark and giving the opposite impression. When l slip in that regard, l always have the image of one or both of them shaking their head or looking up to the heavens. Austin Flynn, as you will read, was hugely instrumental in my career both in starting it and in his example of decency, care and inspirational belief. l hope l have done all three of them proud.

Back to the title of the book, l always truly believed in the law l practiced and its capacity for a just result, regardless of the power or wealth of an opponent. The law is for everyone, whatever your size, gender, sexuality, colour, religion or beliefs. Nothing has ever happened in my career to alter that view. The law will not always get it right and those dealing with it (including me) will often get it wrong, but without the law we would be irredeemably lost.

This book is about my career, those who helped build it, those who tried to derail it and those people that l represented throughout it. It is about the people l met, the things that happened to me and the mixture of good, bad, funny and remarkable that occurs if you hang around long enough. l hope you enjoy it.

CHAPTER 1: A career is born

I can pinpoint the exact moment my career started. It was a geography class in May of 1969 and I was 16 years old, bored and sitting with Jean Laing as a punishment for talking too much with Tommy Gardner, my usual partner for lessons. It has to be said it was not much of a punishment since Jean was not only very attractive, but was wearing a short skirt, nylon stockings and her chest was struggling to break free of her tight fitting white shirt. In fact, if I had known that was going to be the punishment, I would have transgressed much earlier!

Anyway, I digress. There I was in my last year of secondary school, due to leave in a few weeks time to start some sort of life of employment, without having the first idea of what or where. Whilst I was still paying too much attention to Jean Laing's chest, the door opened and in walked my English teacher Mr Austin Flynn, a tall man in his early thirties with a full head of sandy coloured hair and a natural smiling expression. He approached the geography teacher, a middle aged plump lady doing her best, but struggling to keep the attention of the class. Flynn started to talk to her which gave me another chance to talk to Jean whilst trying to look down her shirt without being noticed. There was always a bit of sexual tension in the classroom, particularly now that we were all sixteen or thereabouts, but in fairness most of us had no idea what to do about it. Puberty presented problems for both sexes and often a major distraction, as on this day. I think I may have moved on to the distraction of Jean's half covered legs when to my surprise Mr Flynn turned to me and said,
"McArdle a word please, follow me." God...what was he going to say? 'I saw you looking down Jean Laing's shirt, you dirty little student.' Giving myself time to think I said,
"Who, me Sir? We're in the middle of a fascinating lesson on whatever it is this lesson's about."
"NOW please." he said walking towards the door. Outside the classroom he motioned me to sit beside him on one of the cloakroom benches. There in his right hand was a pamphlet entitled Training to be a Legal Executive, which pictured a middle aged man at a desk clearly giving some instructions to a young girl about a document or some such thing.
"I have the perfect job for you," he said with great confidence and certainty as he began to leaf through the pamphlet showing me what a legal executive did. (I wondered which I was; the middle aged man or the young girl!) The

qualifications seemed to me to be beyond my current career path; I say 'career path' notwithstanding that I had neither a career nor a path, but it seemed a lot for me to achieve. Mr Flynn dismissed any query with a wave of his hand and told me I had nothing to worry about . Still thinking I was playing some part in this decision, I said I would have read the leaflet and think about it.

"What's there to think about?" he asked, "I've got you an interview with a firm of solicitors next Saturday." I tried to inquire what a solicitor did given that my family had managed to get by without one, but he was gone as quickly as he had arrived. Not though, before he told me I was too young to enrol for the legal executive exams and instead he had enrolled me in an A-level law course at Durham Technical College. A-level? I wasn't even doing O-levels at the time. I returned to my class with the pamphlet in my hand and my head spinning a little, but it looked like I might have a job. It's worth mentioning that jobs were easier to come by in the 1960's so I wasn't worried particularly. Most of my worry cells were taken up with whether or not Sunderland Football Club would win on Saturday, or if Anne Reay would go out with me. Anne was a dark haired and shapely classmate who was the subject of my hormonal longing, even more than the lovely Jean. It didn't leave much time to think about what I might do for a living for the rest of my life. On such moments lives are decided, futures determined and destinies settled. At that point I had no idea that a whole career lay ahead of me and that in that career I would encounter almost every human condition, personality and situation imaginable. Anyway, for the moment it was back to ogling Jean.

One fact, which I always felt invaluable, was to have gone to a mixed school. Growing up with both boys and girls, and mixing from an early age is a natural interaction that carries on into adult life. Many a time I have been in the company of men who grew up in a boys school and found they floundered when a woman joined us. They seemed unsure whether to moderate the conversation like some Victorian toff, make unfunny and apparently clever remarks, or mount the poor unsuspecting female as a sign of virility! Not to say that can't happen in someone with a mixed school background, but I suggest it's less common.

When I was 11 years old I was sent to the school boasting the admirable Mr Flynn. It was St Leonard's Comprehensive in Durham and it was the year after the eleven plus was abolished in favour of assessment. My mother, bless her, always said I was wrongly assessed and had I been made to sit the eleven plus, I would have gone to the grammar school; I think she underestimated my laziness! In any event, I found myself very much in the second division of the state educational system and for a time accepted that that was my position.

Note to any young reader: never accept limitations imposed on you by others and always give yourself a chance to succeed, even if that opens up the possibility of failure. My career has shown me that the difference between successful and unsuccessful people is often how they react to apparent failure. One group deems it a sign of their inability, whilst the other as information to use on the next task. St Leonards was a decent school, but Mr Flynn was head and shoulders its best attribute. My junior school on the other hand, Trimdon Catholic School which I attended from five to 11 years of age, would have needed to be heavily promoted to be described as bad! It was set in a field seemingly miles from anywhere and as such open to the elements, which created an unwelcoming climate both inside and outside the building. It was a bus ride away and many years later I was amazed that it was only a few miles from home because, as a five year old I felt I was being taken to a land far away where only misery existed.

It was a large forbidding Victorian building where law and order were hard to find. On reading Mark Twain's 'Tom Sawyer' I was struck that the only difference in his bleak school in America's Deep South was that we were wearing shoes and Tom's classmates weren't. The age range was five to 15 and the older kids looked at us younger ones much as lions might look at young antelope, thinking about the tortures they could inflict at playtime instead of just eating us. Playtime; now that was a misleading term if ever there was one. For the younger kids it was more like survival time, particularly in winter when the snow provided weaponry for the monsters of the final year. They would catch us and throw us into snowdrifts which collected in heights way above us, so that we disappeared completely. One particular torture was to line up a group of us against the main school building, much like prisoners in a war film. The herders would make sure no little prisoner escaped, whilst the firing squad stood a few yards away loaded up with snowballs. I can still hear those snowballs to this day, exploding against the wall having whistled past our ears. Obviously some would strike, resulting in loud cheers from the throwing monsters. Particularly painful were the strikes on bare short trousered legs, especially if the snowball had been laced with ice. Perhaps some of those monsters went on to lives of crime, post school, or maybe became priests; who knows.

The school didn't have a kitchen so every day a small van arrived with the culinary delicacies of the day. The food was awful and I used to wonder if it had been rejected by a local prison and sent to us so that it wasn't wasted. The vegetables were boiled to different coloured mush. The meat, if there was any, was thin and tasteless and the only salvation was an occasional portion of chips. I persuaded my mother that I would starve to death on these meals and she agreed to provide me with a packed lunch, which I would eat with a group of fellow parolees who had also been saved by packed lunches. This was when I noticed for the first time a glimpse of differences in social standing. We were all working class kids, but some were poorer than others. In our rough Catholic school the idea of a uniform would be laughable, but some children wore old worn clothes or ill-fitting hand-me-downs. Although my family had no money to speak of and probably lived from week to week, my father was a police constable and always in work. I never knew hunger, never needed to wear someone else's clothes and, as young as I was, I saw the insensitive indignity of it all. One such humiliation was free school dinners (dinner actually referring to those disgusting lunches). They were recorded during Monday morning registration when pupils had to answer 'yes' when their name was called out. The next segment was the dinner register; names were repeated and this time pupils walked out with their five shillings and handed it to the teacher. If your family was really poor you qualified for free school dinners and had to shout 'free Sir' which was often repeated, as the teacher hadn't heard the self conscious response the first time. At my senior school the names of all the free diners were read out first, therefore putting all the poorest pupils together. I imagine some of them are still in therapy.

This may give the impression that the education system was insensitive, unsupportive and created an unfriendly environment and that impression is correct. Add that my father was a 'copper' and you might imagine the extra problems I had in a very rough environment. The school was far enough away that my father would not have encountered any of the rougher element of the school, but to them he had by association. These hulking 15 year olds would occasionally wander around the playground asking 'which one's the copper's kid?' There was always someone who would attempt to curry favour by pointing me out, whereupon I would receive their welcome of choice. The donkey drop was a curling of the middle finger to display the knuckle and then, in a quick flicking motion, a hit on the top of the head. In the Chinese burn the victim's bare forearm is grasped by the yob who twists in opposite directions causing a painful burning sensation and finally

6

dead leg: where the yob's knee engages with the side of the victim's thigh causing loss of sensation in the leg.

I can't recall whether I told my parents of these incidents, but I suspect I didn't because I had no point of reference. Although I had the burden of my father's job and my own reddish hair, others were bullied for being poor, being fat, skinny, short, tall or anything at all. One boy was often targeted because he had unusually thick lips.

There was a particularly nasty family of brothers of all ages in the school, the youngest of which was in my year. He was an apprentice thug with the attitude of his older brothers and whilst he lacked their size, he had their implied protection. My mother, sensing my unhappiness would often give me a chocolate biscuit or some sweets to take to school. One day the apprentice thug saw my sweets and no doubt emulating his brothers demanded some. To my immediate shame I obliged, but young as I was I realised I was making a rod for my own back. I did tell my parents on that occasion and my Dad said, "I will give you a shilling if you punch him": very Christian and politically correct!

The next few days I avoided the situation by not taking anything to school, but eventually I reverted to taking the treats with me. My luck seemed to be holding as I had managed to avoid any confrontation. However, one day I was eating my treats and he appeared behind me making the huge mistake of pushing me in the back, a mistake because for as long as I can remember I've had a healthy reluctance for physical confrontation as a means of dispute resolution. It may well be founded in a fear of loss of teeth, seeing my own blood or just losing, but that fear disappears if I am attacked or even touched by any assailant. So there it was. I had been pushed so I punched him in the head and knocked him to the ground. I was probably as shocked as he was, but he looked at me from the floor and burst into tears. Before I knew what was happening he'd run off snivelling and the boys around me lifted me up onto their shoulders as though I had just won the world heavyweight boxing title. Rewarding as this was, I was more concerned about the likely visit of one of the older brothers seeking revenge. I must have looked a picture being held aloft, looking around like a meerkat trying to spot a likely attack! In the event no attack came. Perhaps he was too ashamed to tell his brothers or perhaps they were as mean to him as they were to everyone else, but suffice to say my sweets were safe from then on. I even claimed the shilling from my Dad, no doubt by exaggerating the incident out of all recognition and portraying myself as a fearless hero. The incident gave me a certain respect amongst my own age group, but I still had the problem of the older thugs.

I developed a reputation of being a lunatic small kid likely to thrash out if knocked, but the size difference meant the thugs never had anything to fear and when they tired of being amused at my counter attacks, they would revert to the punishment menu as set out previously. Humour turned out to be the weapon that saved me from most harm. I've always had this illogical confidence that I can't really explain. Anyway this day, one of the hulking brutes approached looking for a victim and upon seeing the copper's kid he homed in. As he approached towering over me I said, "I don't want to hurt you, but if I have to I will".

"Eh?" he replied intelligently, completely taken aback.

"Hold me back, hold me back." I put up my fists and started to dance around like a boxer, throwing punches in the air a few feet from him. The sight was too much for the yob who started to laugh. He put his hand on my head and I began to swing wildly like Norman Wisdom to peals of laughter from a now small audience. The next day the biggest and scariest of the monsters sought me out. Pushing my luck I said,

"If you want a fight I will give you a chance and only use one hand." He bent over double laughing and obviously saw great pleasure in this little tic giving him cheek. He lifted me onto his shoulders and carried me around as the ultimate seal of approval and, as it turned out it was an unexpected level of protection as most of the yobs were scared of him. I had a tendency, which I retained throughout my career, to push my luck and sure enough I would occasionally go too far with 'king yob' and he would throw me off or flick my head, but generally I had found a way to survive in this bleakest of places. The savagery that people are capable of when unchecked is remarkable and I was to see a great deal more of it throughout my legal career.

Bullying was rife in that school and one place to be avoided during playtime was the toilets. Set away from the main building they consisted of brick compartments with half doors on one side and a long foul smelling urinal on the other. They attracted the smokers amongst the older boys and therefore other possibilities for torture. My trick was to wait until the bell sounded then dash in when everyone else was leaving, or wait until class then ask to go to the toilet. This worked pretty well until a hapless day in the class of Miss Clifford, an elderly spinster who probably hated children and had the appearance of a Roald Dahl like creation. With teeth of various colours pointing in different directions, her manner was more in keeping with a correction facility than a class of five year olds. Anyway, I put up my hand and asked if I could go to the toilet.

"No! You should have gone at playtime," was her reply. I tried to hold it, but after a while the young muscles could resist no longer and a warm damp feeling spread through my lower clothing. I was sitting with Jeanette Brown and said to her,

"Jeanette, if I tell you something will you promise not to say anything?"

"Yes I promise" she replied. I confessed to her in a very quiet whisper, "I've wet myself." She immediately shot her right hand up like a skyrocket and shouted,

"Please Miss, John McArdle's wet himself." Note to self; never trust a woman particularly if you have just wet yourself.

Today such an incident would no doubt lead to hundreds of forms, counselling of teacher, pupil and parents and a restructuring plan to avoid such calamities reoccurring. No such concerns for Miss Clifford who hauled me out in front of the class. Her preferred method of corporal punishment was to hold the child's hand and to belt it with a fast moving ruler, over and over again, sporting a mad look in her eyes. That done, she made me stand in front of the radiator to dry and told everybody what a dirty little boy I was. My mild mannered mother found this too much and without telling me, took several buses to school and confronted the teacher in private. She never did tell me the whole story, but it was a rare thing for my mother to be confrontational. I think it's unlikely that my mother did what would have satisfied me, namely holding Miss Clifford prisoner at gunpoint until she wet herself and then parading her through the streets of Trimdon!

The headmaster of the school was a small, bald rotund man called Mr Higgingbottom (no, I haven't made that up) and his approach to the problems of the school was to rule by fear. Maybe his diminutive size made him violent, but his answer to everything seemed to be a furious use of the cane. Perhaps hard to imagine now, but permissible in the 50's and 60's was the beating of young children, of either sex, with a long piece of bamboo. This was done on either hand or bottom for a whole variety of misdemeanours. The standard punishment from other teachers was to send you to the headmaster and there was always a line, of mainly boys, standing outside of his office. Out would step this short angry man, who would hit each in turn without much, if any explanation from either child or teacher. This was quite a terrifying sight for a young child and my main aim was to avoid him and the inevitable pain that would follow at all costs. During my entire time there I managed it, although I had a very close escape one day.

I was having my sandwich lunch in the separate room that children who were lucky enough to escape school dinners occupied, when one of the girls squirted her drink at me. Just at the moment of retaliation the teacher on duty walked in and shouted the dreaded phrase,
"McArdle, go to the headmaster's room"
I could scarcely believe my ears and I tried in vain to explain, but no appeal was allowed and no mercy on offer, so I trudged in painful expectation to stand outside the room of death. I was surprised to find that I was the only child there and didn't realise the break that was going to give me. Out stepped Mr Higgingbottom in his usual non communicative way and instead of immediately beating me with the cane he always carried, he must have realised I wasn't one of his regulars and wrongly thought I was on my way somewhere.
"Don't just stand there wasting time boy, get to your class," he said sternly. Well, God had spoken and who was I to tell him that I was there for a beating? Thank you very much and goodnight, I thought as I rushed back to class hands and backside still intact! I wonder if my experiences in this school had a subconscious effect which made me tackle certain inequalities later in life and to challenge bullying in any form it came in. As a lawyer, working for individuals throughout my career, I was to have plenty of opportunities. So that was my first experience of school and things improved marginally at my senior school where I was to meet the teacher who would propel me into my career.

CHAPTER 2: New school; time to wake up

I remember my first day at St Leonard's Comprehensive School in Durham. It was September 1964 and the school was about half a mile from Durham City centre and was a stark contrast to Trimdon Catholic School. It was much bigger for a start and had a very modern look as opposed to the Victorian austerity I had come from. There I was in my brand new bottle green blazer, grey trousers and white shirt with a green striped tie, certainly a bit of a change from Trimdon's jeans and jumpers. In fact, the whole place was a culture shock. It was bigger and more formal, and obviously much more serious about education.

A loud bell sounded and all of the older children stood still as if nailed to the floor. We new kids followed suit and became motionless without really knowing why. A number of older kids started to move around slowly in between the groups, apparently without fear of authority and consequence. God, they must be hard, I thought to myself. Maybe they are gangsters like on TV and rules don't apply to them. Then I noticed that each was wearing a badge that said, 'Prefect'. Wonder what a prefect is, I mused and then decided it was some sort of prisoner turned prison officer. Anyway we were organised into year groups and sent off to be indoctrinated into our new homes for the next five years.

After the introduction from the first year teacher he asked if there were any questions. I put up my hand and no doubt gave him a story to tell his wife that night when I asked,
"Can we move from this school to a grammar school, Sir and if so how do we do it?" I have always had a tactful approach to an enquiry! Instead of saying that I was an uppity ungrateful little git, he rather kindly replied that it was possible, but one had to be in the A stream at this school, studying for GCE exams at both O and A level. I was in the B stream and would study for CSE exams where a grade one was the equivalent of an O level grade C. Not for the last time in my life came a suggestion that walking before flying might be a good idea!

I really would like to explain where my natural confidence came from, but I can't. I certainly couldn't boast any academic success to date. In fact, a few years earlier at Trimdon I had managed to finish 23rd out of a class of 26. I think the three behind me were special needs and required help to put their clothes on and eat their food. Surprisingly, not even that setback seemed to upset me. I did however, suffer an enormous lack of judgement when taking my report card home to be met by my over expectant father. He beamed a smile and said,

"Oh, your report let me see it." I put it behind my back with a bigger smile and said,

"I don't think you want to see this", which was a mistake. He took that as a sign of excitement and said,

"Are you top?" with a gleeful expression.

"Not quite" I replied still smiling.

"Second, then?"

"A bit lower", I said, still thinking that humour was the way.

"Third... fourth... fifth? Give me that BLOODY card"

I handed him the report and the colour drained from his face. "23rd? How can that be?"

These were the days before DNA testing, but had it not been I think I would have been whisked off to the nearest laboratory! My father always had a sort of belief in me despite evidence to the contrary. He used to say of me, "For some reason I don't worry about the little un (my brother is five years older than me). Perhaps he will do something with his hands." I think he had in mind carpentry or something like it, but if he had lived long enough to see my attempts at woodwork and metalwork, he would have despaired of me.

Playtimes, or breaks were less fraught with risk and danger at St. Leonard's and were largely well supervised by both teachers and prefects. That's not to say that danger didn't lurk, because it did. Initially, it was kept at a respectful distance; the reputation of the school I had come from preceded us and we were given something of an early wide berth. However, this soon wore off and the usual run of school bullies made themselves known. There was a little group of three bullies in my year, the worst of which was John Smith. Smaller than the other two, what Smith lacked in size he more than made up for in pure nastiness and raw savagery. For a time he teamed up with quite a pleasant lad in our class called Barry West, who perhaps thought swimming with a shark was better than avoiding one. One day whilst walking with him, a few feet away from me, Smith turned and punched West in the eye with a sickening crack. Why, I don't know. Maybe in Smith's twisted mind West had said something he didn't like, or hadn't answered him quickly enough, but the extent of the violence only served to increase Smith's reputation as someone to avoid.

I managed to avoid him for almost the whole of my time there, but in the penultimate year my friend Tommy Gardner told me a joke about Smith. Nothing unusual about that as Smith was loathed by almost everyone. However a couple of days later Smith approached me and said that I had been telling jokes about him and he wanted to fight me after school. I told him I hadn't and he replied that if I told him who had, he would let me off. Later in the day and to my shame I told him it was Tommy, but I changed the story to make it sound better. I didn't feel relief, but anger at both him and myself. I caught up with Tommy and told him, and as it turned out Tommy's charm and humour was too much for Smith and no beating took place. I vowed to myself that I would never be bullied again and I have always kept that vow. I don't know what became of Smith as I never met him again after school, but for a number of years and in particular when I was doing criminal work in law firms, I imagined I might meet up with him perhaps on remand at Durham prison, where he might be awaiting sentence on some violence related crime. I might have been able to say,
"Ah John Smith, looks like you may be going away for a long time. Have you ever seen Shawshank Redemption? Great film."

School life settled into an acceptable routine although whenever I heard the phrase 'school days are the best days of your life' I concluded that adult life must be pretty bleak. In truth, I never believed that and felt that school was just an obligation that would end sooner rather than later. My first year form teacher was Mr Welch, an amiable enough young teacher, eager to please his pupils and mix in. He was very thin with dark wavy hair and a regular welcoming smile. He was also very quiet and had little impact on me. In the second year Mr Flynn, who was our English teacher, became my form master and although I didn't know it at the time I had met the man who was to have a profound and lasting beneficial effect on my life. He was a rather softly spoken man who carried authority without menace. Clearly passionate about his subject, he tried his best even with the irretrievably thick, to get pupils to understand and to use their language. I suppose he took something of a shine to me because I liked to write essays and never saw them as an unpleasant task. I would be inclined to enter into the spirit of the subject and try and make it interesting, to both him and me. He would often read out my essay in class, which of course would lead to jeering and I would happily play up to the notoriety of it! I had become something of the class clown at this stage, perhaps learning from my beneficial use of humour at the previous school, and found it very effective at defusing taunts. I would stand up and take a theatrical bow to increase the jeering; it also achieved some welcome attention from the girls!

I wasn't always in his good books though. Being quite a good mimic I could impersonate most of the teachers, which was always likely to raise a laugh. One day, on entering Mr Flynn's English class and no doubt distracted by and showing off to the girls, I hadn't noticed him sitting at the back of the room. I sat down and impersonated him for the early morning giggle, which was cut short when he walked up behind me and hit me on the back of the head with the book he was reading. Even he was capable of violence, but it has to be remembered that this was an age when that sort of thing was commonplace and not worthy of comment. Today the teacher would be suspended, the child sent for MRI examinations and Twitter and Facebook would be spinning with the story. The suddenness and unexpected bang to my head not only rendered me speechless, but literally sent stars circling my vision like some Tom and Jerry cartoon moment. The blow by the way raised a bigger laugh than the impersonation. It was playful rather than malevolent, but even a malevolent blow was, in my view better than the premeditated cold blooded violence of the prearranged caning. Young as I was, I could see the injustice and potential for cruel abuse of the cane. I'm not suggesting that most teachers had a cruel streak, but some did and the fact that they were allowed to wield a weapon with which to beat children is quite an indictment of the time. I was caned several times at the senior school, but the one I recall vividly happened when I was fourteen.

Our form master at that time was Barry Mason, the PE teacher. He was an accomplished footballer who played for Durham City and was generally fairly reasonable, but idiosyncratic. When we played football he would join in by playing in one of the teams. He saw that as his opportunity to be Sir Alf Ramsey the then England Manager, stopping play to rearrange the teams' positions, showing us what we should be aiming to do and then restarting the game. This always seemed to end up in a nominated boy feeding a pass through to him, so that he could crack a shot into the roof of the net and scream what a goal! For a better example, watch the film Kes where director Ken Loach obviously had the same experience. The teacher in that film was played by the excellent Brian Glover who was somewhat hapless, whereas Mason was not.

On one occasion I was playing full back and standing on the goal line when the corner was cleared to Mason who volleyed it towards goal with full force, straight into my stomach. Footballs in those days were made of laced up leather and absorbed the moisture from the grass, which added to their weight. When kicked by a young foot they felt like concrete and even worse if you headed the ball and were unlucky enough to make contact with the lace, which left a nice indentation on your head. On this occasion, the ball took every ounce of air out of my body. I hit the ground with a thud and couldn't breathe. The harder I tried to gulp air into my lungs the less success I had and panic began to take hold. Mason picked me up and said, "Well stopped son, it looked a certain goal." Realising I was still not breathing, he calmly controlled the situation and got me to breath slowly, until some air found its way into the flattened lungs.

The caning incident began at the end of a school day when he was sitting at his desk and I must have either done or said something to upset him. Some days he was amiable, others less so and this was evidently a non-amiable day.

"Right, go and get the cane and the punishment book," he said to me angrily. This particular ritual had something of the Victorian era about it. Not only were you about to be subjected to cold blooded violence, but you had to go and collect a book so it could be recorded, plus bring the weapon to your assailant. The adult equivalent would be a judge telling the man in the dock that he will be hanged by the neck until he is dead and instructing him to collect the rope and sling it around the gallows. I trudged to the headmaster's study to collect the items and returned. Mason looked up and said,

"I'm not doing it now. I will do it at 9 o'clock tomorrow morning." I tried to reason with him, but he was not for discussing the matter and sent me off home with the rest of the class.

Somewhat depressed, I got off the bus outside S & M Cleaners (not cleaners for the lovers of sadomasochism; these were much more innocent times and the initials were the owners!). My mother was the manageress of the shop and arranged for me to call in every day after school so that I wasn't returning to an empty house. Bit of a treat really, as I always got a cup of coffee and a chocolate biscuit while sitting amongst the uncollected cleaning in the back shop. My mother's supervisor was there that day and asked me why I was glum, so I told her the sorry tale of my delayed beating. She smiled and said,

"Oh, I know what he is doing. He isn't going to cane you; he's substituting a psychological punishment for a physical one by getting you to worry all night and then letting you off. The worry is the punishment, which is very clever." Of course it is, I thought to myself and immediately saw the plan and relaxed although with a little trepidation. Next day I turned up at school and Mason said,

"Don't you have to go and get something?" I stood up and played along saying,

"Yes, Sir," and with a worried expression I went to collect the equipment of abuse. When I returned he took me outside the classroom and I waited for him to tell me he hoped I had learned my lesson, but instead he opened the book, wrote in it and asked me to extend my right hand. Unsatisfied with a 180 degree extension, he positioned the hand even higher and with all his might brought the bamboo down with a sickening swish across the tips of my fingers. He repeated the dose on the left hand. The tips of your fingers are particularly sensitive, so if your intention is to inflict the most pain then they're an obvious target. Having completed the punishment, two to each hand, he told me to return the cane and book. This made me late for my English lesson and as I walked into the class, the colour having drained from my face, my appearance started a low murmur from a largely disquieted group. Looking back I think it was a shock for them to see me like that and to realise something really bad had happened. In fact, I didn't realise how bad it was until I tried to pick up a pen and simply couldn't hold it. The feeling in my fingers didn't return until much later that day and for days to follow there were after effects, not unlike having been stung on each finger by a bee. Filled with both rage and anger, I threw the pen to the floor and a single tear squeezed out of a reluctant eye. If anyone wanted trouble now I was ready to give it. Sensing the situation, Mr Flynn approached and asked in a soft whisper if I was alright. When he saw my fingers, he gave me a book and asked me to just read quietly whilst he got on with the lesson. He excused himself a little later and I often wondered if he confronted Mason, but I never found out.

I should have realised that Mason was not clever enough to have thought out a psychological punishment and he was perhaps at the extreme end of his academic capability being the PE teacher. Years later when leaving Court in Durham City, I saw Mason with his wife and young children going into a café. I stopped at the door and contemplated going in to confront him. I would have asked him if he remembered when I was much smaller and he appeared to be much bigger, and how would he feel if the children sitting with him were beaten with a weapon by a fully grown man. In the event, I walked away and still can't say whether that was the right thing to do or not.

Teachers at both primary and secondary schools had access to the lawful use of the cane as a punishment in those days. At St Leonard's one of them wore the cane through his belt a like a sword. His punishment was always the cane without any apparent thought to the type of offence. It never occurred to him that some offenders would benefit more from something other than extreme violence. Playtimes were policed by prefects and a duty teacher, and the prefects could place a pupil on 'corridor' for any offence deemed appropriate by them. The duty teacher would then administer the appropriate punishment which was frequently 100 lines or just a telling off. When I was a prefect I took note of who the duty teacher was and if it was the 'cane wearer', or any teacher who regularly used the cane, I would excuse all of the transgressors who had been placed on corridor punishment. I don't claim to be St Leonard's answer to Oscar Schindler, but I was not going to serve up victims to violence. You won't be surprised to hear that I was never aware of Mr Flynn using the cane at all. His personality and natural authority was enough for him to exercise control.

The settling in period at St Leonards took a few weeks and during that time I began to realise that I had to try harder and be competitive with my contemporaries. I never really struggled with English, or with most of the other subjects, with the exception of maths. I would be in the top three of each subject, but in the bottom three for maths. All that changed with a box of breakfast cereal. It contained a free gift of a cricket game, which I played with for hours on end. What it did was to sharpen my mental arithmetic skills and propelled me to the top of that class. See? You can mix sport and academia.

Having moved into the second year at school I had also developed a lifelong love, bordering on obsession (who am I kidding, it is an obsession!) with Sunderland Football Club. I had been to local football matches such as Ferryhill and Durham City and the matches at the small clubs in the northern leagues were exciting, simply because I loved football and the atmosphere of the game. There would be a few hundred people there and everything was at ground level. The fans went through a turnstile at a single storey wall and the pitch was in front of you as you walked in. Then my brother announced that he was going to take me to Sunderland's home ground, Roker Park to my first proper professional first division (now premiership) game. As the day got nearer, my excitement levels grew. I was going to see my heroes in real life. I was a Sunderland fan only because my older brother was, but it made no difference to me why; I was just excited. How many times since I have wished my brother had chosen Manchester United or Chelsea!

We travelled to Sunderland on a special excursion bus, which took more than an hour to get there. Having got off, I walked towards the ground amazed by the number of people going to the match. Roker Park was in the middle of a large housing area and as I turned a corner, there it was standing like a vast Cathedral of football. We joined the lines of people jostling to pay their money at the turnstiles, dropping their coins at the tiny window. Once you'd paid, the turnstile was clicked by the operator and you pushed it open to get in. I was met with an enormous concrete structure and I filed past a number of pungent smells such as pies, Bovril and urine depending on which cubicle you were passing. There were men walking around selling programmes, newspapers and peanuts in the melee, and finally we reached a concrete staircase taking us up. Up where? I wondered. Is the pitch suspended from the ground? Where are we going?

I followed an almost entirely male group, hardly daring to blink until I reached the top of the staircase. Those in front of me peeled off to my left and right leaving me with my first view of the pitch. There it was; a basin of vivid green bathed in bright white floodlights with a circle of tobacco smoke hanging above the crowd like a low lying fog in poor man's San Francisco Bay. The sight took my breath away and my pupils enlarged to try and take it all in. All my dreams and hopes had been exceeded by this magnificent and overwhelming sight. I was smitten and incurably in love. Sometimes it has seemed like a life sentence as the club has struggled from season to season, but it was love at first sight and when the players came out onto the pitch to a deafening ovation, they became live images of the heroes they were to me. This was cemented by them winning 3 - 0 and the noise of the goal roar made the initial entry ovation seem like a whisper.

The colours, my first sight of floodlights, the red and white striped shirts and the unique sounds and smells of a full blown football match was a heady mixture for a young boy. I think my heart pounded for the full match as I was moved in a sea of supporters every time there was any incident. If there was a near miss from the home side, the crowd surged forward like the tide coming in and you were swept up with it. The enormous empty spaces behind you were quickly filled by the tide of supporters flowing back to their original positions. When the first goal was scored, the famous Roker Roar was almost deafening, but infectious and I screamed like everybody else. I was being infected with a narcotic that all football supporters know, and very few can ever lose however hard they try. As it turned out, I was going to need that love and distraction as I had begun to realise that things were changing at home in ways that I knew would be difficult and possibly devastating. I was now 12 years of age and my father was dying.

CHAPTER 3: Childhood ends

It was a Sunday in March 1966 and I was sitting in the living room cutting out photographs of the Sunderland v Spurs match from the newspapers. This was almost a year on from my first ever Sunderland match. Standing in the Roker end the day before, I had watched as Mike Hellawell looped a header over the Spurs goalkeeper and into the net. It was a picture of that very moment that I was pasting into my scrapbook when my mother came into the room and said she needed to talk to me. I had realised that my father was seriously ill, as he had been in bed for weeks and had lost a great deal of weight. In fact I thought he must be dying, but nobody had confirmed it and I hadn't asked. I sensed this was the confirmation that I didn't want to hear.

I suppose I first noticed a problem some months before when my father's regular difficulty with stomach ulcers had resulted in more than usual doctors' appointments. He had spells of being in bed, but recovered and went back to work and looked normal. But this was a much longer period and at one stage he'd gone a yellow colour through jaundice. I could also feel a change in the atmosphere from the adults, who appeared more serious and sometimes stopped talking when I went into the room. All this made me wonder if he was going to die, although I didn't really know what that meant as nobody close to me, up until then had died. As the weeks went on and he became frailer, it was hard to imagine him getting better. In hindsight, I think I believed it was somehow unreal and maybe everything was going to be alright. No adult had said anything to make me believe otherwise, but here was the moment when the unreality was going to turn into a crushing reality and all escape routes to normality were going to be closed off.

"You do realise that your Dad isn't going to get better, don't you?" my mother said in a concerned voice.

"Oh yes he will Mam. Where is your faith?" I blurted out and she just said, "I'm sorry, but he won't." This was as far as my mother's script ran and the end of her ability to cope with telling her youngest son that he was to lose his father and face a very uncertain future. My mother was a very emotional woman who kept her emotions at bay by not displaying them and this was her biggest test so far.

I don't think she knew what to say or do. She'd been carrying the burden of the certain loss of her husband for months. Not only was she going to have to become the breadwinner of the house, but she was to lose the man who was her support and strength, as well as the love of her life. As she said her chosen words I kept pasting in the pictures, not looking up. I noticed tears hitting the scrapbook in front of me as they fell from my eyes. It was as if they belonged to someone else. I wasn't used to crying and there was no noise to accompany the tears. I just watched them hit the book, trying to stifle them and hold myself together. The realisation of something I had often considered hit me hard, almost as though I had not considered it at all. Tightness filled my chest and my hands shook. The tears were squeezed to extinction, but replaced with a sore dryness in my throat and a pounding in my head. The confirmation of my father's likely death washed over me like an unpleasant and unwanted anaesthetic. The next morning I was awoken by the sound of the telephone and I got out of bed to hear my mother speaking to someone on the telephone.

"He died in the early hours of the morning," she said. I walked into the darkened bedroom to see the lifeless body of my father lying as though in a deep sleep. Again the heavy tears squeezed out of my eyes despite my resistance, but through them I continued to look, trying to take in what it all meant. I knew my life had changed forever and the world seemed a little darker and a little more frightening now. Here lay the remnant of the powerful man of the house, a father I loved and beyond doubt the leader of our small pack.

My earliest memory of my father, also called John is of a large imposing figure especially in his police uniform; a man both feared and respected in our village. He actually had a thin frame, but at six feet in height he was considered taller than average for the era. Then add another foot or so for the pointed police helmet officers wore at the time and he was a big man. He was born in 1918 in the iron and steel town of Consett in County Durham and was one of five siblings. His mother died when he was a young child and he had been brought up by his father who was a cold and perhaps bitter man. His eldest sister was Betty and she performed the maternal role in the household, creating a special bond with her brothers and sisters.

In pre-war Britain money was very tight, especially in the North East and although my father was bright and articulate, he had to leave school at 14 to work and help support the family. Betty was allowed to continue her education and became a teacher, picking up a somewhat 'Hyacinth Bouquet' manner! The family managed to get by, but the world was about to go to war again for the second time in just over twenty years. In keeping with a number of young men at the time, my father volunteered to join the armed forces and ended up in the Navy. A strange choice given that he was not a confident swimmer and had a fear of drowning. Nonetheless he was sent off for training to the south of England and wrote letters to his family which catch the flavour of the time, namely uncertainty and anxiety as to what would happen next, mixed with a little excitement.

What happened next was that he set sail for Singapore and Malaysia aboard HMS Sultan on which he served as an able seaman. I have read other accounts of men from the North being sent to the hot and humid climate of the Far East and into what was generally accepted as a military disaster. The Allied forces surrendered to a numerically inferior enemy in the Japanese army and it became the biggest surrender in British military history. On the 20th of April 1942 the Commodore of the Royal Navy Barracks in Devonport sent the following letter to my grandfather, James McArdle.

Dear Sir,

In confirmation of the telegram already sent to you, I deeply regret to have to inform you that your son, John McArdle (Able Seaman D/JX .167248) has been reported missing on war service. There is insufficient evidence at present to show whether your son may be alive or not, but I will write to you again as soon as possible. In the meantime please accept my deep sympathy in your time of anxiety.

Yours sincerely

My father had been captured in Indonesia, along with most of the armed forces in that area and was to face three and half years in a Japanese Prisoner of War camp. He would be subjected to cruelty and neglect that was to nearly kill him and which permanently damaged his health. In common with most former prisoners of the Japanese my father spoke little of his experiences, but he did confide in his family that he and others had been told to dig their own graves in preparation for their execution. Most of the prisoners probably felt they would die of starvation or tropical disease anyway. The horrors of that time and place have been depicted in films over the years, but I can only imagine the darkness, hopelessness and suffering he must have endured. He was allowed to send the odd postcard, which was censored by the Japanese and these precious cards are still with us today. They remain, along with letters sent between him and his sister, the only real history the family has of that time of worry and suffering, but through them the love that existed in a tightly knit family is there to see.

He was in a camp with another soldier called Jimmy Robinson, a small Scotsman with an unshakeable and infectiously positive personality. My father always said that Jimmy kept him alive in those camps. For his part, Jimmy told us that my father suffered more than him because he was tall and a target for the diminutive Japanese guards, who were encouraged to be cruel to an enemy they believed had dishonoured themselves by surrendering, rather than dying for their Country.

I really know so little of his time there, but on a recent visit to Singapore I was able to trace the only record in existence written in his own hand. It was a paper confirming the camps he had been interred in which he completed upon his release. I was able to read on the internet that his camp freed themselves when they overthrew the remaining guards; a British supply airplane had crashed and the guards' cheering was too much for the inmates. It was at the end of the war and the emaciated prisoners drove the Japanese trucks into the nearest town to freedom. How I would have loved to have heard about it from my Dad. When he was rescued he was a little over four stones in weight, having lost two thirds of his body weight in the ordeal. On being dispatched back home by ship, he was pumped full of steroids so far as I can tell, because some time after his return home he is pictured looking almost overweight, before returning to his normal size.

My father was able to find humour in most things. When a medical specialist came from Newcastle to visit him bedridden and at home in the last year of his life, they were left alone for the examination. The specialist left saying his goodbyes to my mother who rushed upstairs and said
"Well what did he say?" My father pondered for a moment and replied,
"He didn't say much, but he did tell me not to read any long books and that we would have a devil of a job getting the coffin through that door!" I could hear the laughter upstairs which I wrongly read as good news.

As I've mentioned previously being a policeman's son had a number of drawbacks particularly at my rough first school, but I was immensely proud of my Dad and the job that he did. It seemed to me that he knew no fear and his brother (my Uncle Jimmy) told me that when my Dad was growing up he would prefer a fight to having his tea. When I was about eight or nine years of age I ventured into the notorious King's Cafe in West Cornforth where we lived. My Dad had told me to keep away because of the yobs who hung out there, being the last knockings of Teddy Boys from the fifties and the newer leather jerkin mob. Despite the warning I ambled in to use the juke box and play Bobby Vee's latest hit *Please Don't Ask about Barbara*. When I opened the door it was like a scene from a Western as the collected yobbery turned to face me in silence. In true gunslinger mode I strode up to the juke box, put in my money and started to listen to Bobby over the dull mutterings of the 'bad guys'. Maybe they were deciding if they should cook me before eating me when the lookout at the door shouted,

"HE'S COMING."

There followed a stampede which left only me and the bartender (ok, shopkeeper) in the place. Intrigued as to what had saved me I went to the door to see them all running at top speed to my left and when I turned to my right, I saw the unmistakable figure of my father in full uniform walking steadily towards the cafe. My feeling of pride was quickly replaced by concern as I realised I shouldn't be there either and I made a dash for it too, but not without thinking that it was my Dad walking like the town sheriff.

A year or so later I was out playing football with a friend when we saw a bright light coming from the High Street in the village and someone ran passed us shouting,

"The Co-op's on fire!" The village Cooperative store was the main shop used by everyone and sold food, clothes, furniture and almost anything you could think of. Everyone was a member and received dividends and tokens for milk and many had a Christmas savings club, too. The relatively large two story building was now well ablaze. We made our way to the High Street and could feel the heat of the inferno as we approached at speed. There was already a crowd and the fire engines were sounding their warning as they beat a path towards the fire. There standing on his own in the middle of the road stopping traffic, directing the public and clearing a path for the fire brigade was my Dad, my hero, looking like the leading man in a film. Bursting with a mixture of pride and excitement I pushed my way to the front of the crowd and shouted,

"Hello Dad!" as I beamed a smile towards him. He looked over in all that havoc and shouted,

"Get home you little bugger, I'm busy." Fair enough. I sloped off home undaunted by the rebuke, still thinking that's my Dad out there saving the day. Many years later I met a man who told me he was there that night. He'd had a few drinks and asked my Dad for a fight. Having been told to clear off three times, he told me that my Dad grabbed hold of him, took him around the back of a building and gave him a good hiding. The man told me that he respected my Dad for that and for dealing with it on the spot. It certainly cut down on the paperwork. I can't help but think that today he would have been suspended and sued by somebody like me. Sorry Dad. Anyway the moral of the story is I knew to bugger off when he told me to!

I never heard my parents argue or fight during my childhood. My father clearly loved my mother and told her often, but not in my hearing. He liked to sing and had a reasonably good singing voice, which he failed to pass on to either of his children. It never even crossed my mind that my parents were anything other than devoted and totally committed to each other. I just thought that was normal, a view which of course in the career that awaited me was to change dramatically. Grief is an emotion not fully felt by a child of twelve years of age, as there is not the depth of experience, knowledge or understanding that comes with adulthood. What are felt are great sadness, fear and anxiety about how the stability of the family unit will be affected.

Tears come easily to children, as do recovery from those tears, whereas an adult knows what lies ahead. In my own case, I have always missed my father and what might have been. I missed him when I got married and particularly when I had children. After the birth of my first child, I took the baby to his grave to introduce his first grandchild and a new generation, and I could feel a lump as big as a football in my throat. However, I missed him most keenly on the day my name and his appeared on the window of the solicitor's firm I started with my business partner. His faith in me, however blind, had proven to be well placed after all and as I looked at that window I hoped that I had made him proud.

So, going back to the start of this tale and my conversation with Mr Flynn, here I was at sixteen years old embarking upon a career or at least an interview for a job, without a father to ask questions of or to prepare me. I was on my own as I took the bus to Durham City and to start out in this new exciting and daunting world.

CHAPTER 4: My first job

My mentor Mr Flynn told me that in an interview you must sound both interested and interesting and the best way of achieving this is by asking sensible questions. With this in mind, I went prepared with three questions to show what a prize interviewee I was. *How long has the firm been in existence? How many people work in this office? What type of legal work does the firm specialise in?* Upon hearing these incisive probing questions they would clearly think they had a genius on their hands and would employ me immediately.

The plan was in ruins within minutes however when my interviewer Mr Larnach sat me down, asked if I wanted a coffee and then said,
"Well let me tell you a little about the firm. We have been going for more than a hundred years and there are about thirteen of us working at this office. We mainly do property work, but also some criminal and matrimonial cases. What else would you like to know?" To always have a Plan B prepared is a good idea; pity I didn't have one. Possible alternative questions that sprang to mind were *How long is the lunch break? When will I get a pay rise? Are there any pretty girls here?* They didn't sound like questions from a budding lawyer though, so I fell upon a skill that was to serve me well in the years ahead. A little voice in my brain sends a message to my mouth saying, *'Brain speaking here, can't come up with anything so over to you, mouth. No idea what you are going to say, but say it now'.* I was pleasantly surprised when I heard myself say,
"So when you say property, what sort of work is involved in that?" I had managed to avoid asking him how old he was, who was the best looking girl he had gone out with or if he was any good at cricket. The enormously charming and friendly Mike Larnach ran with the ball and told me about house buying and selling, as well as giving me time to think up other questions. The job was mine.

As a trainee legal executive I was to earn the mouth-watering salary of five pounds ten shillings per week (£5.50), and after tax and national insurance I got to keep four pounds, nineteen and sixpence (£4.97). I gave my mother two pounds for board and lodging and the rest went on bus fares, lunches, clothes and football matches. At sixteen years of age I thought I was making progress! Now all I had to do was learn how to do the job. Although I was officially a 'trainee legal executive' I was too young (as Mr Flynn had warned me) to enrol on any professional courses so I was effectively the office junior and tea boy. I didn't mind, I was just happy not being at school and earning some money. I made the most of making the tea by adopting my 'class clown' role and using the hot drinks delivery to chat to the older women and to practice my impersonations of members of staff.

To begin with I was placed in reception under the care of Eunice Stokoe a middle aged slim woman with jet black hair and, over the weeks that followed, I was taught how to answer the telephone, deal with clients who came to the office, photocopy documents and deliver mail locally. The office was also an agent for a building society so I was shown how to take money from customers, enter it into a passbook and fill out sheets to be banked. She told me that the last junior at the firm had been sacked for stealing money from clients when they paid money into their accounts. Apparently the girl thought she could help herself to a tip from the cash being deposited and nobody would notice. No danger of that with me as my father would have shot me.

Answering the telephone is a simple enough task you may think, but when you are sixteen and you have been given a line to deliver as well as a selection of buttons to navigate, the combination is very challenging. When Eunice told me I could answer the phone for the very first time I felt like it was my debut on a first night of a Shakespearian play. To Eunice my line was, *'Good Morning, Wilson and Co Solicitors, how can I help you?'* but to me it was the rousing speech of Henry V at the battle of Agincourt. When the phone rang I picked up the large black receiver, as big as a dog's bone and sped through my line in such an indecipherable way that the caller probably thought they'd rung the local Chinese takeaway. So relieved was I to deliver my line triumphantly, that I was temporarily rendered deaf and didn't hear what the caller said. Realising this, panic set in and Eunice rescued me by taking over and transferring the call. Note to self: remember to listen to what the caller says. Despite an unpromising start, I was given the responsibility of answering the telephone solo. I sat looking at it as though it was a spitting cobra likely to strike at any moment. When it finally rang, I grabbed the reptile firmly by the neck and said, 'Good Morning, Wilson and Co Solicitors, how can I help you?' Learning my earlier lesson I listened intently to the caller so that I would get it right. Only two mistakes this time, one it was the afternoon and two it was my boss ringing on the internal line.

John Shepherd was the managing clerk and had been at the firm for many years. Managing clerks were like butlers in stately homes. They had a certain deference to the partners and solicitors, and were in charge of the rest of the staff. Unlike some of his contemporaries, he was a very kindly man with a sense of humour and a willingness to help lesser beings like myself. Twice a day I made tea for everyone and often he would seek to hasten delivery of his tea with calls from his room of, *'There must be a power cut, I can't hear the kettle boiling'* or *'I hope there is some tea coming, I'm feeling faint'* or *'Has that ginger lad left the firm because it must be days since I had a cup of tea'.* He was, in addition, quite the best domestic property lawyer I ever encountered. There was nothing he didn't know about how to buy and sell property, inspect the title and prepare perfectly completed documentation. The old style was to study the history, which in some cases was more than a hundred years old, and type out a detailed history of the property known as an 'abstract of title' which involved legal shorthand. In this way he knew everything about a piece of land or house and would make sure that the client was fully informed. The clients in turn felt comfortable when buying or selling and, unlike today, a good deal of time was spent with them.

I was impatient to learn and be tested and would badger John Shepherd to give me things to do in my desire to push on. He in turn gave me his stamp duty forms to complete. This was a tedious job at the end of a transaction and led to the final document being stamped as no tax payable or with the amount of tax paid. After doing dozens of these I asked him for something more testing and more appropriate for a man of my burning ambition. After pointing out a few mistakes he witheringly replied to my request with, 'Don't you think you should learn to do the forms properly before we move on to something more complicated? Well, you can't win them all.

Had my boss, Mike Larnach, actually been aware of all of my mistakes and embarrassments, he may have had cause for rethinking the employment of this 'bright young thing'. He did however witness a few of them. One in particular was when he had gone to the Magistrates court in the centre of Durham and I had gone into his room to do some filing. He had a very comfortable chair at his large desk, which overlooked the city. It was a cold winter's day and the gas fire was on, giving a very cosy atmosphere in this period building. Having completed most of the filing, I sat in the great man's chair to see what it was like and the combination of the distant moving traffic and the whistling gas fire promptly sent me to sleep. I'm not sure how long I was dozing, but my slumber was interrupted by the unmistakable sound of his heavy footsteps immediately outside the door. I think I must have sprung out of that seat like a frog catching a fly and grabbed some letters just as he walked in. He looked as surprised as me when he opened the door and saw his young charge in frantic activity. Better that than finding me curled up like a cat in his seat though.

Another incident that he witnessed, and one which I sincerely wished he hadn't, was when I was collecting cups from the previous day. The cups were a green moulded heavy plastic and the bottom of one fitted neatly into the top of another. This meant that if carrying a tray you could put a second set on top of the first quite safely. Now for some reason which completely escapes me, I had not brought the tray into the room. There were about eight or nine of these cups in his room and a little voice in my head told me I could carry them all like a beer glass snake downstairs. As I began to pile them up, Larnach looked up from his work with a look of real concern and said, "Don't you think you should make two trips?"
"No I will be alright" I confidently replied and carried on. As I got the ninth cup in place I turned to walk away and my coffee cup snake began to come alive. Seeing a bulge appearing in its middle, I felt that I needed to add a little stabilising pressure from both the bottom and the top. The result of this pressure however, was to explode the cups sending them spinning in all directions, spilling their contents up the walls and over the carpet, not to mention the very unfortunate legal documents. The whole thing seemed to happen in slow motion for me, like a scene from a horror movie. I turned to Larnach and was relieved not to see tea dripping down his face.
"I will go and get a cloth and clean this up" I said meekly.
"Good idea " he said wearily. He persisted with me however and after a few months suggested I take a desk in the corner of his room so we could start some real training. Progress at last, I thought, not that I was struggling to enjoy myself.

Whilst delivering the local mail to other professional firms in the city, I also met a number of my contemporaries and developed a friendship with two who were broadly at the same stage of training as me. They worked at a firm called Ferens and Son, and one of them was to show me an example that I stored away for later use. He was called Richard Nixon (no, I'm not making that up either) and although only a little older than me he'd bought a house for £700, obtained an improvement grant from the Council, had work carried out on it and then sold the property for £1,100 making a whopping

£400 profit. Councils were to tighten up the procedure later to prevent instant profit, but it showed great nerve and was a fortune back then. I am not sure what became of Richard, but I am pretty sure he didn't become the president of the USA.

My firm acted for the Shafto Estates, as in 'Bobby Shafto went to sea, silver buckles on his knee' a well known local song. I hadn't realised that he was a real person, but here was I looking at huge waxed documents of Shafto title to land dating back centuries, all handwritten. I noticed that, although the sums paid centuries ago were only a few pounds expressed as guineas (one pound and one shilling), the land never fell in value. This information meant nothing to me at the time because it wouldn't help Sunderland beat Everton on Saturday, or persuade the girl with the short skirt on the bus home to go out with me, but it was valuable information for the future.

Things were beginning to look up for me. The job was developing, I was due to start at college, a girl nearer my own age had started at Wilson and Co and I knew my way around the city. I definitely felt like I had made progress; that is until the dark cloud of news emerged that someone new was starting. Enter Ian Todd, the nephew of one of the partners, who was starting work as an articled clerk (trainee solicitor). He arrived bouncing into the office, loud, overconfident and brash, bringing with him the ability to end my career before it was even launched. The battle between the heir to the throne and the working class tea boy was surely lost before it was even started.

CHAPTER 5: Career strangled at birth?

The first day Ian Todd came into the office I knew I would never like him. He was something I had not yet encountered in that he was a child born of privilege with an attitude to match. He was tanned, wore a blue blazer, smart trousers and behaved as if he owned the firm rather than having paid for his two years training, which would lead to him becoming a qualified solicitor. He knew not to push John Shepherd or Mike Larnach, but the women in the office were there to be dazzled by his charm and influence and I was not worthy of much more than servant status. He was, in fact, the archetype Flashman from the book Tom Brown's School Days. It is worth pointing out that I had nothing against his background as by now I had met a number of people from the upper middle classes and most were perfectly charming and pleasant, including his uncle. Junior Todd would frequently come into the office wordlessly singing Strangers in the Night by Frank Sinatra; imagine that tune to do *de do de do, da, da da dad da, do de do de do dad da...* etc, etc. Now imagine hearing it twelve times a day, just a little louder than is comfortable. It was irritating! There would also be *'John, can you make me a coffee?'* at a time of day where there would only be him drinking it or *'can you pop this letter into the post office?'* The letter was often personal and the post office was literally across the road, so that even with his upbringing it should have been possible to amble the few yards and drop the letter in the box himself without requiring assistance.

He was a member of the British Skiing team which he gloried in, but his chances of winning a gold medal in that team were similar to my chances of playing cricket for England. That said, it still made him one of the best skiers in the country, but also indicated the sort of life he had experienced. He once told us that he'd been to a party at the weekend, but had hidden his brand new Mini Clubman, what with all the sports cars on display. I would have committed murder for a Mini Clubman (particularly if it was him I was murdering!) and couldn't get my head around his shame of the car. This was part of the world I was joining. It wasn't a major problem to me and Todd wasn't someone who bothered me particularly, as both Kathleen (the new girl) and I thought him a bit of a joke and old fashioned with his blazer and Frank Sinatra songs. After all, it was the trendy Swinging 60's and trendy, Todd definitely was not! One day he stopped me and said,
"John, my beautiful girlfriend is coming over from Holland and I have bought her a dress at the ladies dress shop in town. Here is the ticket,

go and pick it up." Now as a young teenager I really didn't want to go and collect a dress, let alone walk up the street with it so I refused. John Shepherd upon hearing something came out and said to Todd, "Go and get your own dress, he is not here as your servant," to which Todd replied,

"Sorry Shep, of course I will," with a patronising smile. Perhaps that rankled with Todd and led to a more serious incident a few weeks later.

My tea deliveries had gone as normal in the morning and the typist working for Todd was a woman in her thirties called Muriel. She liked a laugh and would tease me in a playful way and I would respond in similar vein, which had never been a problem. On the afternoon tea delivery there was a different atmosphere in the room when I walked in. Muriel was sitting at her desk and Todd was sitting in front, facing me with his legs crossed in that wide angle assertive pose.

"You need to apologise to Muriel for what you said this morning" snarled Todd

"What are you talking about?" I replied aggressively.

"You know what you said, so do as you are told." Todd said raising his voice.

"We were having a laugh and I don't know what Muriel is offended about." I said in a puzzled tone and looked at Muriel who looked a combination of embarrassed and cross. I always thought she was a bit infatuated with Todd, impressed by his background and flattered by his attention. At that point this upper middle class product decided to raise the stakes and said,

"AND get your hands out of your pockets when you are talking to me!"

"Get lost, do you think you are in the army?" came my reply. Not exactly Oscar Wilde I agree, but the first thing that popped into my head. At that point Todd got out of his seat and made a move towards me, focusing on my hands now firmly glued in my pockets. He was about to grab my arm when I looked him in the eye and said,

"Touch that arm and see what happens next" (Clint Eastwood take note!). I now realise that Todd's experience of working class teenagers was as extensive as my experience of upper middle class toffs. I saw a look of concern cloud his face. He was bigger than me, but if he had grabbed my arm I would have hit him or pushed him over. I was used to fighting at the fairly rough schools I had been to and, from time to time, with my brother who was about the same age as Todd. He stopped in his tracks and just yelled,

"GET OUT!" I did indeed get out and felt victory coursing through my veins, which was soon replaced by anxiety as I wondered about the consequences of my actions. That night, travelling home on the bus I replayed the events of the day and simply couldn't see any other outcome but the sack for me. However wrong Todd was, he was related to a partner and he was going to be a solicitor. I, on the other hand, had no influence and I had shown an aggressive side to my nature which was real and maybe not in keeping with this particular career. I told my mother about it and she told me that my Dad would have done exactly the same thing. That was good enough for me, upset though I was at the possibility of losing my job.

The next morning I went to see Mike Larnach to tell him my side of the story, sure in the knowledge that he must have known about it and had already prepared my P45. I asked him if he'd heard about yesterday and he surprised me by confirming he knew nothing of it. I shakily went through the details, including my threat and intention at the end. He could hardly suppress his smile at the tale and at one point I think he was on the brink of laughing.

"I wouldn't worry about it, John. He hasn't said anything to me, but if he does I will deal with it so off you go." I never heard anymore about it, or had any further trouble with Todd. So far as Todd is concerned he qualified and left the firm to take up what appears to have been a very successful career in the Sports Law industry and may, for all I know, have changed into a nice person. What I do know is that for the two years I knew him he was a self-centred, conceited, smug bully and I learned two lessons from my encounters with him: always challenge a bully and never be a bully yourself, particularly if you have power or influence over someone. It is a responsibility not a privilege.

Todd had been joined at the firm by a second articled clerk called Michael Luxmoore who couldn't have been more different. He also enjoyed financial privilege in that his father was a partner in the firm, but Michael was very quiet to the point of being painfully shy and in the main he faded into the background. His father Edmund Luxmoore was a very strange man indeed, the like of which I had up to that point, never encountered. Edmund was the Under Sheriff of County Durham which seemed a fairly prestigious position, but amazingly he exceeded his son's shyness. I don't think he spoke or looked at me for more than a few seconds at a time. It wasn't rudeness, instead being either social discomfort or semi-indifference. The only times I recall him walking into reception were to look in the outgoing post basket, flick through the letters and say in an accent straight out of Downton Abbey, but with eyes averted to the floor,

"Could some of these letters go second class?" Second class, would you not like a man servant to deliver them from a carriage? I wondered. I was amazed when I recently discovered that Edmund is still alive at the age of 101 and perhaps even more surprised that he was only in his fifties when I started working for him. He appeared much older to me in his thick tweed suits and somewhat stooped stance. To my amusement, when talking to the staff he would refer to his son as Mr Michael and the already insufferable Ian Todd as Mr Ian. Young as I was, it was not a game I was going to play and I always answered by referring to them as Michael and Ian. Edmund probably thought that his father would have had me horse whipped for such impertinence!

This is what the legal profession was like in the 1960's, especially in an old city like Durham where firms had been in existence for many years. Solicitors were not used much by the working classes unless they were arrested, and there was little chance of someone from the working classes becoming a solicitor as the hurdles were too high to overcome. You could obtain a grant in those days to sustain yourself at university and obtain a degree in law, but then you had to find a firm to give you a two year term of articles which may be unpaid or require a payment for the privilege. This was beginning to change, but trainees were still a long way off being paid a living wage. The social change in society since then has been quite remarkable. The middle class has grown and the working class has shrunk and, to some extent, divided into those who work and those who do not.

When I started work, very few working class people owned their own homes or even aspired to do so. Many people who had accidents at work, or suffered industrial conditions or injury, simply saw that as part of the job and it was unlikely that they would rush off to see a solicitor, even if they knew they had some right in law which had been infringed. In those early years I didn't see myself as a solicitor, let alone someone who might seek to change things in a small way, but I did feel that the law appeared to be remote from the majority of people and that couldn't be right. It didn't feel remote from me and I was hungry to learn all about it and try out these new skills on anyone and everyone, just as soon as I was given a chance. But however keen I was to learn I was still a teenager and the chance for advancement might have been postponed indefinitely had Edmund Luxmoore been more proactive with the new urchin in his office!

One day, I boasted to a couple of the typists that I felt I could climb through the reception sliding window. The window was set half way up the wall separating reception from the passageway into the office and when a client appeared, the glass would be opened for the 'how can we help you?' welcome. I checked that there were no clients in sight, ran out into the passageway, jumped up to the window and began levering myself through it. My backside became caught in the frame, much to the amusement of the typists, and as I wriggled to free it Edmund came in through the front door to find me sticking out of his reception window, my feet parallel to his chest. He evidently decided to ignore the sight rather than give me a helpful push through.

A couple of years on and I had progressed within the firm, having some work of my own and a young typist to type it. After the firm's Christmas lunch I needed to check on whatever deliveries had come in, plus send off an urgent document before going home. My typist offered to come back with me to help and I didn't think too much about it as we walked back to the office together, which was now closed for the holidays. We went into reception and opened up the new post, found the document and prepared the letter to go, when all of a sudden she grabbed me and we were soon in a passionate tangle. This was definitely a very welcomed move so far as I was concerned, but also a surprise. I did flirt with her on a regular basis, but she had a long standing boyfriend and I assumed she was quite happy with him. Anyway, the temperature was rising and clothes were being removed when I heard the key in the front door lock. Quickly trying to reassemble myself I saw Edmund Luxmoore pass by the reception window on his way either upstairs or into reception. He hadn't been expected in the Durham office that day, still less when the office was closed and two of his younger staff members were semi-naked! I rushed to the door into reception and almost frightened him with a slightly louder than appropriate,

"Hello Mr Luxmoore, we weren't expecting you today." He might have gathered that with my tie half way around my neck, shirt undone, hair pointing north and lipstick all over my face. Looking surprised, he mumbled something or other and quickly bounded upstairs to the safety of his room!

More unwelcome was the attention of the new lady working in the accounts department. She was married, overweight and thought herself rather sexy. She wore quite short skirts displaying ample legs that a rugby player would have been proud of and low cut blouses that struggled to conceal two enormous breasts. I had had a stint of working in the accounts department and those breasts were regularly thrust in my face, or found leaning on my shoulder as she stood behind me reading over me. I didn't find any of this disturbing and, by and large found it quite amusing. She would often bring the conversation around to sexual matters and had a walk not unlike the character played by the late comedian Dick Emery (older readers will remember) who dressed as overtly flirty women, would see double entendres everywhere and use the phrase *'Oh you are awful, but I like you!'* before playfully pushing the man and walking off. One day I was standing at a desk in the accounts department and had my left hand on the corner of the desk as I checked one of the handwritten registers. 'Dick Emery' walked up behind me and put her right hand on my shoulder and straddled the back of my left hand with her crotch saying,

"Is there anything I can help you with?"

"No, I think I am fine." I replied with my hand now unmistakably trapped by her most intimate body part.

"What exactly are you looking for?" she hissed as her breasts edged either side of the back of my left arm.

"Well that's an interesting question," I teased "and I will let you know when I find it." I can't say I was worried or uncomfortable. I was growing up fast and I had developed a personal confidence that, added to the natural amount I already had (however misplaced), probably made me insufferable! I found the situation funny and I was also cross referencing the facts to make sure there was no doubt about her intentions. I was just about to ask for my hand back when the door opened and someone came in, allowing the blood to flow back into my knuckles. The lady didn't stay that long at the firm; I always wondered if she ran off with the milkman!

I was now learning a lot more about life as well as law and with the passage of time I realised that I could do the work well, even though training was minimal. Seeing new people start work allowed me to detect how much progress I was making. Practical matters of the mechanics of buying and selling property had sunk in, as well as an understanding of how the court system worked. Prior to almost being caught semi-naked by Edmund Luxmoore, I was seconded to the Under Sheriff's office to work under the supervision of Noreen, his very formidable assistant. Noreen had the look of Elsie Tanner from Coronation Street. Busty, bright red lipstick and a woman who, in her youth would have been both attractive and I imagine fairly active. She was not someone who would take fools lightly and certainly not someone to get on the wrong side of. Eunice disliked her intensely and the feeling appeared to be mutual. However, I got along with her very well as she liked a bit of banter and was fond of a laugh. My abiding memory of her is seeing her sitting upright at her desk with an open file in her hands, which she would still be holding when I opened her door.

"Oh, it's only you!" she would say putting down the file which held the library book she was reading! Noreen taught me the functions of the Under Sheriff's office which were primarily selecting the juries for the Assize and Quarter Session Courts (now called the Crown Courts) and processing writs issued in the High Court for enforcement by the High Court bailiffs. You might think this to be pretty uninteresting and you would be correct, but it was good to know how these significant aspects of the justice system worked.

I was given the task of going through the electoral registers and selecting the victims for jury service. It was a tedious task selecting at random forty or so names at a time and having done this for a time I decided to spice it up a bit! On one list I selected forty people from all over the area, but all their surnames began with the letter B. Although I wouldn't be there I had some pleasure in imagining the court usher shouting out the names in the corridor of the large Victorian court.

"Would the following jurors come forward: Mr Brown, Mrs Bainbridge, Mr Barrington, Mrs Batley, Mrs Baldock, Mr Bright.......hey, what's going on here?" On another occasion I chose different names, but they all lived at number 14 on their respective street so it would be,

"Mr Smith of 14 Argyle Road, Mr Brown of 14 Queens Terrace, Mr Armitage of 14 Cleveland Avenue....what's going on here ?" For some reason that job was taken away from me (I wonder why!), but I was given a shot at jury release, dealing with the requests to be excused jury duty. They varied enormously from having to go to hospital that week for a serious operation, to having young children and nobody to look after them, to having had a bad hair do which made it impossible to leave the house.

Noreen was very arbitrary in dealing with these requests and it seemed to rest on what sort of mood she was in or whether she liked the tone of the letter. She believed she could tell the difference between genuine and fake from the ink, paper or language used. I was useless at this part and would have let them all off. Learning the detail of enforcement of court orders was, however, very useful for the career ahead. So, I moved out of Noreen's office to a desk of my own and the long awaited work of my own. I was desperate to have a go at anything and that desire was about to be tested as I made my debut in court...as a teenager.

Chapter 6: The boy is given a chance

Before I had risen to the rank of 'own desk' I had been introduced to the court system in the way a number of young trainees were in those days. As a seventeen year old arriving at work and expecting to do some filing and photocopying, I was presented with a file and told to go round to court now, meet the barrister and sit behind him in court. End of instruction. This meant running across the bridge, going into the large Assize Courts beside Durham Prison and into the huge central area where a mixture of barristers, criminals, criminal's families, police officers and solicitors milled around looking for each other prior to the criminal hearings taking place.

On the first occasion I felt an intoxicating mixture of excitement and panic as I wandered aimlessly, trying to tell the difference between the groups. Barristers were easy to identify. They helped by wearing long black gowns like schoolmasters, winged collars like a Dickens character and wigs like something you'd wear to win a bet! Upon asking one of these characters from an eighteenth century play if they knew where Mr or Mrs (barrister's name) was I would be directed to my target. They were generally very charming and friendly, and my job would be to either find the accused in the central area or go down to the cells within the court building to locate him and sit in while his future was discussed. I got the hang of this quite quickly and began to feel important, walking around the building with my file. One day a young woman came up to me and said,
"Are you dealing with the case of Bill Thompson?"
"Yes, I am." I said with a touch of pomposity and pride.
"Well, it doesn't matter then" she responded, letting all of the air out of my over inflated balloon. Not letting the rebuff alter my course, I followed her to her seat and said,
"Would you like me to get the barrister?"
"Yes" she growled, no doubt thinking I should bring my Dad as well!
As with other experiences of being 'thrown into the professional deep end', I quickly found my way around and really enjoyed the front row seats in the courts (well, okay second row seats), until those occasions when the barrister would turn and ask me a random question, expecting an immediate answer: *Did you make a note of what the accused said yesterday about his girlfriend? What did the judge just say? Do you have a copy of the theft act with you? Can you get a psychiatrist here in the next hour?* The answer, after much searching of the file, a possible trip out of the courtroom armed with a very determined look and then much deliberation, was generally no.

Those early encounters at the Assizes and Quarter Sessions were a real eye opener onto a whole range of human behaviours and major role playing by all concerned. The accused knew where to stand in the Victorian Dock and either looked fierce or frightened, and perhaps both were something of a performance. I got to know most of the other clerks who sat in the second row and most of the barristers in the first row, and it didn't take long to realise that some of the barrister 'charm' was aimed at subsequent instructions, rather than a fondness of me. The most elevated location was reserved for the judge, who sat in the highest seat so that he could look down on everyone, both actually and figuratively. The deference shown to judges, particularly by barristers, took some getting used to: *As Your Honour pleases; As Your Lordship pleases; Indeed Your Honour is absolutely right, of course, and I apologise for giving Your Honour any other impression; May I kiss Your Honour's ample backside?* (ok I made that last one up) Also if any member of the judiciary should attempt humour it was met with theatrical laughter and the judge would be complimented on his astonishing wit. The judge was often treated like some mediaeval king and some behaved as such.

One of my favourite early judicial experiences happened at the Assize Courts in Durham when a particularly pompous judge was sitting in a case of a serial burglar. I had by now heard such cases many times and, as this was the case before ours, I had semi switched off. The judge asked the defendant to stand and the prison officer beside him got hold of his arm and pulled him up to receive his sentence. The judge fixed him with a glare and said,

"Albert Maxwell, you are a serial offender who knows no decency. You have been before this Court on numerous occasions and despite the best efforts of the Probation Service, your lawyers, this Court and countless others, you have spurned every chance afforded to you. (Voice begins to rise in anger.) I grow sick and tired of, week after week, having to sit here and listen to accounts of good people wasting their time on the likes of you and the poor victims who suffer at your hands and the hands of others like you. Well my patience is exhausted and you have had your final chance. You are nothing short of a disgrace, an appalling example of mankind and a menace in the society in which you live. A liar, a thief, an abuser of trust and a totally unrepentant criminal, (voice now rising to fury and making me wonder if the judge knows that hanging has been abolished) why even now you look at me with no emotion and a completely blank expression, well I will teach you a lesson. DO YOU UNDERSTAND?" he bellows. Slight pause then again twenty decibels louder "DO YOU UNDERSTAND, MAN?"

"Eh?" Maxwell replies

"What did you say?" explodes the judge

"Eh?" Maxwell repeats

"How dare you, have you not heard what I have said to you?" the judge screams

"No, no, I can't hear what you say cos I'm deaf." Suddenly the judge's anger disappears and sympathy and concern replaces it.

"CAN YOU HEAR ME NOW?" the judge shouts so loud that I suspect people in the city centre can hear him.

"A little bit" Maxwell responds.

"WHY WAS I NOT TOLD?" shouts the judge, frantically looking around for someone to blame.

"Get him to sit down," the judge orders the prison officer, now obviously believing he is dealing with a disabled man.

"I am so sorry, you should have had some assistance," explains the judge, his voice growing hoarse. "Can someone go and help this man?" I could barely contain myself! Within a few minutes a man who looked like he may be flogged now looked like he may be joining the judge for dinner!

"Sentence adjourned" the judge hoarsely concluded.

Going to the criminal courts was only a part of my legal education and I enhanced my learning by being willing and ready to have a go at any task, however unprepared I was. Having absolutely no idea what I was supposed to do didn't bother me too much and if there was nobody to ask, I would just guess. Never a good idea in the competitive world of law and I was caught out many times happily displaying my lack of knowledge and experience.

I think my disproportionate confidence partly stemmed from my first academic success with the 'A' level course I undertook. I had started the course on the advice of Mr Flynn, who had enrolled me, but immediately I found a number of difficulties with it. It was on a Thursday night which meant I missed Top of the Pops and Pans People, who at that time were every male teenagers dream. How would I ever marry one of them if I couldn't even watch them on television? In addition, I was the youngest person in the class by about 20 years it seemed, plus I hadn't got the faintest idea what the lecturer was talking about and went home every week none the wiser. Consequently I decided it was a waste of time. The decision to abandon the course was made easier for me by a pipe smoking middle aged man (looking back he may have only been in his mid thirties) who approached me during a lesson break. I thought he was going to invite me to have coffee with his little group but instead he said,

"Are you sure you have the right class? This is an 'A' level class; wouldn't you be more comfortable in an O-level class?"

"No, I know which class it is thank you." I replied wanting to ask him if he would be more comfortable with his pipe sticking up his anal passage. With my mind made up I felt I owed Mr Flynn the courtesy of telling him, so one lunchtime I walked from Durham City centre to my old school, practicing my little speech and perfecting it. It would go something like:-

"Oh hello Mr Flynn I just thought I would tell you the job is going well and I'm really enjoying it. I wanted to thank you again and oh, by the way, the 'A' level course didn't work out. It's too advanced if you haven't done the 'O' level, so I will concentrate on the legal executive exams next year instead." In my head he would agree, tell me it was a sound decision and release me from the clutches of the pipe smoking middle aged bore, to the arms of Babs from Pan's People. In reality he dismissed my concerns, told me not to be silly and to complete the course and do the exam. It would all make sense in the end and I would be fine. Before I knew where I was, I was walking back to the office having agreed to continue. In one respect he was wrong in that I never did make any sense of it. At the end of the course I really hadn't gleaned much extra knowledge or indeed learned how to revise properly. In the many exams that followed I developed an almost foolproof way of revising, but having only just turned seventeen I was, at that time, somewhat hapless.

On the night before the second paper, England was playing Brazil in the World Cup of 1970. I had been sitting in my room reading the text books, hoping for some inspiration. Totally lost, I gave in to temptation and went downstairs to watch the match. The game turned out to be famous for the brilliant performance of the England captain Bobby Moore and the save of the century from England goalkeeper Gordon Banks. The match was very close, but England lost which seemed somewhat ominous for what lay ahead in tomorrow's exam. I went back upstairs, re opened the book I was reading and in my utter frustration shouted out for some divine help. I was reading a page about orders in the high court and had neither come across them in the office or ever heard of them, let alone knew what they were. For some reason, out of three hundred pages in the book, I read and re read this page six times. The next day I gloomily went into the examination hall and at the appointed hour turned over the exam sheet. Question three asked me to identify the three high court orders I had been reading about the previous night and to explain their purpose. Whilst I would have struggled to have a conversation about them, I could almost see the page in my mind and I copied down the image onto the paper.

Some weeks later, my results fell onto the mat. The school system assessment of me was one of unsuitable for 'O' levels and I had accepted that. I believed I was academically second division and with that, closed off to certain careers or positions. I opened the letter expecting a failure, but instead I saw the word PASSED. Although I had scraped through by the skin of my teeth, I was now the proud holder of an 'A' level a full year earlier than if I had gone into the sixth form. Not only did I have the euphoria of the moment and one of the many professional qualifications I would need, but most importantly of all the barriers, whether visible or invisible, had been torn down and my world changed forever there and then.

There was a downside of course as I now felt I could do anything on minimal instruction. Give me six lessons and I will have a go at flying or give me that file and I will take on that partner in court. At eighteen years old I had saved up enough money to learn to drive and I remember my first driving lesson, in which I felt that now familiar cocktail of anxiety and excitement. At the end of it the instructor told me it had gone well. I imagine he dined out for weeks on my comment of;
"Shall I apply for the test?"
"Not quite yet" he replied through a grin. In fact I applied after six lessons and sat my test after ten. There used to be a list of thirty or so boxes which the examiner completed during the driving test, and two or three ticked meant a failure. I think in my case there were only two or three that escaped a tick and I'm sure the examiner was relieved to have lived through the experience! Undaunted, I immediately reapplied and four lessons later we were back. This time it was much better and I really did think I had passed, but was as disappointed to hear the words, "That is your driving test completed and I am sorry to say you have not reached the standard required". I just could not believe it and had I been armed, I may well have shot the examiner!

On my third attempt, there waiting for me was the first examiner no doubt recently released from therapy. My instructor had made the mistake of telling me that he was the least friendly or forgiving of all of them and also advised me to apply for a test elsewhere, as Durham City was a difficult place to sit the test because of the narrow city roads. I didn't take his advice because the waiting list was shorter in the city, for obvious reasons. I set off and noticed the examiner jotting down one or two things. On one occasion I overtook a parked car, causing the oncoming car to brake. In addition, the emergency stop wasn't all I had hoped for. The examiner said, "When I tap the dashboard, I want you to perform an emergency stop." When he did, I braked so hard that, had he been fitted with false teeth, they would probably have flown through the windscreen! Back at the test centre and convinced I had failed again, I reversed straight into the first available space without the usual careful judging and slow precise manoeuvre. He then asked the Highway Code questions, which I answered in a monotone reply, followed by,

"What would you do if faced with a parked car and an oncoming vehicle?" I told him I realised I had made that mistake and that I should have stopped. I looked out of my window and away from him as he said,

"That is your driving test and I am happy to say you have reached the standard required." For a moment I couldn't believe my ears. He completed some paperwork and said, "McArdle. That is an unusual name; do you have relatives in Framwellgate Moor? " At this point I couldn't remember if I had any relatives at all and when he asked me to sign the form, my hand was shaking so much I could scarcely hold the pen. I had done it! Now where's that airport and the flying lessons?

My appearances as an advocate followed a similar path. My boss took me to the County Court to show me how it was done and asked me if I wanted to do the next one. I think I was eighteen and I said yes. I walked across to the county court building with the file and sat amongst the solicitors and barristers. When my case was called I walked into the judge's chambers, which is a fairly informal court and appeared before Mr Curry who would be a district judge today, but in those days was called a Registrar. Mr Curry was a very nice and kind judge who was both patient and helpful. This was unusual, but quite important, as I knew very little. I spluttered out my prepared statement and when he asked me if I had the necessary form, he realised that he had exceeded my area of competence. Asking me for the file, he removed the form and kindly refrained from saying what a plonker I was!

Over the months that followed I appeared in that court many times and developed a relationship with most of the court staff. The chief clerk at the court was a very experienced man with an unfriendly aggressiveness about him, however I would go into the court office with a document I had drafted and ask him if he thought it was correct. To begin with he would shake his head and tell me where I was going wrong, but eventually he started to show me where I would find a precedent I could use. What he said he liked was that I asked them rather than just did it, but the truth was I had nobody else to ask. Be that as it may, it meant I had a good relationship with the staff. This proved very beneficial as we had no automated system at the firm and in fact, no system at all for recording important dates or court appointments, so that it was not uncommon for him to ring me and say,

"Good morning Mr McArdle, didn't you have an appointment at court this morning? Ten minutes ago."

"Oh my God, which one?" I would scream.

"Jones v Baxter. Don't worry I have moved it down the list, but I expect you are on your way." I would grab the file and belt across the bridge to the court.

On one occasion I turned up and my opponent was a senior partner from an established Newcastle firm. When I spoke to him outside he was both unfriendly and dismissive. We were called in and as I responded to his remarks, he interrupted and made reference to my lack of experience and poor preparation. I was ready for a fight, but could see his point. The mild mannered Mr Curry went for this senior partner, instructing him that he was not going to allow him to come into his Court and be offensive, whereby he promptly dismissed the senior partner's objections along with his application. Looking back, I don't believe this was favouritism or parochial behaviour on Mr Curry's part, but a refusal to allow bullying. It must have left a mark on me, because in the long career ahead of me I had a reputation for being aggressive in litigation, but I never took advantage of those in training or generally inexperienced. If you were of the same level of experience, or more so then that was different, but I think I followed Mr Curry's example on junior opponents.

I'm afraid bullying was all too apparent on the legal scene, but not so much with me as with junior barristers in court. The presiding judge in Durham was Judge Sharp who was, without doubt one of the most offensive people I have ever met. An aggressive manner was his standard behaviour and inexperienced barristers who had the misfortune to appear before him were regularly tortured in his courts. One poor soul was a very charming young barrister named Mr Sunderland, a name I've always remembered for obvious reasons. Having met him outside of the court room I asked him if everything was in order and, as an aside, mentioned his ill luck at the judge being none other than Sharp.

"Yes, the papers are in order, the matter is straightforward and Sharp is fine really. I always get along with him well." he said like a sheep stumbling into the lion's den.

"Mr Sunderland, what is the meaning of this application? Did you serve it on the defendants?" boomed Sharp.

"I will just take instructions, Your Honour." he said turning to me to enquire. I told him it was served and acknowledged.

"Mr Sunderland, do you not know that in my Court I like three copies of each document?"

"I will just take instructions, Your Honour." still smiling he turned to me and I gave him extra copies.

"Mr Sunderland, have you not even bothered to enquire of the defendant's employment status?"

"I will just take instructions, Your Honour," another turn and a faltering smile as he asks me. After another two or three more of these Sharp, turning a mixture of blue and red, launches another attack.

"Mr Sunderland, did you ask your client to attend today?"

" I will just take instructions, Your Honour" This time the unfortunate advocate turned and as he looked at my file a line of perspiration ran down the bridge of his nose from his brow and plopped onto the file cover.

"Get out of the way man." screeched Sharp as he instructed Sunderland to move aside so he could speak to me directly. Caught in the direct line of fire, Sharp asked me the question which I answered and the barrister's humiliation was complete.

Thankfully, I had a somewhat charmed life with the ferocious Judge Sharp. I once stopped at the gate controlled court car park to ask if I could park my car and panic ensued when the police officers realised that Judge Sharp was behind me and was being kept waiting. They had to let me in to turn around before he could pass me, with me looking in the other direction so he couldn't tell who was making him late. I then found myself appearing in open court without a right of audience due to not yet being qualified on THREE separate occasions. On the first I stood up and explained I had thought the matter was being heard in chambers and to my amazement he said,

"No matter; what is the application about?"

On the second occasion I found I had made exactly the same mistake with the same surprising result.

The third was not really my fault as I was told that the judge was just reading out a judgement in open court and all I needed to do was take a note of it, as the barrister would not be attending. I was chatting to the solicitor on the other side, who I knew well, when in walked Judge Sharp who said,

"Not wearing your gowns gentlemen? I expect a detailed argument on costs." I toyed with the idea of replying that I wasn't wearing a gown because I didn't have one and the very good reason for that was because I wasn't qualified; I dismissed the thought and blagged it!

Whilst sitting in criminal matters Sharp was always scathing of car owners who left their cars unlocked and had them stolen. Serve them right for being so careless was his view, although not sparing the villain who stole the car. It was reported at the time that Judge Sharp had driven home to collect something in his lunch break and not only left his car unlocked, but the keys in it. As luck would have it, a local villain was passing and promptly jumped into the car and sped off. Delightful proof of the existence of God or the power of fate!

CHAPTER 7: Pastures new

At the grand old age of twenty I had been handling my own cases for a while. They were fairly varied and intermittent, and I approached each one with enthusiasm and vigour, hoping it would compensate for my lack of knowledge and experience. My staple diet of work was for the admirably named Brandon and Byshottles District Council for whom I acted in completing paperwork for mortgages. It wasn't difficult work, thanks to the skills John Shepherd had taught me and the work also gave me a new and invaluable 'people' skill.

The council officer responsible for local searches was by reputation a very difficult man. A local search is done in virtually every conveyance and flags up any plans that may affect the property, so it is pretty essential. The searches seemed to take an age back then, holding up completion and often necessitating a telephone call asking the Council to expedite the search. Many times I engaged this gruff and outwardly unfriendly council officer in conversation and over a period of calls managed a very slight thaw in him. During one of our conversations he told me that on receiving a request to expedite a search, he'd go out of his way to find the application and put it to the bottom of the pile. This valuable piece of information gave me a strategy. If I had the need of a quick search, I would ring him for a normal chat and then say 'When you have a minute can you check where my search is in the pile, so I have an idea when to expect it?' This almost always led to him finding it and doing it straight away. I was learning that there was more than one way to skin a rabbit.

And so it happened that my accumulated experiences led me to believe that I had to leave the sleepy city of Durham in search of more excitement and advancement. This feeling was cemented into decision by one of the partners of Wilson and Co, my own employer, who prevented me from winning a case. It concerned a horse which had been sold by a very nice lady client to an Irish purchaser. The purchaser used an excuse for delaying payment whilst taking the horse, thus leaving the owner out of pocket. It was clear he never intended to pay for the animal, which led the unfortunate lady to seek legal advice. I started a civil action against the dishonest purchaser, also believing that if we could establish that he had no intention of paying, it was theft. I read the theft act and convinced myself (and her) that it was so and off we went to the police station to make the criminal complaint.

At the desk I was insistent on seeing a senior officer and we were led into an Inspector's office where I proceeded to explain the position and the law, no doubt to the irritation of the Inspector. Anyway, I was in full flow and was aware that the client was both impressed and relieved that someone so apparently in control was dealing with her case. So sure of myself was I, that I had not heard the door open behind me and knew nothing until an arm was wrapped round my throat, pulling me backwards with the owner of the arm shouting,

"I have him Sarge. Fetch the cuffs and get the cell ready, this boy is dangerous!"

Just as I was being pulled over the back of the chair, I registered my client's startled expression. As I landed on the floor I recognised the voice of my Dad's old pal Ken Wilson, who was an officer at that particular station.

"Hello Ken!" I said getting to my feet and trying to straighten my clothes and hair, which was now pointing in several different directions, as well as trying to find my car keys and take the pink blush from my cheeks

"How are you doing son? I haven't seen you in ages," replied Ken, obviously to the relief of the client who probably thought she was next (another lesson: never take yourself too seriously as someone will always bring you back to reality!). Undaunted by the embarrassment, I pressed on and persuaded the Police to investigate whilst I continued with the civil proceedings. At an early application I met the "thief" who tried to persuade me that he was in fact the brother of the real culprit and he was here to help sort it out.

"Well, tell your brother from me that I intend to not only recover the horse, but have him put in prison and, when he is in prison, find his assets and sell them."

"Fair enough, I will tell him," said the man

"Is he your twin?" I ended sarcastically. I had traced the horse, which was still in England and I planned to ask the Police to seize it and return it to my client. I felt I could persuade them that, as the thief had sold it on it was evidence of dishonesty. I returned to the office and rang my client, telling her that I thought we were close.

A few days later Mr Todd, uncle of the odious Ian asked to see me which was very unusual. He was a shy but charming and polite man.

"Ah John, take a seat. I gather you are dealing with a case involving a horse," he said.

I was convinced he was going to praise me and bestow more cases on me (ever the optimist!), but to my astonishment he said, "I'm afraid you are going to have to drop the case as it turns out the horse is in the possession of good clients of the firm." I was absolutely crushed. I was on the verge of success and despite my age, I knew the client had come to rely on me. I did my best to argue the point, but there was a conflict of interest and although I didn't see it at the time, it was a reasonable request. I felt betrayed and stifled and rang the client to break the news. She was as devastated as me. I arranged for her to be transferred to another firm and I never did find out what happened, but I never forgot the experience. What was implanted in me from then on was a burning desire to make my own decisions and practice law the way I wanted to, although I was too young to think about the practicalities of it then, it was time to leave. I was to abandon this safe haven and go to a firm which specialised in turmoil, both inside and out.

Completely at random I wrote to a firm in Sunderland called Richard Reed and Co for no other reason than I liked the name. Sunderland, although a town then, was much larger than Durham City and would offer different challenges. I received an invitation to an interview and, having nothing to lose I felt no nerves. In fact, I was quite excited at the prospect. I was interviewed by three of the partners including Tony Palmer, a man in his thirties and obviously the dominant partner in the room. Palmer told me that they didn't have a vacancy, but that legal executives were hard to come by and my letter had made them think about a small expansion.
"Which department are you expanding?" I enquired
"Civil litigation" Palmer answered. "What work do you specialise in?"
"Civil litigation" I replied. I would have 'specialised' in any department he mentioned and in reality civil litigation was the subject I least specialised in at that time, but I decided I could wing it whilst I picked it up. The interview went fairly well and I left feeling reasonably confident. I duly received a letter offering me the job, which more or less doubled my salary to the dizzy heights of £30 per week. I went to see Mike Larnach with something of a heavy heart, telling him of my decision to leave. He acted as nicely and as fairly as he always did and wished me well, saying that he was sorry to see me go. He also said he'd heard some tales of the firm I was joining and if I found I didn't like it there, he would be happy to welcome me back. He was such a nice man, a caring boss and someone I never forgot. He once told me that he trusted me and if I needed any time off for illness, I didn't need a doctor's certificate to prove it, I just needed to phone in. It may be why in four years I wasn't off sick once and I think I would have struggled in if I had been shot! As happy and excited as I was at the challenge of a new job, I will always remember closing that ancient heavy door of Wilson and Co's office for the last time and upon hearing that final loud click of the lock, hoping nervously that I was doing the right thing.

One final point about the offer letter; I didn't open it myself but my new girlfriend did. Driving to work I had noticed a strikingly good looking brunette who always waited at a bus stop in a nearby village. One day I saw the bus pulling away with the girl giving vain chase, so taking this fine chance I stopped beside her and offered her a lift. She smiled, thanked me and got into the car. She was even better looking than I had thought! We had a chat about not much in particular, before I enquired about her personal life. She told me she was engaged, but wasn't happy with her fiancée. Oh, back in with a chance! When I dropped her off she walked away and I decided that if she was interested, she would turn and wave. If not, she would just walk on to her office. After fifty paces or so she turned and waved leaving me determined to reach the bus stop before the bus tomorrow. I duly beat the bus, picked her up and asked her out. She accepted and we became an item. On the day the letter arrived I was late so I asked her to open it and read it to me. She read the letter confirming the job offer and salary as I struggled to hide my smugness. What she didn't tell me was that the man she was engaged to (and had now dumped) was the brother of Tony Palmer, my new boss. Small world and looking uncomfortably smaller as I realised that Palmer was the driving force of Richard Reed & Co; a man with an awful temper and feared by most of the staff. He was to tell me a few weeks later that his brother was very upset because 'some twat has waltzed off with his fiancée.'

On my first day I was met by a very friendly receptionist, Lillian Huntley. There was a real buzz about the place and more importantly there were several girls my age working there. I was taken up to Geoff Cardwell's office, who I knew from college. He was away for two weeks, so I was allocated his office and his work, whilst my office and work were sorted out. The first person to come and chat to me was Malcolm Donnelly, an articled clerk (trainee solicitor) who was, as it turned out, to play an enormous part in my future. He was friendly, but a little miserable as he said,
"Well, I suppose I had better show you around and introduce you to everybody, but afterwards you will have to fend for yourself because nobody (he meant the partners) will do anything for you." That didn't worry me; I was used to doing things for myself and anyway, I was pretending to be an experienced litigator so not having close scrutiny was useful.

At one o'clock I was introduced to the lunch regime. You either ate your own sandwiches or bought them nearby and everyone took turns to make the tea or coffee. Malcolm Donnelly was joined by fellow articled clerk

Gordon Wellham and surprisingly the fearsome partner Tony Palmer. A very leggy attractive clerk called Catherine (not her real name for discretion) also joined us, which was a bit of a treat as she wore very short skirts and was great company. Lunchtimes were quite lively with food, banter and games of cards. I may have been the new boy, but I had learned that being a shrinking violet was unhealthy and anyway, I was glad of the challenging atmosphere. Despite Palmer being loud and to some extent menacing, I really quite liked him and I was impressed that he didn't seem in anyway pompous or uncomfortable about eating with the staff. He had an edge about him though, which I saw more and more of, but he never used it on me. I'm not sure he knew how to take me and I think he sensed in me someone likely to react to anything he might say or any attack he might launch. One day in the lunch room he said,

"Can I have another cup of tea, Freckles?"

"You certainly can, Ugly" I replied. There was silence as I poured the tea. Later, one of my colleagues suggested it was very dangerous to talk to Tony like that and I was lucky he hadn't gone for me. I wasn't worried and explained that when he became personal with me, he surrendered the privilege of avoiding me being personal to him. And I was happy to tell him so. I was adamant about it and in the years that followed, I didn't change that view point even as an employer.

I could relay many examples of Palmer's temper, but the following are typical. He once shouted at a secretary about the quality of her work, marched her into the typing pool and told her that's where she belonged. I can't imagine how embarrassed she was. Both Malcolm and Geoff had experiences of him bursting into their rooms complaining about some work, with no regard for the clients who were with them, which was incredibly unprofessional. That never happened to me, but some months into the job he did ask to see me and told me one of the partners was unhappy that Geoff and I talked to each other in our offices.

"Oh, who was that?" I enquired.

"Not prepared to tell you," he responded.

"Are they frightened of me and unable to speak to me directly?" I somewhat sarcastically answered.

"No, but even you must accept that a partner is entitled to raise an issue like this" he bristled.

"Is there any complaint about my work or my billing?" I asked.

"No, actually both are very good as you well know," he retorted.

I did know because Geoff and I had, completely off our own bat, taken over a great many files which had been left to rot by predecessors, and turned them into profit as opposed to negligence claims against the firm.

"Well, in that case I see myself as selling my time to you as an employer and how I spend that time is up to me as long as I get the results," I said proving that pomposity is not limited to those in power, but can be assumed by a young man who should think a little more before he speaks. Palmer laughed and asked if in my 'high and mightiness' I might find it in me to be a little more subtle in my conversations with Geoff. I agreed that I might. Geoff Cardwell has always referred to me as the world's worst employee and he may have a point!

Richard Reed himself was an interesting character. He'd become wheelchair bound following a disease after the war, but depending on which story was told, was either pushed out of the firm he worked for because of his incapacity or declined a demotion to set up his own firm. Either way he was a very effective advocate and a man of great charisma. The firm he had started was doing well and had a very large following. He was a criminal advocate and had a much used trick in the Magistrates Court when he would say 'Your Worships will forgive me for not rising' which apparently had them eating out of his hand. The other thing he was very good at was pretending he remembered somebody when he clearly did not. I was told by his former assistant that a young police officer came up to him after a court hearing and said,

"Hello Mr Reed, I just wanted to thank you for your help a few months ago."

"Ah yes it is Derek, isn't it?"

"No Colin, Sir"

"Yes of course it is Colin; you are stationed in Sunderland aren't you?"

"No Durham, Sir"

"Yes of course, and how's your wife?"

"I'm not married Mr Reed"

"No, I'm thinking of your brother "

"Sister Sir?"

"Yes, how is she doing?"

"Very well sir and thank you for asking"

"Anyway lovely to see you Derek, er Colin and you take care."

I was told the young officer was glowing and so impressed that a man as busy as Mr Reed had remembered him amongst all the people he must deal with. This was the man Richard Reed, extremely charming, charismatic and on the face of it someone who had not only come to terms with his disability, but had learned to use it to his advantage. However, I was to see a very different side of him in my time with his firm.

In fact I saw nothing at all of him in the first few weeks at the firm, before finally receiving a request to go to his room and meet him. He had spoken to me on the telephone previously, but only to ask me if I was Mrs Moore! Geoff Cardwell had told me of his introduction, which resulted in Mr Reed calling him Eric for the next few months. Almost all of Reed's employees were in awe of him and I had been told he liked to be called Sir. Well he could like all he wanted, but the rebellious side of me was sure I wouldn't be doing it. I wouldn't go in and say 'How are you doing Dick?', but Mr Reed would be his name to me, not Sir, a relic from a bygone age. I went into his room to find it empty and after a couple of minutes was told that Mr Reed was in his car in the car park and I was to meet him there. It was a winter's day and a light snow was beginning to fall outside. As I approached his white Jaguar the electric window slowly opened and Reed extended his hand from it saying,

"Hello son, I'm Richard Reed, pleased to meet you"

I shook his hand and said, "Hello, I'm John McArdle"

"What do you prefer to be called, John or Mac?" he enquired.

"Well nobody calls me Mac, so I suppose I would have to say John" I responded.

"Well I think I will call you Mac," he said after a few seconds.

It crossed my mind to ask him if I could call him Reedie or Dickie, but I thought better of it. Anyway after a few pleasantries he was off to court and I was back in the office wiping the snow off me.

Obviously, because of his disability he was confined to the ground floor meaning that we on the first floor were safe from him turning up without warning. If he wanted to see you he would rarely ask directly. Your summons would come from reception. I was to have a poor relationship with Mr Reed, which was certainly as much my fault as his and was perhaps a collision of two worlds that were changing. He was from an established middle class background and part of an old guard legal profession, whilst I was from a working class background and part of a new breed of lawyer ready to challenge old values and status, although I was not aware of it in those terms at the time.

I was now settled in my new room and into life in Sunderland. My strategy on filling in the blanks on my litigation knowledge was to go into Geoff Cardwell's room and check whether the way he did things was the same as I had been taught at Wilson and Co. I neglected to tell him that I had in fact been taught nothing, but just picked it up as I went along as I was doing with him. I was getting by without too much of a hitch until the partner in charge of us, John Cooper, asked me to pop down for a chat. He asked me to take a seat and told me it was good for them to have somebody who had worked somewhere else and had different experiences. I played along and agreed that there may be benefits. He then said,

"I just want to check some things to see if we are getting it right. For example, what is your position on the disclosure of medical reports in a personal injury action?"

Now he may as well have asked me about my position on Einstein's theory of relativity. My one personal injury case, up to this point, didn't give me a lot of knowledge as he was in danger of finding out. I tried to look intelligent and answered,

"Well there are two schools of thought, aren't there? The first is that you should disclose, then you've let the opponent see the report; the other that you shouldn't disclose so that you can keep it for later, when it might have more effect."

"Yes, but what do you do?" he enquired

Giving myself a little time to think, I said

"I have always gone with ....disclosing the report as I think it is more appropriate."

"Good, that is what we do" he said approvingly as I dodged the bullet.

He seemed genuinely pleased that he was getting it right with disclosure, as opposed to concluding that I didn't know what I was talking about. Undaunted by this near miss, I continued on my merry way of collecting knowledge until, having formed a solid friendship and sound working relationship with Geoff I felt confident enough to admit my previous limited experience and my sponge like approach to the first few weeks at Reeds. Between us we covered most aspects of civil litigation and had both been to court many times, and indeed it was not unusual in those days to have as many as three or four court applications in one day.

The court system didn't allow for convenience or efficiency, so that appointments were never consecutive and you were often backwards and forwards to court several times a day. Consequently, the working day flew by for me. I would drive to Sunderland from my mother's house a few miles outside Durham City, and settle in to my room after some chatting to what was a lively bunch of people. Importantly there were a lot more of them than in my previous job. A little bit of flirting was also a good way of starting the day and it often carried on throughout it! Once I actually made it to my room there was always plenty of work to do interspersed with regular interruptions by the telephone. Twice a day our tea lady would do her rounds. She was a little eccentric to put it kindly and seemed to live in a world of her own. I imagine she was in her fifties or sixties, but it was hard to tell. She would wear ill fitting wigs and would come in singing or muttering to herself,

"What are you having today?" she would ask.

"A pint of lager please or a tequila sunrise" I would tease.

"Eee what are you like?" she'd say as she handed me the cup she'd already poured before asking me the question. It made no difference if I had clients with me, her patter remained unchanged and she would be completely oblivious to their possible need for a cuppa. One day when I had three clients with me she came in singing, plopped a cup of coffee on my desk and said,

"Eee that Mr Cardwell was lying across his desk pretending to be dead when I took him his tea. He had a note in his hand that said the tea'd killed him. Eee, what is he like?"

As she left, I turned to three confused clients and smiled and said ,

"Right, where were we?"

I didn't always need someone's assistance to embarrass myself, though. My office was on the first floor overlooking Frederick Street and I sat with my back to the window. I had a very large Victorian mahogany desk with a heavy wooden separate top covered in leather. I was in the habit of tilting my wooden seat and swinging backwards and forwards on it, catching the desk top with my knees to send me forwards when I had tilted backwards. One summer's day, the window wide open only a few feet behind me, I was not only swinging on the chair but also being insufferably smug as I broke the news to a young married couple with my success in my last court appearance for them. I could see they were impressed and delighted with the result, when my knees missed the desk in the backswing and I had to throw out both arms and kick the heavy desk top with my feet to save myself from falling out of the window. I kicked the desk top so hard, that it lifted from the base and crashed back down with a noise like a shotgun being fired, which caused both of them to shout out in shock. I can remember the terrified look in their eyes; they had absolutely no idea what had happened. I consoled myself with the thought of what might have been had I missed the desk and gone backwards out of the window, and decided that life was too precious to continue with my dangerous habit.

However not long afterwards and again with clients opposite me, I had drifted into the old habit. With my chair leg inadvertently sitting on a wire on the floor, the chair slipped off mid-swing giving me a small jolt. Obviously still traumatised from the previous near miss, I let out a shout mid-sentence, opening my eyes to their widest point. That was met with mutual shouts from both of clients, similar to a noise a startled child might make. I don't think they were any clearer when I told them I thought I was falling off my chair.

It was very busy at Reed's and regular contact with clients was increasing weekly. We all had a full list of clients every afternoon and here I was in the hub of a very busy and hectic schedule, encountering new challenges and situations every day, along with a good smattering of life's eccentrics. Bring it on...!

CHAPTER 8: Settling down

There were five partners and maybe eight or nine other lawyers in the firm, who all seemed to have full lists covering most types of work. Since I had announced my 'expertise' in civil litigation, my appointments tended to be people who had been injured in accidents at work, in cars, in the street or almost anywhere. I also saw people who had disputes with their bank, their neighbours, family, employers or almost anybody. Other lawyers dealt with matrimonial, criminal, property, trusts and probate; this was what I had left Wilson & Co to experience and I found that the days flew by, and my knowledge increased almost on a daily basis.

I was enjoying the daily routine and feeling good about my decision to move from a happy but slow paced firm to a very busy and what seemed dynamic firm. That would all change in about a year, but for now the variety of crises that the general public manufactured took up most of my energy.

There was a particular type of client who tended to make either a 2.30pm or 3.00pm appointment who we called the 'after the pub' client. This was somebody who would take a liquid lunch and fit in the solicitor's appointment when the pub or working men's club closed at 2pm. They were quite often entertaining and sometimes even lucid. Even the non pub clients could amaze with the diversity of incident they could conjure up! Here are but a few from that first year in Sunderland:-

Mr A was a short, middle aged man with thinning hair, a slight limp and a very cheerful disposition. He came in to ask if he could make a claim against the large department store in the town. When I asked him what had happened, he told me that he had gone into the store in the early morning and had slipped on a pool of water in one of the aisles, injuring his back.
"Which aisle was it?" I enquired
"It was the DIY aisle," replied Mr A
"Was the water at the beginning of the aisle?"
"No, it was right at the end"
"So you had a chance to see the water as you walked towards it?" I clarified
"Oh yes, I did see it but I thought I could jump over it"
"You mean you saw it and decided to take a jump at it, rather than go another way?" I asked bemused.
"Yes, I took a few steps back and took a run at it," replied Mr A confidently
"So you were running before the jump that caused you to fall?"

"Aye and I would have made it if I hadn't got the dog on a lead, cos it pulled me back" "So let me get this right. You saw the pool of water ran towards it and tried to jump over it whilst you had your dog with you on a lead?" "Aye that's right, how much do you think I'll get?"

Mrs B was a lady in her late sixties or early seventies, a little overweight with something of a rolling gait. She enquired about making a case against the Council because of the injury to her legs and back.
"Where were you when you were injured?" I asked
"I was at the graveyard visiting my husband's grave," she answered
"What happened?"
"Well as I bent down to put some flowers on Bert's grave the headstone next to his fell over on top of me," she explained
"What? Of its own accord?"
"Yes there was no warning or wind or anything it just fell over on me"
I wanted to ask if she and Bert had been happily married, but I decided against it!

Mr C was a bald man in his late fifties; more than a little overweight. He had the look of a man who'd had a long paper round and the reddish nose of a man who liked a pint or two. He arranged an appointment and asked what he could do about a domestic incident at his home, which led to a serious injury.
"I had been on nightshift and got home early morning" began Mr C
"Yes, go on" I encouraged
"Well I normally make myself a cup of tea before the wife gets up"
"OK" I coaxed him to continue
"I had my cup of tea and then I generally go to the toilet before she gets up"
"I see," I said wondering where we were going with this
"Well, I always have a sneaky cigarette in the toilet while I'm sitting there so I lit one up"
"Yes?"
"Well, I didn't know the wife had put cleaning powder in the toilet and when I dropped the match there was this flash of light and this explosion"
"Were you injured?"
"Injured? Me balls were on fire"

Sadly not all cases had a funny side and often we were faced with tragedy; none more so than when the death of a child was involved. One case is burned into my memory where a five year old boy went out playing and didn't return home. A woman walking in the street near to the boy's home saw a pair of children's shoes lying upside down on top of a broken drain cover and bent down to pick them up. As she did so she screamed as the child was still attached to the shoes, having somehow fallen head first into the full drain and drowned. Remarkably, in her shock the woman dropped the boy back into the drain and ran away screaming. I always wondered if the child was capable of revival at that point, but probably not and the point was not raised at the inquest. The boy's home was not the best and I often dealt with his drunken father enquiring about compensation. In cases I was to deal with in the future, the death of a child was totally devastating to parents who often never recovered from the grief or if they did so, never removed the sadness. This was a double loss to other children in the family who not only lost a brother or sister, but happy parents. Fortunately these dramatically catastrophic cases were relatively rare.

The number and variety of cases kept arriving on a daily basis. Looking back, it should have been a tremendously successful firm because of the sheer number of people who came through the door. It has to be remembered that no form of advertising was allowed in those days and solicitors were not even allowed to hold themselves out as specialists in any kind of legal field or to suggest that they were in any way better than any other firm. The kind of footfall at RR & Co would today cost a fortune in advertising or marketing. Despite this, I doubt that the firm was enormously profitable and I think this came down to two factors, one being that the work was not done particularly efficiently and the second was that the five partners didn't seem to like each other very much.

Richard Reed was something of a loner who perhaps believed he was the top dog and the firm belonged to him. Tommy Slack was a man in his fifties who had been a legal executive and struck me as having a chip on his shoulder about his local accent, as well as seeming uncomfortable with his rise in stature as a solicitor and then partner. He once confided in Geoff Cardwell that he sometimes wished he had stayed a legal executive. John Cooper was my immediate boss and he was a short man with black curly hair and almost a split personality. You could pass him on the stairs and he would tell you a joke and wander off laughing, but an hour later he could be thunderous and snarling. Tony Palmer was, as I have indicated, a man much feared in the office. He worked very hard, but in a self induced pressure cooker which spilled over from time to time. He thought he was the best lawyer in the firm and the most successful, which he may have been, but he was something of a loose cannon which was always likely to go off and was to do so spectacularly in the future. Peter Thubron was the newest and youngest partner, and in fact only became a partner after I joined. He was reasonably pleasant and although he did not join in with us at lunchtime, he would often pop in at the end despite the piss taking he would endure. The combination of these five probably did not work when it came to running a business and none of them seemed to be friends. I was to find later in my own business that it is not essential that your partners are friends, but it is so much better if they are.

My first year at the firm had been my most enjoyable so far in my short career. Not only had I developed as a young lawyer with a full and diverse caseload, but I had enjoyed good relationships with almost all of the staff. In Geoff Cardwell and Malcolm Donnelly I had started lifetime friendships that would grow into business relationships and I had also enjoyed relationships of a different kind with a few of the girls in the office. I had now passed all of the examinations I needed to qualify as a legal executive, but I was too young to be enrolled and that had led me to the decision to try and qualify as a solicitor. I had investigated it and found that it would be difficult because of financial circumstances. Therefore, I would only get one attempt at it and I decided to go for it. Yes, my cup seemed full and life was really enjoyable at this firm with everything seeming to be running smoothly. That was all to change dramatically and having experienced my best year to date, I was to follow it with the worst year, not only to date, but as it turned out in my whole career. I would leave in the most acrimonious of circumstances and battle to save my career.

CHAPTER 9: Things turn sour

It is hard to say when things started to change at Richard Reed's or indeed if the problems that surfaced were always there, but the mood of the place seemed to be altering significantly. Tony Palmer's behaviour was also something to be concerned about. He still joined us at lunch, but it became obvious that his relationship with Catherine was developing. They would share a joke between themselves or start playfully hitting each other, which could end with them wrestling on the floor. Palmer had an array of cars which he brought to the office, but when he started bringing his camper van we were all a little suspicious. Then when he stopped joining us for lunch and left by the back door to drive the camper to the end of the street where Catherine, having left by the front door would get in, our suspicions were confirmed.

One day Palmer came into my room when one of the office girls was being a little playful with me. Actually, I had her shoe in my hand and upon seeing him she limped out of the room whilst I placed the shoe behind me.
"Have I come at a bad time?" he said smirking.
"No, not at all" I replied.
"Look, I know you've been out with a few girls from the office, but I would just suggest a little more discretion." he said with a serious voice. The irony of the moment was evidently reflected in my expression as he added, "I know that's rich coming from me."
"Yes, that's what I was thinking," I couldn't help replying.
"Anyway moving on, the reason I came to see you was about this case." he responded with a smile. That was him; unusual, aggressive, but with a sense of humour and never pompous. Not with me anyway.

On another occasion Palmer told me that Tommy Slack had a problem with me, a surprise as I had had very little, if any contact with him. Apparently Slack felt I was metaphorically putting two fingers up at him when I saw him and laughing at him. I wasn't, although I did a pretty good impersonation of him, but then again I did a reasonably good one of most of the partners. Palmer went on to explain that my personality probably rubbed Slack up the wrong way because he was shy, lacking in self belief and confidence, and here was this young ginger kid coming into the office with far too much of it. His warning portended the end for me, but at the time I didn't pay that much attention to the warning. To compound matters, two separate incidents served to set the senior partner, Richard Reed against me. The second was, with the benefit of hindsight, at least as much my fault as his, however, the first was in my view entirely his fault.

When Reed told an insurance rep (who had an appointment to see me) that I shouldn't be dealing with my own case load, I reacted badly. The fact that I had been competently doing so and signing my own post for some time seemed irrelevant. It was made doubly embarrassing as the rep was our opponent and he told me about it during a case meeting. I thought Reed was appallingly unprofessional, not to mention guilty of undermining his own staff. Consequently I went to see John Cooper, my immediate boss, absolutely full of hell. John confirmed that I didn't need supervision, but told me that if asked I should say that he, Cooper, signed my post even though he didn't. I refused and went see Mr Reed. I told him I knew about his conversation with the insurance rep and had he wanted to check on my work or post, he should have said. Reed was put very much on the back foot and unused to challenge. He spluttered something about me not getting offended and would sort something out with Mr Cooper, but I told him I had been embarrassed by the incident.

The second incident involved me buying a part for my mini from a Sunderland garage called Byers Dunn Turvey, which was quite a large car dealership. In those days I tried to do basic maintenance on my car for financial reasons and when I fitted the part, it didn't work. For anyone reading this that knows me and may be aware of previous failings in that department, it wasn't how I fitted it! I took the part back asking for a replacement or refund, only to be told by the smart arse at the counter that he would send it back for the manufacturer to consider. After explaining that my contract was with the dealership, not the manufacturer I ended up (and not for the first or last time in retail establishments) telling him that he either gave me a refund or I would sue the dealership. Please your self was the response from Mr Arse, so I went back to the office and issued proceedings for my £10.

Shortly afterwards, the owner of Byers Dunn Turvey telephoned his friend Mr Reed who assured him the problem would go away, which resulted in John Cooper approaching me about the matter. He rightly said I shouldn't have used the firm's name on the proceedings and I agreed. I left his room, had the firm's name removed from the proceedings, entered judgement in my own name and later sent the bailiffs in to collect my £10, plus interest and cost of the proceedings. I accept I was at fault here for being headstrong, but it was my father's genes in me making me unprepared to take shit from anyone, whatever the risk. Strangely the subject was never raised again, but I had been marked down as trouble which when provoked, I agree I can be. In the not too distant future, Reed would attempt to strangle my career without having the courage to face me directly. Perhaps his view was that I wasn't worth the personal contact, but I was evidently worth the time trying to destroy. The act would fail and leave me with no respect for him.

It's worth explaining that my career had taken a turn at this stage. I had passed the intermediate legal executive examinations and, by taking correspondence courses and working at home in the evenings, I had also passed the fellowship examinations meaning that I was academically qualified. However, the minimum age of admittance to the Institute of Legal Executives was 25; I was only 21 and therefore too young. So I decided to try and qualify as a solicitor which meant entering into a four year term of articles. If I passed the examinations I would be a solicitor at the age of twenty five, more or less the age I would have qualified had I gone to university and, ironically, around about the same time I would have been enrolled as a Fellow of the Institute of Legal Executives. Reed had agreed to the articles and therefore we had entered into a four year contract with each other. Perhaps both parties were beginning to doubt the wisdom of the deal.

Despite deciding to do my articles, I very much saw Geoff Cardwell and myself as being at more or less the same level and certainly, we were doing the same work. Having persuaded Geoff that we deserved a pay rise, we made a joint approach to John Cooper. Following that conversation Palmer tried to divide us. He attempted to persuade me that I was in a totally different league to Geoff and was heir to a partnership. When that failed he offered me a large pay rise to take on Geoff's work as well as my own. Looking back now, I don't think he realised how much work we did. I knew we both had to get out, although I didn't tell Geoff of the conversation until he was safely employed elsewhere.

My route out would take a lot longer because of my four year agreement with Reed, but I saw an advertisement for a legal executive's job at Tyne and Wear County Council which I suggested Geoff apply for. On the day of the application deadline Geoff admitted he hadn't completed the application form I had given him, so I sat with him whilst he filled it in and then drove him to Newcastle to deliver it. He must have thought he was using the wrong deodorant such was my determination for him to leave! There were many candidates for the job, but he was successful and duly left to take up his job with Tyne and Wear County Council on twice his former salary.

Geoff wasn't replaced, so I ended up with his work as well as my own anyway, with only the small pay rise we'd both received. Others had also left so when I saw a job advertised at another council for a legal executive on double the salary I was getting, I decided to apply for it. When I went for the interview I found I was shortlisted with ten other candidates. After the last interview the clerk came out and asked me and one of the other candidates to wait, instructing the others to claim their expenses and leave.

Summoned back in, I wondered if I would be taking on the other candidate in unarmed combat for the position! Instead the very charming chairman said they were impressed by me and the job was mine, but only if I gave up the articles which they couldn't offer at this stage. I was now committed to my chosen path and so I refused the job. I never regretted the decision but began to hate life at Reeds. Despite telling the partners my case load was too great and that I couldn't guarantee mistakes wouldn't happen, no effort was made to recruit or control the work. I knew it was time to go, but I was tied by the articles and transferring this type of contract to another firm was rare. However, my hand was forced in the unlikely form of Tommy Slack who caused me to resign and bugger the consequences.

The incident was about a case that Slack had started. He called me into his room and sitting there smoking a pipe, he explained a little about the client and the case. Slack was in his fifties and had a thick crop of wavy, unusually black hair for a man of his age. He was very tall and had something of an eye twitch which may have been caused by the thick smoke emanating from the furnace at the end of his pipe. He also had a very deep voice and a pronounced South Shields accent as well as an air of self consciousness which bordered on low self esteem. It wasn't something I thought much about despite Palmer's comments because if someone is a solicitor, a partner and pretty well off, what could possibly deflate their self esteem?

Despite already having complained about my heavy workload I took the file and went back to my room, which was overflowing with files. There was the usual crop of afternoon clients to see, but at some stage I rang Tommy Slack's client (who was unavailable) and left a message with the telephonist that I had called. The next day Slack summoned me to his room. He had the file in his hand and had obviously worked himself up for confrontation, which I imagine was alien to him. Squinting more than usual he raised his voice and said,

"I told you to ring this man yesterday and you completely ignored me."

"No, I did not. I rang him and left a message." I replied

"No you didn't, just do as you are told and ring him." he shouted.

"I have just told you that I did ring him and I left a message despite having a full list of clients." I responded. At that, a now out of control Slack flung the file across the desk demanding I did as I was told. I had had enough. I stormed out of his room straight into John Cooper's office, told him of the exchange and that I was resigning. Cooper jumped up and said he was sure something could be worked out, but it couldn't. It wasn't just this incident but the firm's failure to replace staff which simply placed more burdens on the remaining staff, not just me. I was soon due to sit my first Solicitors examination and was off from that night for study leave, so I gave a month's notice effective from my return.

I went home that night acutely aware that I had just one month to find a new employer. I was relieved things had reached a head, but little did I know that there was a partners' meeting taking place at Reed's where they concluded that I was likely to sue them. Nor did I know that they were conspiring to create a different set of circumstances with which to defend themselves, and that Reed, a man who was established and reasonably wealthy, would take the time and energy to try and end my career.

CHAPTER 10: Time to move again

I rang my brother Brian that evening asking if he knew of any firms in Newcastle who were recruiting. Ironically, Brian had telephoned me a year earlier with the same question and I had arranged an interview with what were to become his current employers. Brian said he would make some calls the following day and I said I would do the same.

I was on leave to take the accounts module of the Solicitors examination, which was the only one that could be taken on its own, but my search for an employer who would agree to the transfer of my articles term left little time for revising. I managed to get an interview with a firm called Hay and Kilner, and Brian arranged one with Mincoff, Science and Gold, both Newcastle firms.

I duly turned up at Hay and Kilner to be interviewed by three partners, who already knew of me from court appearances and cases where I was up against them. The interview went well and I explained why I was leaving and told them most of what had happened, but not laying it on too thickly as it is easy to sound paranoid. They thanked me for being honest and more or less said they weren't surprised to hear of turmoil at Reeds. The senior partner said they were very pleased to receive my application and were sure I would fit in with the team which was expanding. So well were things going that they showed me my room and where I would be working. Both salary and articles were agreed. I said I had an interview with another firm later in the week and they said they would get a formal offer out to me. However, just before I went for the interview at Mincoffs, the senior partner from Hay and Kilner rang me and was clearly very uncomfortable. He stuttered and stammered through an explanation of not being in a position to offer me a job, as there were no vacancies at the moment. Totally surprised, I reminded him of the expansion comment and the room showing, which increased his discomfort, but there was no doubt that the promised job was withdrawn.

I went for my interview with Mincoffs and met Harry Mincoff, a lawyer who had received national acclaim for representing Linda Desramault in an international child custody dispute with the French courts, which had involved a meeting with the British Prime Minister. He was joined in the interview by his partner Austen Science. The offices were in the centre of Newcastle and again the interview went well. Harry Mincoff was a short man in his sixties who wore thick glasses which gave him the look of Mr Magoo the cartoon character, but he was a clever advocate of immense charm and likeability. Science had a more serious disposition, was in his forties and was more searching in his questions. Again I was told that I was the type of lawyer they were looking for and they would get back to me.

The setback with Hay and Kilner concerned me and it was clear that something had happened involving Reeds. It became clearer when I received a letter from Reeds inviting me to attend a partners meeting to discuss my handling of a case that had caused them some concern. The letter failed to mention my resignation and ended with the phrase, 'The partners hope you will take this opportunity to restore a proper relationship. As best as I can remember this was my reply:-

Dear Sirs,

I refer to your letter dated the 8th of the month which arrived on the 13th, the day after the meeting you invited me to attend. You will of course understand that it was impossibility for me to attend the meeting. It came as a surprise to receive your letter as I did in fact resign my employment on the day I left for study leave, for reasons fully explained to Mr Cooper. If the case causing concern is the case of ******* given to me by Mr Slack, the concern expressed by him was that I had not telephoned the client when in fact I had and had left a message with the client. I intend to serve out my notice upon my return from study leave.

Yours faithfully

A call then came from Austen Science asking me to go for a second interview the following day. He asked me one or two minor questions and then said, "Well John, we were impressed with you on interview but Harry Mincoff has received a call from Richard Reed. We made no contact with them, but Mr Reed chose to ring Harry telling him not to employ you, as you are a trouble maker and somebody to avoid. He told Harry that he has also telephoned Hay and Kilner and warned them off." As I struggled to disguise my amazement and fury he continued, "Of course you told us of the problems which was to your credit. Anyway we don't like people trying to tell us what to do, so the job is yours if you want it." I have never forgotten that moment or the sentiment. Austen Science and I did not always see eye to eye on everything, but I always respected him (and the firm) for their stance against Reed's despicable and cowardly act of revenge. I did go back to Reeds and on the first morning walked into John Cooper's room with a written resignation and said,

"There seems to have been some confusion in your mind as to our last conversation, so for the avoidance of doubt this is my written resignation."

"Thank you" was his meek reply as he looked to the ground.

I proceeded to work my last four weeks, placing progress notes on each file and adding my recommendations to all my cases. I must confess that I quite enjoyed working my notice as the partners were clearly uncomfortable and not one of them had the courage to either come and see me or send me home; a small revenge. After I left, one of the secretaries confirmed the panic my resignation caused and their attempts to engineer concerns about my work, as a defence against the proceedings they were sure I would bring against them. In fact I never had any such intention and was just delighted to be out of such an oppressive and unfriendly atmosphere. I knew I would never be a party to any such atmosphere in any firm that I started or was involved in.

A couple of years later, the poisonous atmosphere boiled over between the partners leading to Tony Palmer leaving to set up on his own, and I am afraid the story had the most unhappy of endings for Palmer. Tragically one of Tony's children died and then to add to his misery, he was reported to the Law Society for misconduct. I spoke to him about it and there was no suggestion of theft, but concerned misleading a firm of solicitors on a property transaction which just seemed to get out of hand. The upshot was that he was suspended for a year which meant he could not work.

Many times I have corrected clients who've said 'things can't get any worse', reminding them that things can always get worse and to guard against it. In Tony's case 'worse' was the diagnosis of a brain tumour which was said to be both terminal and inoperable. Typical of him, he researched it and found a surgeon prepared to operate. I was appearing in a court in Newcastle and was talking to my opponent when I heard Tony's unmistakable loud voice, who, having recognised my voice boomed,

"Is that Ginger, pretending to be a solicitor?"

I turned to give him an appropriate response to see him gazing into space and holding a white stick. The operation had removed most of the tumour, but had rendered him blind. As I struggled to say something, he said with alarming cheerfulness,

"Yes I am a blind twat, but I am still here." He was not to survive long and died at a terribly young age.

The partners at Reeds taught me two things: that bickering between themselves or having a poor relationship with each other was counterproductive, and that treating staff poorly or a failing to ensure staff were happy at work damaged the fabric of the firm, however many clients it had. I was so happy to be out of the Sunderland practice that even today I can remember my first morning in Newcastle with my new employer, Mincoff, Science and Gold. I remember parking my car in a car park and walking over the bridge to their offices in the centre of the city and it was all I could do to stop myself skipping through the morning throng. I was in a new city and it was a new start, but as ever it wouldn't be straightforward.

CHAPTER 11: In the city

It was the summer of 1976 and my new office was Plummer House on Market Street in Newcastle's city centre. On my first day I was introduced to three articled clerks, one of whom was Gordon Brown, not the future prime minister but a trainee starting on the same day. Gordon and I hit it off immediately and were to spend the next two years having a great time which would include forming sports teams, inventing games in the office mainly for the two of us to play, and occasionally finding some time for work and clients. We were both very keen sportsmen and soon joined a newly formed sports club at the Eldon Square Centre. The firm supported us with a Mincoffs five-a-side football team as well as a badminton night once a week. We also formed a cricket team and invited young lawyers and businessmen from the city to both play for and against us. They were something of an eclectic mix, ranging from the fairly gifted to the physically challenged and the combination led to some great and some not quite so great sporting days.

I remember one football match we had organised against the local barristers, our future judges, who were playing a game that was probably totally unfamiliar to them. One such barrister, a man in his late thirties, educated in a public school and as polite as it is possible for a person to be, was running, or strolling quickly down the right wing with his right hand extended and calling out *'TO ME IF YOU CAN, TO ME IF YOU CAN'* which was not a phrase I had ever heard on Match of the Day! I was played through by Brown and for once managed to control the ball and slide it past the goalkeeper to put us one up. A few minutes later I found myself in the same position and this time decided to go around the keeper. I moved to my right, the goalkeeper dived but missed me and I rolled the ball passed him. Just as I was shaping to side-foot the ball into the empty net my legs were taken from me and I slid without the ball, swallowing mud as I ploughed a few yards on my stomach,
"PENALTY" I roared, spitting out most of the debris.
"NONSENSE" was the reply from my assailant who was to sit on the judicial benches for many years afterwards. The referee, sensibly investing for his legal future called no foul, instead deciding that in sight of an empty net, I must have been hit by a bolt of invisible lightening that had taken my legs from under from me. I mean, if it wasn't a foul, what other explanation could there possibly be? But hey, if that's what a judge decides so be it.

Brown and I invented a lot of games such as knocking a coin off a desk with a sponge ball, flicking rubber bands at flies on the window using one hand only, plus indoor cricket or football in the basement. On one particular summer's day Gordon told me he was a master of the paper aeroplane and naturally, this led to a challenge. The contest to see who could build the best looking plane and fly the furthest began. We had moved to our new palatial Jesmond office in 1977 and being on the top floor had plenty of air current available. After floating eight or nine of these inventions, Gordon sent one swirling into the sun filled street, but we lost sight of it after a few seconds. A couple of minutes later Austen Science's secretary rang to ask us if we knew anything about paper aeroplanes. When we asked why, she said that Mr Science was in a meeting with an important client and he and the client were shocked when a paper plane flew through the open window and twice around his desk. I think that was the winner!

I'm a pretty decent mimic and, in my view, anyone who takes themselves too seriously is fair game. A new articled clerk joined the firm, a pleasant enough but serious lad who worked in the room next to me. I could see him from my desk and would ring him on the internal telephone, doing a very passable impersonation of Peter Hedworth, one of the partners.

"Come down Boy" I said, which was a phrase Hedworth used.

The young lawyer would say he was on his way and would return perplexed a few minutes later. I knew that the eccentric Hedworth would in all probability continue with his work when his surprise guest arrived, as well as ignore him and that the guest was unlikely to ask what he wanted. Over a period of two or three weeks I did this several times until Hedworth, passing me in the corridor said,

"Would I be right in assuming you are responsible for Smith coming into my room on a regular basis?" I paused for a second or two and then said, "You would."

"Thought so," he replied as he walked off.

There were three Jewish and two non Jewish partners at Mincoffs and it was an interesting mix. The Jewish partners were much more part of their own community, although friendly enough with everyone else. I got a little taste of that at one of the Christmas parties (yes, strange that a predominantly Jewish firm had a Christmas party). Mincoffs Christmas parties had something of a reputation in the city for being lively affairs. We were asked to go and collect the booze for the night, which comprised huge quantities of beer and wine. No spirits were provided and on asking why, Howard Gold told me they'd made a policy decision not to do so because people got too drunk and made fools of themselves. One of the staff subsequently told me that a local bank manager had been caught with a girl on Harry Mincoff's desk. Anyway, enjoying the party I spotted a striking Jewish girl of about my own age with long black hair, shapely body and cheeky grin. During the course of the evening we got talking, then dancing and then discreetly I thought, kissing in the corner. I knew she was a friend of the receptionist and as we parted I said I would be in touch. The following Monday, the receptionist spoke to me and said she had been told by one of the partners not to give me the girl's number. The girl had been spoken to and told not to see me again, but to look for a good Jewish boy. She said it was nothing personal and certainly nobody would speak to me about it as it was a community matter and that would be improper. Anyway, I never saw her again.

I was enjoying this new life and all that it entailed. I had rented a flat in Fawdon just outside Newcastle, which was perfect for me. It was small, but the block was recently built and the rent included the services. The flat comprised a kitchen area with a sitting room, a bedroom with a small balcony overlooking the area and as I was on the fifteenth floor it had a great view. There was a separate bathroom and even a garage for my car. I had bought some furniture and a television, and loved the fact that I was independent. One night whilst at home with a girlfriend I heard a disturbance in the street below. I opened the balcony doors and saw three or four youths knocking over dustbins and trying car door handles to see if they would open. Reverting to my village life personality I bellowed at them so loudly that they scattered in all directions, looking up as they ran to see this enraged madman with a foghorn voice. What I hadn't seen was my middle aged gay neighbour watching them from his balcony, unaware of my presence until I shouted and I think I nearly frightened him to death. As I stormed back in to put on my shoes, he turned to my girlfriend and said in a Larry Grayson voice, *'Ooo, hasn't he got a powerful voice?'* He probably thought he was living next door to a homicidal maniac!

My morning drive into work was much shorter now and I also had easier access to Newcastle's night life, which was a bonus. The firm had moved to premises in Jesmond, which is a very nice part of Newcastle just outside the city centre. Spread over several floors, we saw the premises as opulent and life seemed to be good for everyone. When I first joined Mincoff, Science and Gold there were five partners, Harry Mincoff, Austen Science, Howard Gold, Peter Hedworth and Mike Smith. The other partner in the firm's name, Howard Gold, was the other Jewish partner. He was in his thirties, trendy and very affable. He was the property partner and had an open door policy where people walked in and out of his huge office all day. Always smiling, he was obviously very popular with his clients and I cannot remember ever seeing him in a bad mood. Peter Hedworth on the other hand was a strange personality altogether. He was tall and slim, wore spectacles and was always smartly dressed for his role as a criminal partner. Criminal practice in this city was very different to what I had been used to in Durham City or Sunderland. This was proper crime involving criminal families and was on a much bigger scale, but more of Hedworth later.

The other partner and the youngest was Mike Smith who was the matrimonial partner. He wore a beard and almost tried too hard to be friendly with the staff and the trainees. He seemed to lack confidence and, smelling too much of it in me, would ask me to do his more difficult applications at court. When asked why, he would explain there was a difficult opponent, or an unhelpful judge, or some problem that required a personality like mine to deal with it. One time I said,

"Do you mean you need a twat to do it?"

He said yes and then added, "You are different to me John, you don't care what people think and you're not bothered who is on the other side."

"Oh, you mean you need an arrogant twat?" I added! That told me more about him than me. He was likeable however and I always obliged when he asked me to do anything. Sometimes that meant being handed a case file that was due in court in an hour. It came with a five minute explanation and off I went. They didn't all run smoothly however. I met up with one of his female clients for a contested maintenance hearing in the County Court in Newcastle, went briefly through the facts with her and then we were in front of the judge. She went into the witness box and I took her through her evidence without a hitch. When she was cross examined by my opponent all was going well until he asked,

"Mrs X, you are not working are you?"

"No, I have children to look after." she replied.

"Well you say that, but you were working when you lived with your husband and your children were younger."

"I don't know what you mean." she meekly responded.

"What I mean is that after starting these proceedings you gave up your job."

"Well yes, but that is because my lawyer told me to as I would get more money off my husband."

The floor opened and a hole emerged to swallow me up!

Harry Mincoff was my principal and I felt very fortunate. He had started the firm and along with his partners had built it up into an impressive business. He was always friendly, called me either son or boy in a fatherly way and would introduce me as *'a firebrand we have recently taken on to shake people up'*. I hadn't been at the firm long when the first Law Society dinner took place in Newcastle and the articled clerks were taken along. At the end of the evening we were invited to go on to Greys Club, which was then a very trendy nightclub and casino, and somewhere we would not normally be able to afford. Off we went in our dinner suits thinking of ourselves as a collection of James Bonds. Very cool it was too, with its mood lighting and gambling tables. Several of what must have been regular frequenters of Greys kept asking each other if Harry was in tonight and I made a joke to Gordon Brown that maybe they were talking about our boss. A few minutes later a door opened and there was Mincoff with a good looking girl on each arm. The assembled crowd gravitated towards him as though the Emperor had walked in and they could have walked into the open mouths of Brown and me.

Although Harry was short, middle aged, bespectacled and limping, he was charismatic. He had in his time been a very good racket sports player and once told me he got most of his first group of clients from the tennis club. He even joined us once on the badminton night at Eldon Square. In he came with his 'Eric Morecambe' shorts on, bandaged knees and extra thick glasses and asked Gordon and myself if we wouldn't mind playing an old man. Gordon and I were in our early twenties, fit and the best two players in the group. Anxious not to embarrass a boss for whom we had a lot of affection and wondering how we could make him look good, we played him in turn. We really had nothing to worry about. He positioned himself in the middle of the court and unless our shot was on the back line or dropped dead at the net, he would reach out and with immense skill flick the shuttlecock to all parts of our court. Every now and again he would say *'Good shot Son'*, but in the main he ran us around like we were being chased by a lion. We were covered in sweat, red faced and we both lost! I am not sure Harry had a style of management, but he was such a nice guy that you didn't want to disappoint him. He once asked me to instruct a barrister for him on a new matter and I prepared the very briefest of briefs. He called me down to his room and had my work in his hand.
 "What exactly is this, Son?" he said gently.
"Instructions to Counsel" I replied.
"Yes, but there are no instructions, no narrative as to what it's about and no help for the barrister." he pleaded.

"I did think of that, but I just felt it best to outline the facts and get an unbiased opinion rather than cloud his judgement with too much information or repeating the documents that are there." I answered with my normal readiness to fight a corner.

"Oh Son you know what I want, can you just do it please? I don't want to fight."

"Of course" I said as I slinked out of the room half the size I was when I went in.

In the first year at Mincoffs I worked on Peter Hedworth's criminal team. Hedworth was very different and I can't say I disliked him, but he was eccentric to say the least. In some ways he was like Tony Palmer in that he was outspoken, assertive and sometimes very rude. He had a strange sense of humour that could be caustic, but on the whole was much more relaxed than Palmer. Hedworth and another Newcastle lawyer called Brad Stephens acted for almost all of the major criminals in the city, which made both of them very unpopular with the police in a way that Harry Mincoff never was.

I always felt conflicted on criminal issues at Mincoffs, presumably because of my father. I had no problem representing criminals, but too close an association was unacceptable to me. Hedworth told me that if he went out anywhere he would leave a contact number at home, so that he could be reached if any of these criminal families needed him. I found this incredible and asked him if he didn't think he should have some free time and that his family was entitled to that. He just told me that his family's bills were paid by this work and if he didn't take the calls they would simply move to Brad Stephens. You have to remember that these were the days before mobile phones.

In the first year at Mincoffs I worked on Hedworth's criminal team and dealt with every type of crime you can think of including murder, rape, incest, fraud and protection racketeering. Every day I would be at a police station, prison or Crown Court and sometimes all three. Criminal law was then something that young lawyers experienced almost straight away, as Crown Court duty didn't require any great expertise and often we would just sit behind a barrister in court. It is a subject most members of the public are familiar with too, thanks to television and film. I never really intended to specialise in criminal work, but I'm glad I experienced the work. The next chapter highlights some of the antics of being on the other side of my father's side of the fence and I can still very much feel him frowning.

CHAPTER 12: A life of crime

My first experience of criminal law was as a young teenager, somewhat adrift amongst the criminals and the court system at Durham Assize Courts. Here at Mincoffs some years on, l was now very experienced both in the system of law and with its practitioners. However, this was a much bigger league of criminal practice with a more extreme type of criminal. The casual or occasional criminal and the totally committed but inept criminal family of three generations of thieves were also represented at Mincoffs, but alongside were the more efficient and professional criminals. These varied from families that ran protection rackets with a ferocious and ruthless determination, to extremely violent individuals who had committed random acts of violence, including murder.

On an early meeting with Harry Mincoff he said to me,
"Have you seen my photographs Son?"
"No l don't think l have" l replied, wondering what he meant.
"Have a look at this one; he was involved in a fight." Out of his desk drawer Harry pulled a photograph of the face and torso of a man who had one eye closed with a massive swelling, crushed nose, split ear and a gouged slash across his chest as though he'd been hit with an axe.
"Wow, he looks in a bad way." l offered
"He was the winner. Do you want to see the loser?" asked Harry excitedly with a big smile on his face.
"Yes please... l think." l tentatively responded.
Harry produced his second photograph of a man, obviously unconscious, whose face was so swollen that there were no discernible features to see. The head had been so badly beaten that the ears had disappeared into the swollen ball of a head which had also swallowed up the eyes. The lips had grown to more than twice their normal size, which made him look like an eyeless fish.
"Nice." l added, handing back the photograph as he pulled out another.
"l acted for this lady's husband." Harry said, as he handed me another snap this time of a dead woman sitting against a wall with her arms limp by her side and her head tilted to her left as though she was asleep. To the right of her bloodstains extended from her head rising ten feet up to the ceiling, making her look like an exaggerated peacock.
"He killed her with a big breadknife, hitting her on top of her head which is why the bloodstains are shooting up the walls."

"Had he never heard of divorce?" I responded, to Harry's amusement.

My first few months at Mincoffs saw me involved in all aspects of its large criminal practice. As I knew my way around the courts and had a car, I was the obvious choice amongst the articled clerks to go to police stations, prisons, Crown Courts and occasionally criminals' homes if they were the subject of arrests or search warrants. I remember an early occasion when Peter Hedworth asked me to go immediately to an address in Newcastle, where one of his regulars was just about to have his house searched. I drove to the address, got there before the police and asked the man if he knew what they might be looking for. Of course he had no idea and was mystified as to why the police thought he might have something that didn't belong to him. Probably the hundreds of previous convictions for theft and handling stolen goods may have had something to do with it! Anyway, two police cars arrived and two detectives plus two uniformed officers walked in. For those of you who watched the BBC series Life on Mars, set in the 1970's, I can assure you it was quite accurate as to the exchanges between police and criminals.

"Oh, we have a brief here today lads." one of the detectives said, looking at me as if I had stolen his wife.

"Indeed you do, can I see your warrant please?" I replied giving him full eye contact.

"Give him the paper Stan," he said to his colleague and the warrant was thrust into my hand. I read it carefully as it was quite likely to be a shopping list or a warrant for somebody else. In fact it was in order and I told them to continue. I sat with the client and his wife for the next twenty minutes or so as they answered the odd question put to them as the officers rumbled through the furniture.

"Is this a loft Billy?" one of the detectives shouted from upstairs.

"Yes" said Billy the bad boy.

I heard the noise of a chair being scraped across the floor and the loft door being pushed open. There was then the clear sound of a man being pushed up into the loft, a moment's pause and then

"Aye, aye Billy, any reason why there are five new television sets up here? Oh hang on and six car radios? And what's this? Oh, some more televisions."

Billy and his wife looked at me without a moment's embarrassment as I gave the standard advice to say nothing unless Billy had an innocent explanation. Needless to say he didn't. A detective came downstairs, arrested Billy and very politely asked me if I wanted to go to the station with him. I replied that I did and I wanted to be there when he was questioned. The detective said they were taking him to the police station in the west of the city and I said I would meet them there. I went to my car and waited as they put him into one of the cars and set off. When we reached the first junction the car carrying my client stopped and waited, even though there was no traffic. After a few seconds, the car pulled out and sped off to the left. They'd been waiting for traffic to arrive and had pulled out in front of it so that I was left waiting for the junction to clear. I thought that their tactics were a waste of time, as I knew the station very well. I couldn't speed because of the other police car, but got to the station in reasonable time anyway. I approached the desk and asked to see my client, only to be told that he wasn't there and neither were the detectives. They'd lied to me and taken him elsewhere. After much argument, the desk sergeant discovered that Billy had been taken to a station in the north of the city. By the time I got there he had been interviewed, had admitted all offences and been charged. When I got the chance to talk to him, I asked why he hadn't waited and he said,

"Well in the car the copper said 'let's get rid of the brief first' and then they lost you in traffic. Then they got me in here and bounced me."

"Bounced you?" I enquired, a little bemused.

"Yeah" he sighed, still thinking I knew what he meant.

"What do you mean?"

"You know, pick yer off the chair by yer lapels and bounce yer off the seat a few times. It knocks all the air out of yer."

So this was the world of criminals, criminal law and police stations in the 1970's. When the PACE regulations were brought in, which regulated treatment in a police station and gave what seemed to be ground breaking rights to those arrested, we all wondered how convictions would ever be achieved.

My business partner to be, Malcolm Donnelly told me that when he worked as a lawyer for the Police Prosecutions Department (a forerunner of the Crown Prosecutions Service) he was going through a number of files with a couple of police officers and commented on the number of confessions there were and that without them, there was not much in the way of evidence. The sergeant asked him what he meant and he replied that he just couldn't understand why so many had confessed when, if they kept quiet, they may get away with it. The sergeant asked Malcolm if he really wanted to know why they'd confessed and he said he did. With that the burly police officer put his forearm under Malcolm's chin and in one movement, lifted him off the chair and pinned him against the wall by his throat.

"Feel like confessing now?" he was asked.

Malcolm also told me that he had appeared at crown court on a prosecution and sat behind the barrister representing what was a fairly normal case. The principal police officer, giving evidence against the accused, was being cross examined by the barrister for the defence.

"Tell me Officer, how can you be so sure that my client used the exact words you gave in your evidence?"

"Because I wrote them in my pocket book as soon as I could," he replied.

"Was that on the same day?"

"Yes sir it was."

"Can you remind me of what my client said when you arrested him?"

"May I check my pocket book, Your Honour?" the officer asked the judge who nodded that he could. The officer proceeded to take the note book from his top pocket and flicked through a number of pages. "Yes here it is, on the 20th of April I entered the address 15 Station Street and upon seeing David Brown told him I was arresting him on suspicion of aggravated assault. I read him his rights and he said 'I knew you'd be coming, but you can fuck off because Jimmy got what he deserved'. He then said 'he has been asking for that for a long time and a lot of people will be happy'."

"You say you wrote that down that day Officer?"

"Yes sir."

"What about the interview at the police station?"

"May I check my pocket book again, Your Honour?" the officer politely and correctly asked.

"Yes here it is. I repeated his rights and David Brown replied 'you can fuck off, I am not saying anymore because I don't want to do time for that fat bastard'."

"Did you record the time of the interview?"

"May I check my pocket book, Your Honour?" The judge nodded again in some exasperation.

"Ah yes we arrived at 7.36 pm and the interview commenced at 7.56 pm."

"May I see the pocket book?" the barrister asked extending his right hand and the court clerk walked over to the policeman, collected the book and slowly ambled to the barrister presenting the book as a butler might present a parcel to his master. The barrister flicked through the book for a few seconds and then looked up at the policeman in the witness box. Fixing him with a stare, he said,

"This book is completely empty Officer."

The accused may have said those things, but nothing was in the book and yes the officer was perjuring himself. Neither I nor Malcolm can remember what happened to the policeman, but this was a sign of the times. We didn't live in a police state and certainly the vast majority of police officers were honest, but there was a feeling which still may prevail today that they were fighting a war against an enemy that knew how to exploit the system and to stand a chance of winning, they would have to do the same. I suppose my background made me an uncomfortable aide to the other side, but I had a job to do and I would do it.

The police stations in and around Newcastle at the time were representative of the area in which they were situated. If I had to go to Gosforth police station, an affluent part of the city, I would find a semi open plan office with a smiling policeman at a comfortable desk politely enquiring how he could help me. On the other hand if I went to a rougher part of the city, the station would be like the security wing of a prison with a closed wooden reception window and bars everywhere. One such visit involved the arrest of one of the firm's regulars and in I went to the fortified station and knocked on the wooden shutter. Having asked to see my client, the shutter was slammed so quickly that I felt a breeze across my face. On my second request a few minutes later I was told to wait and this time the shutter was nearly pulled off its hinges. On my third request I played my trump card and said I was making a formal complaint. This involved the senior officer having to see me which he duly did. He was a charming inspector, who said to me,
"Let me tell you something Mr McArdle, we have had nine official complaints this year and eight of them are from your firm."
Having told him he could avoid a tenth by letting me see my client, he duly obliged but I was given a look of 'your brake lights better be in order' as I left the room. The routine of a criminal defence lawyer involves all parts of the process of the crime apart from actually committing it. You are called upon at the time of arrest or sometimes before, as in the case of a search, then at the police station, at the Magistrates Court, then prison if they are remanded in custody and finally if the crime is serious enough, at the Crown Court for trial.

There were several Crown Courts in Newcastle at that time ranging from a Victorian court called The Moot Hall, a Georgian building restored in 1875 into a criminal court, to Kenton Bar Crown Court which was a modern building. Each had their own characteristics and I always had difficulty persuading clients in civil trials at The Moot Hall that they were not in trouble. The conference room was a Victorian cell with high windows and evidence was given in a Victorian Dock with iron spikes all around it. It was pretty intimidating. At Kenton Bar the difficulty I had was staying awake, particularly in winter when the central heating was on and the low hum of the fluorescent lights had us all drifting off through evidence and speeches. I adopted a technique of sitting behind my defence barrister and propping a file on my knee with the file leaning against the desk, open at a document. I would then place my right hand against my right temple as though deep in thought and doze off in controlled circumstances. Adopting this position in one trial, I was awoken by loud snoring. Initially thinking it was me I was relieved when I realised it was coming from behind me. Turning, I saw an obese prison officer with his ample head buried into his even more ample chest. His snoring was rhythmical and developed into a huge nasal elephant-like intake of breath and a lip quivering exhale capable of blowing an in-range barrister's wig off! This increasing noise alerted the jury who started to giggle and finally the Judge turned to the Usher.

"I think we need to do something about that," he said pointing at the unfortunate snorer. Our eyes followed the Usher as he slowly approached the man and tugged his sleeve. On the third tug the uniformed walrus roused with a final snort and looked around in complete shock, turning quickly to make sure the prisoner he was guarding was still there and evidently wondering if anyone noticed he was asleep!

My real abiding memory of that court was a case involving a man from Blyth in Northumberland who, shall we say, was no stranger to the courts. He'd only been out of prison for a few months and was charged with another serious offence of violence, which he vehemently denied. Our barrister that day was a somewhat portly ex dentist named Gerard Harkins who went on to become a judge. Mr Harkins was very familiar to me as a somewhat theatrical lawyer who liked to flounce into conference rooms and flounce even more so into the court room. Harkins breezed into our meeting before the court appearance, nodded at me, dropped his papers onto the desk with a troubled expression on his face and addressed our client.

"Well Paul, I have looked at the papers very carefully and I'm afraid we have no chance at all of an acquittal and I fear with your record you are facing a very long sentence. If you change your plea to guilty I feel I can persuade this judge to be lenient."

"NOT GUILTY" responded Paul from Blyth, without a change of expression.

"Paul, I'm afraid you don't understand. You will be found guilty and will go to prison for a very long time, whereas I can halve it if you let me."

"NOT GUILTY" stated Paul from Blyth again.

"Look you have to trust me on this; I know what I am doing"

"NOT GUILTY" Paul from Blyth said emphatically.

"FOR GOODNESS SAKE MAN YOU SHOULD DO AS I TELL YOU, I HAVE A TRAINED MIND," said the exasperated brief. I chipped in that the client had given instructions and we had to act on them, which created a mega flounce, and off we went into the court room. The trial started and it was clear that the prosecution case was a shambles and there was little or no evidence to prove beyond a doubt that our client was guilty. Eventually the judge, adopting an irritated tone, turned to the prosecution barrister and asked him if this really was all of the evidence the prosecution had against the defendant or if they had anything else. When the prosecutor confirmed there was nothing else the judge turned to Harkins and said,

"Mr Harkins in the light of what we have both heard, I imagine you have an application to make to me."

Harkins somewhat taken aback popped up and said,

"Err yes Your Honour, I submit there is no case to answer and the defendant should be discharged."

"Application granted, case dismissed, the defendant is free to go." said the judge.

The advice given to Paul from Blyth only a couple of hours earlier was a little wide of the mark and I could hardly contain the smirk on my face as we trooped off back to the conference room. Harkins stomped into the room, took off his wig, dropped the papers with a thud onto the desk and turned to the client saying,

"Well there it is. I didn't think I could pull it off, but I have." Priceless! Without any change of expression Paul from Blyth shook his hand, then mine and was gone. The interesting part of a jury hearing is that the jury has all of the power. They often look like a collection of people from the street, which I suppose they are, but they really do decide the outcome of a criminal trial despite the best efforts of the lawyers and the judge. The same Mr Harkins was again conducting the defence for us in a jury trial and was facing a judge who appeared unimpressed with him and, in addition, was massively pro the police. Generally a judge wouldn't interrupt very much and would rarely do so when Counsel was addressing the jury, but the judge did so when Harkins made his opening remarks to the jury. Harkins had been polite and deferential to the judge however a pressure cooker had been ignited. When Harkins was cross examining the police officer, the judge interrupted him again saying,

"Just so that I understand the position Mr Harkins, are you saying that this police officer of twenty years standing is making the WHOLE thing up and telling this jury a pack of lies?"

Harkins: "I am putting to the officer an alternative position, Your Honour."

Judge: "Carry on."

After a few more questions the Judge again interrupts,

"So Mr Harkins, are you saying that this officer of twenty years standing, not only made the whole thing up but went to the police station and persuaded his colleagues, no doubt all very experienced officers, to tell a pack of lies?"

Harkins: "Yes"

Judge: "Very well carry on"

After another two or three interruptions Harkins eventually exploded, turned to the jury on his left and with a bright red face and droplets of spittle firing from his mouth shrieked,

"THERE YOU HAVE IT MEMBERS OF THE JURY. I AM NOT EVEN ALLOWED TO ASK QUESTIONS" and sat down. The judge remained very calm, no doubt feeling that he was winning the day and invited Mr Harkins to continue. At the end of the trial the judge summed up after both Counsel and said,

"Members of the jury, you have heard all of the evidence in this case and it is entirely a matter for you to decide which evidence you prefer. You heard from three police officers, who you might think were very impressive and convincing in their evidence. On the other hand you have the evidence of the defendant and his witnesses and you may think they were a good deal less impressive. It is entirely a matter for you. You have heard Mr Harkins suggest that the police officers were telling lies (eyes raised to the sky) and that they somehow all got together and concocted a story (hands now upturned in bemusement) and you may wonder why such public servants would do such a thing. It is entirely a matter for you....... finally ladies and gentleman of the jury if the evidence of the prosecution is correct, then the defendant is guilty whereas if the evidence of the defence is to be believed, there is a case for saying that the defendant is still guilty for the reasons I described earlier. It is entirely a matter for you. Please now follow the Court Usher and have your deliberations."

Two hours later the jury returned and in answer to the Clerk's question of how do you find the defendant, guilty or not guilty, the foreman stood his full five feet seven inches and said,

"NOT GUILTY".

For what it's worth, I didn't believe that the defendant was guilty on this occasion and formed the view that the police officers twisted the evidence to fit. This was not an uncommon procedure in those days but the result, along with a number of others reinforced my faith in the jury system. They may often be an odd mixture of people, sometimes asleep, sometimes confused, often distracted, but there is some magic that happens to pull this group of strangers together to try and do what they think is right. I would always want to be tried by a random set of people than by a professional group who think they know just by looking at people, if they are telling the truth and believe they are able to work it all out from limited information. I would include myself in that dangerous group.

I attended court one day to find one of my colleagues from Mincoffs there on a very serious criminal case. One of the bigger criminal clients was charged with a number of offences arising from their protection business in the city. I asked him how long the trial would take and he told me he didn't know because with these people, trials often failed because the witnesses didn't turn up. When I asked if the witnesses had been summoned to appear, he told me that they tended to go missing and may well be in a concrete flyover support somewhere on the M1. I am not sure if that was true, but I knew this was not the work for me. I was not going to spend the rest of my career spinning my father in his grave and being on first name terms with clients whose day job was crime.

Just as my time in the criminal department was coming to an end (I was managing to get some civil litigation work) Mincoffs took on a new case. It was a huge case that, if mishandled it would bankrupt the partners, the firm would close and we would all be out of work. I was twenty two, still three years away from being qualified and they gave it to me.

CHAPTER 13: The firm in my hands

Howard Gold, who was Mincoffs property partner, called me into his office one day saying he had a civil litigation case that was right up my street. Mincoffs was largely a firm that specialised in criminal, property and matrimonial work not civil litigation, but for some reason the case had fallen into Howard's lap. I had already started to bring in some civil litigation cases, but apart from a legal exec that had been with the firm for years, I was the only person doing that kind of work and Howard seemed to have accepted the case with a view to me handling it.

I won't bore you with the detail of the case, but suffice to say that the largest part of it was worth £3.8 million (£36 million today) and my employers had professional indemnity insurance of just £100,000, which was less than 3% of the risk. That the case was taken on was ill judged to say the least; it wasn't Mincoff's area of expertise and they gave it to someone who wasn't qualified. Most firms would have run a mile. Peter Hedworth said to me one day, "I hope you don't cock that case up, because if you do we are all fucked."

No doubt because of the blind confidence of youth I really didn't worry about it and felt pretty confident in handling it. The procedures were the same as in normal value litigation; it was just that everything was on a different scale. To the parties in the case, money was no object and calling me to London for the following day was never the subject of enquiry about expense. These were the days before the internet, email and even the fax machine, which were all still some years off development. Mincoffs had a teletext machine which printed out a ticker tape thin sheet of horizontal message. It proved to be a popular form of communication with Shell's lawyers (Shell was one of the parties involved), who would from time to time drop a bombshell on us of an emergency application in the Supreme Court, or a sudden change of direction on an existing application, all geared to put marbles under our feet.

The first time I was summoned to London I thought it was very glamorous. The head secretary booked my flight from Newcastle Airport to Heathrow and arranged an open train ticket for my return. With full English breakfast served on the plane by a pretty stewardess, what was there not to like? After five or six of these trips I found quite a lot not to like. Getting to the airport for 5.30am, flight delays, taxi rides into the centre of London, aggravation in the Supreme Court, delayed trains and late nights, were but a few. However, l liked the case and enjoyed crossing swords with a different league of lawyer. Our principal barrister was Brian Knight who l hadn't met before. He was a stout man with a large personality, great court presence and a quick wit. He knew his way around the Supreme Court and thought nothing of launching a ferocious attack on his opponents. He had that usual friendly approach to the representative of his instructing solicitor which would be akin to a member of the aristocracy to his estate manager, very polite and friendly on the basis of need, but always retaining an air of superiority. Despite this, l got along with him very well. l made it clear from the beginning that l was not just there to deliver papers to him and that l would be in touch on a regular basis by telephone to discuss tactics and procedure, so that we didn't have any misunderstandings at hearings. Barristers are prone to stand up and give coded messages to judges that say 'this cock up is nothing to do with me. l'm doing my best with very poor instructions from a firm from outside The City and worse than that, a firm from the North!' In case you think l'm an inverted snob, this City of London snobbishness has existed for ever. It used to be that you couldn't make an application in London courts unless you had a London agent. l'm afraid the law has always appealed to those with superiority complexes and it still retains ancient rituals and selection processes to this day.

Early on in the case l received notification of an application and sent instructions to Brian Knight. l flew down to London the next day and arrived just in time to sit behind him in the High Court, awaiting the judge. As l settled in Knight turned to me, already wearing his court wig and said, "Just made it then"
"Yes, taxi stuck in traffic" l replied. l opened the High Court practice book l had brought from the office, known as the White Book and went to the section l had been reading on the plane.
"What do you make of their application?" l whispered to Knight.
"Oh l suppose they are entitled to it" he retorted.
"Not according to Section 29 Rule 5 Paragraph 6" l said, not expecting much of a response.
"Do you have it open on that page?" he enquired as the judge walked in.
l handed the White Book over to him as he rose to his feet with the rest of us, a sign of respect to the judge and we all bowed with Knight still reading the rule.

The judge said good morning to both barristers and invited our opponent to make his application. As he did so, Knight rose to his feet and with a mean sarcastic edge addressed the judge.

"Your Honour I hesitate to speak out of turn, but before we hear the detail of the application I wonder if my learned friend would care to explain how he intends to overcome Section 29 Rule 5 Paragraph 6, which Your Honour will know, precludes this application in its entirety." He sat down with the smug self satisfied grin of a general who had just won a great battle and looked towards his now panicking opponent. There followed a frantic search of the passage within the White Book and a further search of other sections of the book which might conflict before our opponent asked for an adjournment to reconsider.

The judge turned to Knight.

"Do you have any objection to an adjournment Mr Knight?"

"Not at all Your Honour, on the basis that the costs of today are ours."

"I cannot resist a costs order Your Honour" stated our opponent.

The judge duly ordered our opponents to pay our costs of the application and within the hour it was over. Knight turned to me having taken all the plaudits and said,

"That will teach them!"

"You were brilliant and he had no answer," I replied

"Thank you very much," he said with an actor's swagger.

"Good job you thought of that rule" I said with a smile.

"Yes it is" he smiled back.

This was of course a mere skirmish in a long running battle. I got a call from our client's representative, a very engaging managing director who was always ultra polite and correct, and never sought to enquire why someone young enough to be his son was dealing with his large company's case. I imagine he thought I was working under the supervision of one of the partners and of course, I would never have told him that there would be little point in that unless he was thinking of getting divorced, selling his house or getting arrested.

The call was to inform me that some of the other directors were coming into the UK and would like to meet me, Mr Knight and our Queen's Counsel, Mr Keating. By now I was fed up with all of the travelling, but agreed to arrange it despite the fact that I would miss a football match (I kept that bit to myself). I rang Keating's chambers in London to hear what I thought was the good news, that Mr Keating was sitting as a judge in Singapore on a trial that would last six weeks and was therefore unavailable. I rang the managing director and to my horror he asked me to organise the conference in Singapore and we would all fly out there. What? How many football matches would that exclude me from?? Singapore? How far is that? Where the hell is it anyway? I explained that Mr Keating may not be able to accommodate us, but promised to speak to his clerk. Again to my horror, the clerk said that Mr Keating had agreed. It's funny I suppose that my reaction was one of horror as such a trip would have been exciting a few years later, but at the time it was all a massive pain in the arse. Anyway just as the trip was being arranged, Keating's case settled and he was on his way back to London where the meeting eventually took place.

Another factor that was beginning to loom in this case was my forthcoming leave of absence. When I took the job, Mincoffs had agreed to unpaid leave so that I could undertake my Solicitors examinations and the mandatory course at the College of Law. This was a six month period for which I had obtained a grant from the Government to see me through. One of the partners asked me if I would consider postponing the course because of the case, but as there was no guarantee that it wouldn't go on for years, I couldn't. What I agreed to was the appointment of a locum who I would work with before I left. As I had other cases ongoing, a locum seemed like a good idea. The person appointed was Faith Levy, wife of newly appointed partner David. I got along pretty well with Faith, but she was not everyone's cup of tea and irritated the other trainees with a somewhat distant and superior attitude. I tackled this early on and we managed to work together without falling out.

Before her appointment, I told Howard Gold that the case was going well and I thought the client would be expecting an interim bill. Howard wasn't keen and just implored me not to 'fuck it up'. However, the following day Peter Hedworth asked me about the conversation with Howard and asked what I had in mind. I told him I thought £10,000 (approximately £94,000 today) would be about right.
"WHAT?" he exclaimed! I replied that I thought that would be correct and what did he imagine Shell was paying? Almost without hesitation he told me to send it. Hedworth asked me about it regularly over the next couple of weeks and so I rang the managing director to chase it up. He assured me he'd passed it for payment and a few days later payment duly arrived. I thought there may be a bonus, particularly as Hedworth had said they would look after me if I got it in, but nothing was forthcoming. Prior to leaving for college I repeated the process and another £10,000 arrived, but again nothing extra appeared into my meagre bank account.

When I returned from study leave the case was picking up pace and we were asked to work on it exclusively, which was something I had never done. The idea of working the same case day in and day out was unattractive, but I could see the sense of it. An early conference in London with the clients and both barristers brought me up to speed. We were getting ready for trial and Faith had prepared bundles of documents in hard backed folders for the conference and also the forthcoming trial. The meeting held around Mr Keating's desk included three client representatives as well as Faith, me and Brian Knight. As we all settled in, Keating turned to me and said,

"Err, Mr McArdle can I say that these bundles are a bit of a mess. I do not like them presented in this fashion. I like all the documents paginated and properly photocopied. I also like each file to be clearly marked as to its contents. Can you note that for future reference?" I looked at Faith expecting her to say that she had prepared the documents, but she just looked to the floor. It crossed my mind to say that I hadn't prepared the documents, but decided against it and to accept the staring of the clients with a nod. It also crossed my mind to say, 'Oh do you? I like breakfast in bed, my football team winning five nil, and waking up with an attractive woman beside me, but sometimes I have to settle for a lot less. I decided against that one as well! At the end of the conference I sought out Brian Knight and told him that I hadn't prepared the documents and he took the wind out of my sails when he retorted,

"I know you didn't, but I told Keating to have a go at you if he had anything critical to say as I think Faith is on the edge of cracking up. She can't take criticism at the moment, but you're thick skinned. I'm really glad you are back."

He walked away leaving me a little bemused, not knowing whether to still be angry or flattered. I was already very experienced in the tactics of court, but there was ruthlessness about this bigger litigation which taught me a lot.

Our client's managing director told me that he'd received information that Shell had instructed a private investigator to look into the backgrounds of everyone involved in the case, including him and me. I told him that they might use the fact that I'm a Sunderland supporter or a lapsed Catholic against us, but outside that they would be a little bored with me! We pressed on to trial and to the beginning of a hearing that was due to last six weeks. Arriving at the Supreme Court with Faith I recall a room the size of a normal living room, the floor of which was entirely covered with the boxes of documents needed for the case; the result of months of work. However, as often happens in the face of all of this preparation, the trial was delayed as the parties discussed terms. Ultimately the case was settled to the satisfaction of our clients with Shell picking up most, if not all of the cost. My last job on this case was to work on the final bill, which totalled £80,000 (a whopping £752,000 today), which our client paid in full. A promised bonus was talked about a great deal by my colleagues and, as I was approaching my wedding day and had just bought my first house, it would have been useful. The smart money was on £5,000 but in the event that was out by.... £5,000! I received nothing at all. I really wasn't bitter about the situation, as I knew I would not be staying at the firm and the payment of a handsome bonus would have made me feel a little guilty. In addition, I was still grateful for the way the partners responded to the attempt by Richard Reed to scupper my career. It taught me that young lawyers won't always want to stay with the firm they've been trained by, and to never to take someone's strong contribution to your business for granted. In the years that followed I set up several bonus schemes in my own firm and never failed to deliver on them.

I'm not sure if it was the success of the case or the fact that I was the only one in the firm remotely experienced in litigation, but Howard Gold called me in again and told me he was concerned that I might get bored and had therefore secured another massive case for me. This time it involved the city's football team Newcastle United. A group of businessmen, all committed Newcastle United fans, were rebelling against the running of the club and had launched high court proceedings against the club's directors. One of the businessmen was a solicitor who had used his own firm to launch the action, but his partners were now concerned and, feeling out of his depth so was he. They had instructed a local Queen's Counsel, James Chadwin to deal with the matter and legal proceedings were now underway. I told Howard that James Chadwin was a criminal lawyer and as far as I was aware this wasn't his area of expertise. Howard said that I would get my chance to tell him that, as I was to attend a conference with Chadwin and the rebel supporters that night. The dispute was in the news every night on local television, all the local radio stations and in the national press. Talk about a high profile case and once again I was given the advice not to 'fuck it up'.

"Do they know I'm a Sunderland supporter?" I asked Howard.

"No, that's something else you can deal with at the conference" he said laughing.

Just to explain, this was like a lawyer appointed to represent the Palestinian Liberation Organisation saying, *'Hello gentlemen, just before we go any further can I mention that I'm Jewish!'*

So having read what passed for a file of papers, off I went into James Chadwin's chambers in the city to meet our clients. All that was in the file was a writ with a simple explanation that the plaintiffs had no faith in the directors of Newcastle United Football Club. A very detailed explanation in a subsequent document called a 'statement of claim' was promised. Now call me a stickler for detail, but just being a shareholder of a company, whether or not that company is a football club, does not give you a say in how it is run, especially if you are a minority shareholder. If I bought shares in Marks and Spencer I wouldn't be able to go into their stores and demand they change their design of underpants. This was even more so for a private company, which Newcastle United was at the time. It left me feeling I was missing something.

I was reasonably familiar with a number of the rebel supporters through their appearances on television. There was Alex Gibson, who assumed a lead role and was often seen driving away from the cameras in his Rolls Royce. He was a dark haired charming Scottish oil man in his late thirties or early forties and his most recognisable ally was Malcolm Dix, a proprietor of a family business in Newcastle and long outspoken opponent of the directors of the club. I was introduced to everyone and straight away declared my disability of being a lifelong supporter of their dreaded enemy, Sunderland! One or two laughs, one or two glances at each other and then a general well nobody is perfect shrug. So in we went and there was Mr James Chadwin as I remembered him, a small friendly very engaging criminal lawyer. I introduced myself to him and explained that having read the writ I had some concerns about the case, especially the point about having no right of action. Mr Chadwin explained to me that they were all supporters of the club and they were confident that having started these proceedings, the club would see sense and negotiate some sort of deal. Indeed they had received inside information that the club was considering just that.

I was amazed at this revelation as I held the strong belief then, and kept it throughout my career, that you never started civil proceedings on any basis other than a preparedness to see it through to a hearing. It is one thing to threaten proceedings, but quite another to launch them. In fact, in the years that followed I would very rarely even threaten proceedings unless I had clear instructions to follow through on the threat, as I did not want to get a reputation as a paper tiger. Nothing in the conference persuaded me that we had anything but a ticking bomb and the next day I reported back to Howard that, if we were to take over the case, we had to switch to a specialist company law barrister and I knew one in London. He agreed and I sent off the papers. I received a call from said barrister a couple of days later which confirmed my fears. They were added to when he said the club could successfully make an application to strike out the proceedings for showing no cause of action. What he was able to do was amend the writ and prepare a statement of claim to give us something to argue about, but his advice was to get out of the litigation.

I called a meeting with the clients and told them of the position, but they were determined to carry on the fight especially against the information that the club was worried. We amended the claim and set about an enquiry process to try and strengthen the case, finding plenty of people who were willing to help. My investigations found that the company's share register seemed to be in a mess and wasn't up to date. As each breach of company law legislation could lead to a fine and help the vote of no confidence, this was duly noted. In those days, directors of football clubs couldn't benefit from their positions and so I undertook to look at the club's internal dealings to see if there had been a breach of compliance. The views of former players and managers kept up the press interest which applied pressure for change. Over the next few months I spoke to lots of ex players, including Malcolm McDonald, as well as ex managers. Their tales were all very interesting, but didn't amount to grounds for involuntary removal of directors in a private company. One story I do remember is of the Newcastle players complaining of no heating in the training ground changing rooms so four or five electric bar heaters were brought in and placed around.....the communal bath! One slip from a wet foot and millions of pounds worth of players would have been fried.

We thought we had the most dramatic of breakthroughs when reception took a call from someone who wanted to speak to the lawyer dealing with the football case. I took the call and he asked me if I knew there was a contract out on Malcolm Dix. Visions of horses' heads in his bed or machine gun riddled cars sprang to mind as I treated this with a pinch of salt, but the caller gave me the name and address of somebody who had been offered the contract. Now I'm not sure what I thought I was doing, but the next day I drove out to one of the roughest parts of the city to interview this former gangster. I had been told that he was the former bodyguard of a gangster who had famously been murdered a few years before and rather than thinking this might be dangerous, which I should have done, I just thought that it wasn't much of a CV to be the bodyguard of someone who was murdered. Some logic was beginning to return when I parked my car in the sort of place where they end up on bricks, minus tyres and walked down an unwelcoming path to an equally unwelcoming door. I knocked and there was no answer other than my father's voice in my head telling me to make a run for it. Another knock and then the sound of many bolts being released and locks undone until the door opened. Standing in front of me was a man in his fifties with untamed grey hair that hadn't seen a comb in recent times, six feet tall with a large frame where some of the muscles of yesteryear had descended to a large stomach, visible through his string vest. He wore brown trousers (which I should have been wearing and might soon be) with braces hanging to the side, like handles.

"Yeah" growled Mr H.

"Hello, I'm from Mincoffs and understand you might have some information about Newcastle United" I said in a friendly, but not over friendly way.

"Why should I talk to you?" said Mr H looking me up and down.

"You don't have to but I would like to talk to you."

"What's to stop you going to the cops?" he asked menacingly

"I think you know my firm and would know if we did that, we would lose most of our clients." There was a pause whilst this clearly still very dangerous man glared at me and without saying anything, moved to the side with the door opening further as my cue to enter. My working class upbringing was always helpful in this type of situation, giving me the knowledge not to antagonise, but also crucially not to appear afraid or to panic which would certainly ignite reaction. In fact once inside, Mr H was happy to talk and after making me a cup of tea he explained that a criminal contact had approached him and that a contract was available to sort out Malcolm Dix, but he had said he wasn't interested. I asked him what the contract meant and he explained,

"Well it's not to kill him like, if that's what you are asking. The first step would be to offer him money to fuck off. If he said no then there would be nitromors (paint remover) chucked on his car and if that didn't get the message across they would gloss his house."

"Gloss his house?" I enquired visualising a team of decorators painting his windows.

"Yeah, a tin of gloss paint thrown at the house, gloss paint is a bastard to get off."

"Oh, then what?"

"Well if he hasn't got the message by then, it will start on him. He might be in a pub and somebody will say he has spilt their drink and then they'll give him a good hiding."

"And if that doesn't work?"

"Why if that doesn't do it, they will break his fucking legs."

Obviously I can't say that any of this is true or who the instigator of it was, but I reported back to a somewhat shell-shocked Malcolm Dix suggesting he take some precautions and possibly speak to the police. I also made a detailed note for the file in case something happened, which it didn't.

There were regular press conferences and radio interviews, and I got to know the journalists pretty well. The Club's AGM was coming up and I had an idea. I suggested Malcolm Dix, who was the only shareholder amongst the rebels, get me into the meeting as proxy and I would try and create something. We would put forward a motion of no confidence in the board and get them to react. With the proxy papers and the motion prepared, I went to the AGM. The directors, who included my brother's former boss solicitor Gordon McKeag, took their places on the top table. The room was filled with shareholders, most of whom were angry at the Club (things don't seem to have changed much over the years). I had warned the rebels that the directors had block votes that would defeat the motion, but at least we could bring matters to a wider audience. The meeting was very short and the directors somewhat arrogantly, and to my surprise, ignored the motion and wound up the meeting. I rushed to a microphone in the centre of the large room and asked them why they had not dealt with the motion, only to be ignored. I repeated my question which started a murmur in the room and one or two people shouting out loudly, but they walked off. I addressed the room saying we were still able to deal with the motion in their absence and dismiss the board with a show of hands, which led to a large cheer. Although they would have been dismissed, I knew they could issue a fresh motion and have themselves reinstated by the majority block vote the next day, but the embarrassment would have been huge. The news must have filtered back and sadly the board came back, dealt with the motion and used the block vote to defeat it, but we all felt a moral victory had been achieved. And by a Sunderland supporter!

My time on the case was coming to an end as I had given Mincoffs notice that I was leaving. Before I left I arranged for the misguided legal proceedings to be discontinued. The information the rebels now had gave them enough ammunition to keep up the pressure and to retain public support. As it turned out, we received information that the club insider had been feeding false information to the rebels about the board's concerns regarding legal proceedings. The board had in fact received advice that the club was bound to win. The board's objective was to create an enormous defeat with huge costs and cripple the rebels. I don't know if that's true, but they instructed very expensive counsel to attend the hearing when we arranged to withdraw and presented an enormous bill for their costs. By this time I had moved on, but offered to deal with the costs hearing myself, free of charge, and was able to have a great deal of the costs disallowed.

The pressure of all of these events started to show on those in charge of the club and when Sir John Hall joined the group of rebels after I left, momentum was gained. Although I never met him I recall his appearances on the media saying he wanted to 'democratise the club' and some of the rebels worked tirelessly to trace shareholders who would sell him their private shares. In the event I didn't see much democracy as the Hall family seemed to end up owning the club, but change of sorts had been achieved. Turmoil at Newcastle United has continued, but I was really impressed by the selfless dedication of those local businessmen who gave up huge amounts of time and energy for the love of their football team. Nobody was more impressive than Alan Rooney who was a chartered surveyor partner in a firm in the city. He never sought the limelight, but was never afraid to put himself in jeopardy or take on others who he felt were wrong. Although passionate about his team, he always took advice on board and tried to act rationally, but always selflessly.

It was the end of 1978 and my time was coming to an end at Mincoffs. After nine years at work and having passed my examinations by studying part time, I was now qualified and was off to the great adventure of starting a firm of solicitors with my pal. We had no money, an overdraft facility of £5,000 and I just couldn't wait. However there would be two early attempts to destroy this fledgling business.

CHAPTER 14: Qualification

When I started work at the age of sixteen I really didn't plan on becoming a solicitor. The fact that I became one at roughly the same age as a law graduate was something I was very proud of. When my son was eighteen he also decided to try for the life of a lawyer. Asking me if he should do it the way I did, without hesitation I said no and advised him to go to university. I felt this would give him a more structured and fun way to qualifying, as mixing work and study as well as giving up lots of free time isn't an easy route. That's not to say that I didn't have fun and without the working experience I gained, I definitely wouldn't have been able to start the firm with Malcolm Donnelly at the very young age of 25.

Passing an 'A' level at sixteen broke the spell of educational restriction and I was pleased to find I wasn't intimidated by future courses and examinations. I took the Associate course on day release at Newcastle Polytechnic (now Northumbria University) and found myself mixing with friends and colleagues from the legal circuit, which was nice. However, the college option was not available for the Fellowship qualification so I had to embark on correspondence courses. It has to be said this is a fairly soulless and lonely experience. The Fellowship was different from the Associate qualification in that one had to choose three subjects to study on a more in depth basis, with a suggestion that students do one a year. I was in a hurry so I decided to do two each year, picking off four of the five of the subjects I would need for the Solicitors Part I examination. My evenings were spent studying and the summers were always associated with revision and the sitting of exams. I discovered a way to compromise with my natural laziness (and the easy distraction of girls and sport) by taking intensive but short periods of study time with breaks in between. I would come home from work, eat, revise for an hour then stop for coffee. Then I would revise for another hour and stop for the evening. When I had intensive study leave before an exam I would expand this through the day, getting ready as if I was going to work and then using the same hourly schedules to keep my short attention span in check. I would never work late into the evening, as I believe complete relaxation is important. I passed all four exam papers over the next two years and was technically qualified as a Fellow of the Institute of Legal Executives. My young age precluded me from being enrolled, but in any event I was now committed to at least trying to qualify as a solicitor. As far as the Solicitors Part 1 qualification was concerned I was already four fifths of the way there and with a further correspondence course through the Law Society I passed the remaining paper in constitutional law, which gave me the same qualification standard that a university law degree would have earned me.

All law students reach the same point of having to enrol for the Solicitors Part 2 qualification at an accredited law faculty, so I entered my four year articles of clerkship (trainee solicitor) with Richard Reed and Co, and completed it with Mincoff Science and Gold. The Part 2 exams comprised of seven subjects and you had to pass at least three of them in one sitting for them to count. If you did that, you could resit the others over a period of time if necessary. If however you only passed two, you had to start again. The one exception was the accounts module which could be taken on its own, presumably because most lawyers can't count and need all their concentration to get through it. I knew I had only one chance of qualifying because I had limited money and time off work. I did the accounts course at the time of my stressful resignation from Reeds (always a master of timing!) and somehow passed the exam. I then made a decision, borne out of my knowledge of having only one chance at Part 2, which almost derailed my plans and cost me my career.

My friend Gordon Brown at Mincoffs had already passed his exams and had a set of immaculately handwritten notes which he had made at the College of Law, Chester. With my experience of correspondence courses I decided to use his notes to try and steal an edge for the upcoming course. My master plan was to sit four of the exams BEFORE I began my course. If I could pass at least three it would almost guarantee that I would qualify, as I would only have the balance to sit at the end of my course and the chance of re-sits if necessary. This may not seem such a bad idea, but I hadn't taken into account two very significant factors; the examinations coincided with the start of the course which meant I missed the first two weeks, and the results of the exams were not out for almost three months so I was undertaking work on subjects unaware of whether or not I would need to sit the exam. In the event, Gordon's notes were very clear and I felt the exams went well. I was confident that I had passed at least three of the subjects and felt there was a reasonable chance I had all four. I made up the lost time when I started the course in Newcastle and waited for the news of the results.

Results were in those days given in the cruellest of ways. They were published in certain newspapers and if your name wasn't there, you had failed. It reminded me of that old army joke of a sergeant major ordered to tactfully tell Private Smith that his mother had died. He calls out the troop and makes them stand on parade then says, *'All those with mothers take one step forward...not you Smith'* I got up very early on the day of the exam results and drove to the train station to buy the early edition of The Times. Nervously, I walked back to my car with the newspaper. I opened it to the appropriate page and to my devastation my name wasn't there, which meant I had failed. It took a while to sink in as I was sure I had done well enough to pass, but there was no doubting the absence of my name. The actual results came by post a couple of days later and worst of all I had passed two of them and failed the other two by the slimmest of margins. By letting me know how close I had come, the cruelty was complete. I was as low as I could remember being. My confidence and self assurance were in tatters as I contemplated the consequences of the decision I had made. It was apparent to me that, not only did I not have the advantage of securing a base of exam passes, but I probably hadn't been concentrating as much as I should on the subjects I thought I had passed. I was deeply wounded. Worst of all I didn't understand how I had failed. Coming so close was harder to bear than being a mile off.

Those first few days were dreadful and I felt utterly alone. I had a girlfriend, lots of friends and a loving mother, but I suppose I missed the guiding hand of a father at that point; somebody who could come in with natural authority, totally on my side and tell me where I had gone wrong, what I should do and make me pull myself together. I decided to ditch two of the six courses and concentrate on the remaining four to try and salvage the situation, but my brother Brian talked me out of it. What he persuaded me to do was to concentrate on four, but to sit all six exams on a 'puncher's chance' that I might just squeeze through on one of the two that I wasn't working on. Once I had formulated a plan I started to recover. I wanted this really badly and there was no point in dwelling over what went wrong, so I found the determination to pick myself up, dust myself down and get on with plan B. I didn't have a second chance.

Having completed the course and the revision period, I drove to Birmingham (my allotted examination centre) where I was staying at my brother's house for a week as the exams were taken over a four day period. Every day I grappled with Spaghetti Junction to reach the university and every day people stood around outside looking nervous and ill. I still remember a girl walking quickly from her desk at the front of the exam hall to the exit at the back, desperately trying to contain her vomit in her fingers as her step quickened. For me it was different. I was always glad to be there because I was fed up with revising. I wanted to get the exam over with, empty my head of all that information and replace it with sport, women and booze (what an intellectual - well I was young!). I would sit at my desk in the exam hall and visualise it as my ship whilst ignoring everything going on around me, apart from one exam as the man opposite me occasionally squeaked like a mouse as he read his questions, no doubt realising he didn't know the answers. I employed my now strict tactic; ten minutes of question reading and noting down the answer and the relevant act of parliament or case example. Not to do that is a mistake because you are quite likely to find your brain has misplaced the information when you come to write the answer. Then I allowed myself a strict number of minutes on each answer and a final ten minutes of re reading and review. So focused was I that, had there been a fire I probably would have been completely oblivious and emerged with smouldering clothes and singed hair, holding a completed exam paper!

One of the two neglected subjects was taxation law which I hadn't been interested in and barely understood. On the day of that exam, the selection of seven questions out of ten was easy, as I had no idea at all about the ones I discarded. My knowledge was so sparse on the subject that on the three discarded questions, my answers could have been *'unfortunately, I can't help you with the information you seek, but if you ever want to know the Beatles No 1's in sequence or every player to play for Sunderland AFC in the last ten years then please feel free to give me a call!'* I knew enough about three of the questions to answer confidently, but not enough to expand or waffle. The remaining four were short educated guesses and my normal ten minute review at the end was expanded to an hour as I had so little to read when looking at my answers.

I felt that my core subjects had gone well and on the last day, a Thursday morning, I set off with a light heart in the knowledge that it was soon to be over. It had started to lightly snow as I pulled into the car park and by the time the bell rang to signify the end of the matrimonial law exam, the snow was a thick carpet of white. I drove back to my brother's empty house, the falling snow still heavy, stopping at Greggs to buy a pasty and sausage roll for some self indulgence. Once inside the house I made myself a coffee, opened up the greasy bag containing my food and watched Little House on the Prairie on television; a programme I couldn't stand, but now that I had so much free time I blissfully felt I could waste some watching rubbish! With the snow falling, my brother's fire burning and my stomach full of pastry, I fell into a deep satisfying sleep.

Over the next few weeks I settled back into the office, managing not to think too much about the enormity of the awaited results. Results day was the 6th of May 1978; cup final day. In those days the cup final was the pinnacle of the footballing season and had particular significance to me as I was born at home on cup final day in 1953, whilst my Dad watched the match. It was the famous 'Matthews Final' between Blackpool and Bolton Wanderers when Stanley Matthews finally won a cup final medal after a glittering career in a spectacular game which ended 4-3. No wonder I've always had football in my blood. The previous night Gordon Brown, his wife-to-be, Lyndsey, and my girlfriend and I had gone to our local for a meal. The pub held a raffle that night and for the only time in my life I won it, which Gordon proclaimed to be a good omen. Once home I managed to get to sleep and was woken by the alarm at 4.30am. Straight out of bed, into my clothes and off I drove in the darkness to the train station to buy a newspaper. When I arrived, I took a second to look at the piles of newspapers freshly delivered by train and, taking a very deep breath, bought The Times and The Daily Telegraph. I walked back to the car with my whole destiny in the pages of those newspapers. Sitting in the car, heart thumping, mouth dry as sandpaper, I turned the pages to the relevant section, found Birmingham and then looked for my name under M. If the name was there, I had at least passed four of the subjects and I would almost certainly qualify by knocking off the other papers in the next year or so. If my name wasn't there my plans to start a firm with Malcolm Donnelly, or indeed anyone else, were gone.

The names of the successful examinees were followed by numbers within a range of 1 to 7, each number corresponding to a single subject passed. I found the section and, with my heart now pounding so loudly that I could actually hear it, my eyes ran down the Birmingham section. There it was; my name was the last name in its column. The numbers 1, 3 and 4 appeared after my name and, when my eyes moved to the next column, the numbers 5, 6 and 7 followed. Having already passed number 2 (accounts), I realised to my utter relief that I had passed all seven subjects and was definitely going to be a solicitor, as long as I managed to live until November! The pleasure, relief and satisfaction were total. It swept over me like a warm bath and engulfed me in ecstasy. It was too important to cry, shout, or scream; it was a narcotic filling my veins and my head with the deepest delight I have ever experienced. Against a great many odds, here I was about to become a solicitor in my own business, free to represent people the way I wanted to and not answerable to anyone in the direction of the business. I was so excited and had no fears whatsoever. Oh, the blindness of youth! The rest of the day was just perfect. There were the telephone calls, the congratulatory visits, the cup final itself where I felt drunk watching it without even having a drink and then a meal out in the city to celebrate. My mother was on holiday at the time and was the only one who brought a tear to my eye when she sent me my one and only telegram in my life. It read *'Just got the news, my heart is bursting with pride, well done, love Mam.'*

On Monday I went into the office for more congratulations and pats on the back, even from the partners. Peter Hedworth took me to one side and told me that now that I had got that nonsense out of the way I had to concentrate on being a partner at Mincoffs. What he actually said was "Now look. There are eight of us and three of us want you to be a partner, three don't and two are undecided."

"Who are the three who don't want me?" I asked and he told me they were the two recent additions, David Levy and Stuart Winskill and a little surprisingly Mike Smith the family partner, who used to send me on his difficult applications. I wasn't too concerned as I knew I was leaving anyway, but Hedworth told me I should go out of my way to win over the ones who didn't want me. A few days later I was in a bar in Cramlington, where I was now living, having a few drinks with Gordon Brown and a few others when Stuart Winskill walked in. I said hello, but deliberately didn't offer to buy him a drink when I was ordering. I continued to talk to him and was friendly, but no doubt he was bemused by the absence of the offer of a drink which I would normally have made. A couple of weeks later I was about to leave the office to drive to my now weekly stint at our North Shields office, when David Levy ran after me asking if he could have a lift there. I said yes and he jumped in the passenger seat. After a few minutes chat he said,

"John, do you mind if I give you some advice?"

"No" I said with a certain absence of sincerity.

"John, I think you are a very talented lawyer, but you can rub people up the wrong way and you might like to think of a slight change of approach as you can seem quite aggressive and threatening."

"David, do you mind if I give you a piece of advice?"

"No John that's fine"

"If I were you, I would avoid upsetting somebody giving you a lift as it's a long way to North Shields from here on foot."

"Fair enough" he replied good-heartedly.

A few days later, Hedworth passed me in the corridor,

"I see you're pulling out all the stops to curry favour"

"Doing what I can" I said smiling. In fact whatever the reservations were, the offer came. I was offered a one year deal with a view to a partnership. A lesson I learned from that was that nobody had actually asked me if I wanted a partnership and if they had I would have told them the truth. It was just assumed, but I was happy to take the job until our new firm, which was now up and running, could support two lawyers. I never presumed in the years that followed that people working for me would always want to stay, or that those training would see themselves as partners of the future. That was for me to find out and to enquire about.

When my term of articles was completed in October 1978, I formerly qualified and was admitted to the Role of Solicitors on the 1st of December of that year. Mine and Malcolm Donnelly's new practice had started in May of that year, with Malcolm working on his own and me assisting from the wings with a view to joining him when there was enough work to justify both of us being there. In fact, Malcolm said that he would prefer me to come sooner rather than later and we decided that I would join him in our firm on the 15th of January 1979. I went to see Peter Hedworth and told him of my decision and plans. He was somewhat taken aback and suggested I needed my head examining. He said that starting up a new firm of solicitors was all but impossible and asked me to name one which had started in the last 30 years and had succeeded. But I was very confident and I wanted to try. He then played the guilt card and said he had fought for me to get this job and the potential partnership, but I couldn't help saying that he never asked me if I wanted it and in any event had told me that three of my 'future partners' didn't want me. He replied that was only because they were scared of me, but I said the reason mattered less than the feeling. The truth was that I wasn't really concerned about their reactions as I was so determined to try this new adventure. Here I was sailing into the unknown, completely in charge of my own destiny with no money at all, as all of my savings had been spent on my wedding and our first home, which was furnished with bits and pieces from my flat and orange crates with table clothes over them. I was so excited!

CHAPTER 15: Nobody said it would be easy

Malcolm was living in Norton, near Stockton in those days. Prior to launching our firm, I would go and stay with him and his first wife for business planning and updates. We would go in to Hartlepool to look at potential office sites and occasionally we drove past houses belonging to local lawyers and estate agents. It was evident they had made quite a bit of money from the town. My philosophy was simple; I didn't think too much about the money because I thought that if I did the job well the money would follow. Blind as that might have been, it's more or less the advice I have given to lots of start up businesses since. Get the product or service right before worrying too much about the financial implications. They are important too, of course, but you have nothing without the product or service. I was too young to consider all of the implications of starting our own business, but I was desperate to have a go. I had qualified as a solicitor against all expectations and I wasn't going to waste all of that effort. I wasn't intimidated by other lawyers and had enjoyed a lot of success with the cases that I had taken on. I had a huge amount of experience for one so young and I was beginning to see the effect that my confidence had on others and how useful it was in my career.

We survived an early scare when Malcolm changed his mind and accepted an offer from his existing firm, before changing it back again. His first wife blamed me for that. I had the distraction of sitting my examinations and waiting for the results, but once I knew I had passed it was all systems go. Trading under the name of Malcolm Donnelly & Co we rented premises which, although a little off the High Street, were priced at a rent we could afford. However, Malcolm had a problem as there was a rule stating that a sole practitioner, as he technically was, had to have been qualified for a minimum of three years before he could practice. Malcolm applied to the Law Society for permission to trade earlier and the Law Society in London said it would leave the decision to the local Law Society in Hartlepool. Bearing in mind that it comprised those solicitors practicing in Hartlepool, predictably the request was refused. Perhaps the refusal betrayed a fear of competition, but in any event it resulted in a few months wasted rent. That fear and protectionism was to re surface when I joined Malcolm at the firm and consequently an outbreak of war ensued, but more of that later.

As it was, on the 15th of May 1978, to coincide with Malcolm's third anniversary of qualification, the doors opened and we were up and running. Costing out how much business was needed to run the office, plus Malcolm's salary, he instigated a points-per-client system to keep us on track. He gave one point to a new criminal matter, one point for a divorce and two points for a new property instruction. We didn't have a target for what was needed for me to join, and in any event we had no real means of doing anything about it. Looking back it seems incredible that solicitors were not allowed to advertise, tout for business or describe themselves as experts or specialists of any kind. The letters on the windows could be no bigger than five inches in height and to breach any of these rules was a serious disciplinary matter. You could guarantee, with the welcome we had received, that any transgression would have been reported with great enthusiasm by the local lawyers. The prohibition of description of specialist seemed a particularly nonsensical rule since it deprived the client of information as to who would be the best choice for them and their particular problem. I held a fairly strong view that the Law Society, at that time, managed to neither serve the public nor the solicitors it governed.

After the call came from Malcolm to join him I served my notice at Mincoffs, sold my house in Cramlington near Newcastle and bought a house in Billingham, just a ten minute drive to the office in Hartlepool. My first wife and I had bought the house in Cramlington for £12,000 and a year later sold it for £14,000. The house in Billingham was a step up from the semi-detached we were leaving, to a link detached which was very similar but joined by a garage rather than a wall. The house cost £15,500 and again buying on a 100% mortgage, we had almost £2000 to spend on furniture after paying off the previous mortgage. I managed to organise the move to coincide with starting work in Hartlepool and I was raring to go. I had been to the office several times, but on that first day I was very conscious of the significance of being there full time. The office had a shop front window that led into the front office, which sported a counter with a seating area behind and a small reception area in front. Behind that was my office which was fairly spacious, but a little dark as the only window was to the dark backyard. Malcolm's office was upstairs beside a small kitchen and toilet. The staff comprised Malcolm's first mother-in-law Doris, plus Christine a 19 year old office junior, who was also the receptionist, head typist and anything else we needed all rolled into one. So there we were, just the four of us in the firm which was now called Donnelly McArdle & Co. I cannot overemphasise how proud I was when the sign writer had finished and my name was up there along with my pal, as solicitors ready to take on the world. In those first few weeks, whenever I walked away from the office,

I always stopped to look back at the window and felt a surge of pride and excitement course through my veins. All the talking and planning was done, and here I was in Hartlepool with my name on the window of my own firm.

On my first day, Malcolm was due at court and I declined an invitation to go with him, instead wanting to look at target areas for work. As he was leaving I asked him about a pile of files in the corner. They were completed property transactions that hadn't yet been registered, he said, primarily because he didn't know how to do it. That wasn't ideal and I managed to complete them all and keep us on the building society panels. In the first couple of weeks two other issues caught my attention. The first concerned our two sets of account books, which is an important part of a solicitors practice due to the need to account correctly (to the penny) for clients' money, and to keep separate accounts for the running of the office. I looked at the clients' ledger (these were the days before computers and everything was written by hand), then at the office ledger and noted that everything appeared to be in order except that the debits were all written where the credits should be and vice versa. Malcolm said he just followed the accountant's instructions, that the accountant had checked the books recently and declared that everything was fine. I suggested we may need to change accountants and re wrote the ledgers correctly! At least there had been an attempt to write up the books, which was more than I could say for the wage details. We only had two staff and they were paid weekly. Malcolm told me that Christine was paid £25 per week and said,
"Well I reckon there will be about £2 tax and £1 national insurance, so I give her £22". When I asked how he recorded this he replied, "I don't. Some bloke came in from the tax office and left me some books, but I couldn't make head or tail of them. They are over there in the corner".

My experience in property work meant I could sort out the property problems, and my experience in the accounts department at Wilson and Co meant I could rectify the accounts books however I hadn't done wage calculation or recording. I picked up the pile of books left by the local Inland Revenue man, looked through them and managed to work out how to do it. It was easier than it looked and I brought nine months of books up to date. I sorted out the discrepancy with the two staff, but Malcolm's gut instinct on the tax and national insurance was not far out. A few days later I received a call from the local Revenue office asking if they could come and inspect the records. I said yes, they could pop in tomorrow and the man seemed surprised saying that it was not urgent and next week would be fine if I liked. I said tomorrow was convenient and he duly turned up. Other than being concerned he might smudge the hardly dry ink in the books, I just sat and watched him go through the records. When he had finished he looked up and said,

"Well thank you Mr McArdle. Everything seems to be in order and there don't seem to be any problems. I must say I was surprised that you invited me in straight away as we normally give people a couple of weeks to write the records up after we telephone." He sort of chuckled when he said that and with a completely straight face and appalling cheek I said,

"Do you mean some people don't write up the records straight away and haven't done anything until you call?"

"Yes, amazing isn't it, but no such problem here" he responded as I continued my theatrical bewilderment. If he had called a week ago he would have had to blow the dust off the blank books and start from scratch. I had known Malcolm pretty well for a few years so none of this alarmed me, although I was surprised he hadn't asked me to help him before arriving on a full time basis. I could tell he was stressed about a number of things and I felt I had arrived just in time to prevent smaller organisational matters destroying this embryonic business. Malcolm was very good at bringing in work and was popular in the town with both clients and other professionals. He had done a great job in getting us underway on his own with only a little help from me, so tardy paperwork was very forgivable.

I didn't want to be a magistrates court criminal solicitor so I spent part of my time meeting fellow lawyers, building society managers, bank managers, estate agents and insurance brokers identifying target areas of work and following them up. I continued to resist the easier option of sharing Malcolm's criminal work, although I did fill in for him from time to time. On one occasion when Malcolm was on holiday I went into the court cells to meet one of his regulars, a man in his forties with shoulder length hair and tattoos on his fingers. He was a career criminal who was a regular at both the courts and the prisons. Predictably, he told me that he hadn't done the crime, but had instead been fitted up by the police. This is a curious phenomenon in the criminal brotherhood where denial in the most ridiculous of circumstances is a matter of course. He asked if I would apply for bail and I said I would if he liked, but I thought there was currently no chance and it might be better to apply to a judge later. He said that was fine and then leaned forward and said,

"Malcolm always gives me 20 Benson and Hedges" whilst extending his hand.

"Well, I'm not Malcolm and it's illegal to give you cigarettes, sorry" When I told Malcolm he said,
"Cheeky bastard, he must have thought you looked dim!"

On the subject of denial by the criminal, the desk sergeant at Hartlepool police station was a very funny man called Eric Hudson, who was destined to work for us and become a friend. On one notable occasion Sgt. Hudson, on seeing Malcolm entering the police station said,
"Ah Mr Donnelly, we have a guest staying with us this evening who is one of your clients. He is in his underpants in the cells as we have taken his clothes for forensic examination. There was a burglary tonight when a man, whose description exactly matches your client, threw a brick through a jeweller's window, climbed through the broken glass and stole some jewellery. When your client was apprehended a few hundred yards from the scene, the officers noticed his clothing was covered in fragments of glass. Your client has told us that it is not glass, but ice particles caused by the current very cold weather, so we have placed his clothing beside the radiator to see if the glass melts!" Those early criminal cases also illustrated a certain lack of intelligence in a number of criminal clients who were totally mystified as to why they were suspects, despite the fact that they committed the same type of offence, in exactly the same way, time and time again!

A criminal lawyer and good friend of mine, Graham Sylvester, once told me that he was representing a thief who stole empty prams and who had a number of previous convictions for the offence. He had an appointment to see Graham and was in the process of giving his instructions when Graham's wife popped into his office, which was on the first floor. She had a young child at the time and left her pram on the ground floor. On leaving, Graham's client passed her and you've guessed it, he stole the pram on the way out no doubt amazed that anyone would ever suspect him! I was also called to a man who was arrested after failing to answer his bail curfew. I went to see him in the police station and he was sitting in his cell with what can best be described as a vacant expression. He had an unfortunate large gap between his eyes, which was accentuated by a tattoo, and his eyes looked in slightly different directions. A Ricky Gervais style interview went something like this,
"Hello Mr X. I gather you failed to comply with your bail conditions"
"Eh?"
"I'm saying you didn't go to the police station"
"Which police station?"

"Any police station. You were supposed to go before 5 o clock"

"When?"

"Every day"

"Oh right"

"Well did you?"

"Did l what?"

"Go to the police station?"

"When?"

"Yesterday"

"What day was it yesterday?"

"Tuesday"

"Oh right"

"Well did you?"

"Did l what?"

"Go to the police station, yesterday which was Tuesday"

"No"

"Why not?"

"Why not what?"

"Why didn't you go to the police station, yesterday, which was Tuesday?"

"Oh l was in the pictures like and l fell asleep"

"What time did you go to the pictures?"

"Before 5"

"What time did the film end?"

"About 7"

"So you wouldn't have been able to go to the police station even if you hadn't fallen asleep"

"Eh?"

"Never mind" Upon his return, l was more than happy to hand the criminal practice back to Malcolm and concentrate on other things.

Property transactions were still the staple diet of most provincial firms in the 1970's and we lived off the odd call from a building society or less common, an estate agent. Our favourite incoming call began with the phrase 'Hello, l have a new sale and purchase for you.' Property transactions were a big step towards our weekly target and a good way of building a client base. We were young, very friendly and spent time with our clients making sure that they understood and were fully informed every step of the way. Despite this we didn't charge anymore than anyone else and soon became popular with younger clients and the less established businesses in the town. However, our small success hadn't gone unnoticed by the town's other law firms.

I had also noticed that one of the established estate agents in Hartlepool, Norman Hope and Partners had a very strange way of trading. It became apparent to me that they were accepting multiple offers on properties and sending all the proposed purchasers to apply for mortgages. Each transaction was therefore an inadvertent contract race which left a lot of purchasers disappointed, angry and once more searching for a property. I rang and spoke to one of the partners, who confirmed that my impression was correct. I told him that it was unfair and misleading, and if they didn't change I would be advising my clients to withdraw. Who was I, an upstart, to tell them how to sell properties was more or less their response, and certainly they had never been challenged before. I duly advised every client, particularly young clients, to look elsewhere which didn't endear me to Norman Hope and Partners, but a bigger challenge lay ahead.

One of our business clients and a friend of Malcolm's told me shortly after I arrived that Hartlepool was a strange place and if I wanted to succeed I would have to do what he had done, and that was to adapt. He advised me to tell the locals what they wanted to hear, not what I thought was right otherwise they would go elsewhere. He also said there was an 'establishment' of local professional people in the town who ran things their way, and it was as well not to get on the wrong side of them. I asked if any of them were connected to the mafia, as unless they were going to shoot me, I really didn't see that I had to conform to anybody else's idea of a lawyer. He wished me the best of luck, but I am sure he felt I would change. I didn't. I had put a great deal of effort into getting where I was and I wasn't about to be inhibited as to the type of advice I would give, or to be in any way intimidated by those who thought themselves in power. If I failed and I was unable to make a living, I was young enough to regroup. I was recently married, as yet without children and lived in a modest house so starting again, if need be, was no big deal.

The estate agent experience showed there was some truth in the warning, which other experiences served to amplify. However, I didn't find the people of Hartlepool difficult and if anything found them very responsive to straight talking. There were however certain Hartlepool characteristics which I encountered quite a bit. The Hartlepool Mail was the local newspaper which almost everyone received and often in conversations with clients, they would refer to an article or advertisement in it. If I hadn't seen it or worse still said that I hadn't read the paper, they would look at me with total bemusement as though I had said that I didn't own a television set or I didn't eat hot food. As part of my protection of house buyers I not only warned them of the problem with Norman Hope and Partners accepting multiple bids, but would suggest spreading their search for a property to nearby places like Billingham where properties were cheaper. This was often met with total incredulity. I would explain that it only took me eight minutes to travel into town from Billingham and there was no passport control to worry about or a force field to penetrate. Even so, the majority of clients wanted to stay in Hartlepool so badly that they would pay more and put up with the problems they would surely encounter.

To add to the mix, Hartlepool was divided into two regions, one being the Headland or Old Hartlepool and the other being the Town or West Hartlepool. The same desire to stay in their own region existed between the two parts of Hartlepool. The Headland is the craggy coast of the town which is a magnificent sight, especially in rough seas when the waves crash against the sea defences. It also has the dubious honour of being the recipient of the first German shell to land on UK soil in 1914 when the German navy launched an attack against sea towns to draw out the British fleet. If the German fleet had tried to land, they may have found more than they bargained for in the Hartlepool direct approach and the war might have been shorter.

 As an example of the Hartlepool direct approach, I went into an electrical store in the town called Rumbelows which was a chain store similar to Currys. The manager was a small, thin, balding man who wore dark spectacles. He was always very busy rushing around replacing goods that customers had moved, and would serve those waiting only when he was ready. His favoured means of serving customers was to look up from his counter and perform an upward flick of his head in the direction of the next customer, which indicated that he was ready to receive them. He was not particularly unfriendly, but there was no smiling or affectionate chit chat. On one occasion I was in the store standing behind a middle aged man clutching his newly bought toaster. Having received the upward flick at the counter the conversation went like this,
"Hello, I bought this toaster two weeks ago and it's not working," explained the customer
"What's wrong with it?"
"It doesn't toast the bread"
"Why?" asked the manager
"I don't know, it just doesn't toast the bread"

"Give it here and let's have a look at it" With that, the manager pulled out a screwdriver from his counter draw and started to dismantle the toaster, dropping bits of stale bread onto the counter. The man turned to me and gave a look of dismay which I returned.

"There you are that's the problem" said the manager "you've dropped a piece of wire in the toaster"

"I HAVEN'T DROPPED WIRE IN THERE," shrieked the customer

"Well it's fixed now....next" came the reply with an upward flick in my direction. The man stormed out of the shop in disgust and I took a second or two to gather my thoughts before airing my enquiry.

Over the years I was to develop a fondness for the town and its people and will always look upon both with great affection as the place where our business started. However, at this early stage a dark cloud was hovering as the new boys had caused a stirring in the old guard. Apparently there was a meeting arranged of all of the town's law firms, apart from us, to discuss us and how best to get rid of us. We were going to war and the only question was for how long.

CHAPTER 16: Hostilities begin

We were tipped off about the meeting by a young lawyer from another firm. He told us that one or two of the local law practices were stoking up the others under the cover of apparent protection of professional standards, with the intention of trying to close us down. I should make it clear that neither Malcolm nor I would ever have contemplated doing anything unethical and we both knew that the concerns were another mouth feeding in the legal pond and a result of our failure to show any deference. What I didn't know until some years later was that Malcolm had been inadvertently stoking up a fire by saying that I would shake everybody up when I joined him and more or less, that I liked eating babies and savaging people for the fun of it. When he did eventually tell me, he explained that he thought the good cop, bad cop thing would be a good idea and they might be better with him for fear of me. In truth, I don't think this was the problem, rather a very parochial attempt by one or two lawyers to destroy competition and retain perceived status. I didn't need much provoking and wrote a letter to the senior partner of every firm in the town which to the best of my recollection was as follows,

> *Dear Sir,*
>
> *We understand that you attended a meeting recently to discuss this firm and apparent concerns about our practice and transactions that we have been involved in. To date we have not received any complaints from clients, other law firms or any other organisation and therefore insist that you confirm in writing any concerns that you may have and in particular any that you have expressed to anyone else.*
>
> *We also wish to make it clear that in the event of unfounded remarks being made against this firm proceedings will be brought for damages in defamation and a complaint will be made to the Law Society.*
>
> *Yours faithfully*

The letter produced an immediate response from about half of the firms to say they had no concerns and hadn't expressed any objections at the meeting. After a week or so there were only three firms who maintained they had a problem and it was always my view that Ivor Walker of Levinsons was a major factor. There was a threat that these firms wouldn't accept our cheques and we retaliated by saying we wouldn't accept their cheques either, meaning that each party had to go to the trouble of bankers drafts. The other two firms came to a peace deal quickly amid claims of a misunderstanding, but Levinsons stood firm. I doubt that most of their partners wanted this level of trouble but Walker was an archetypal bully. The essence of a bully is that often they are unopposed or challenged because they choose their victims on the basis of least resistance. Walker had been a solicitor in the town for many years, building up a reputation in criminal work. He had a favourite seat in the magistrate's court and would tell younger lawyers to move if they happened to be sitting there when he walked in. He expected his cases to have preference and was very much a big fish in a little pond. He knew Malcolm from attendances at court but didn't know me at all. I had seen him once or twice when filling in for Malcolm and noticed his swagger. He was a balding aggressive looking middle aged man who spoke with a local accent and displayed an attitude. I wasn't looking for a fight, but my background and the civil litigation that I handled had the effect of making me indifferent to it.

The inevitable flashpoint came when he took advantage of our young trainee's naivety in completing a property transaction and sent her back to the office in tears. I rang him and after an early exchange, I told him he was a small minded bully and in future he would be dealing with me, not someone who was learning the law. In answer to his charge of incompetence, I told him I had much to learn from him, as he appeared to practice it every day. He slammed down the phone. His partner Sol Levinson was a much more likeable character and I regret the argument with him when he tried to defend his partner in a conversation with me a few days later. After an exchange with him, he told me that no solicitor had spoken to him in the way I had in 30 years and my glib answer was that it was therefore long overdue. He was deserving of better, unlike his partner. In the event, the antipathy towards us by some firms of lawyers and estate agents actually brought us business from newer agents, brokers and younger people happy to use an alternative. Peace even broke out with Levinsons, although Walker retained his apparent hatred of me which gave me great pleasure. Malcolm remained on reasonable terms with him at court and would relish his comments about me because he could tell that I had rattled him. The short war was over, we had survived and in fact thrived, but another battle lay ahead.

I wouldn't want to give the impression that these were unpleasant times because trouble was something I was very used to dealing with in the area of law that I specialised in. It was hard to fathom that some senior lawyers would go out of their way to try and destroy our embryonic firm, but as the earlier chapters show it wasn't the first time someone had tried to derail my career. That aside we were having a great time, we didn't take ourselves too seriously and had fallen into a very enjoyable routine. Malcolm would go off to court at about 9.45am and I would deal with property and litigation matters, after which I would do a bit of prospecting for further work. Malcolm would normally return at about one o'clock and we would go out for lunch at one of the local pubs. We ate a huge amount of food every day as we always had a hot lunch, including pudding, and then repeated the intake in the evening when we went to our respective homes. I never put on a pound in weight so I must have been burning up a lot of calories! Sometimes lunch was given up to a business meeting with bank/building society managers, insurance brokers or agents of one sort or another. In the early months we did this regularly and were becoming a little bored with it. One of these lunch meetings was with someone we were introduced to; he talked incessantly, laughed uncontrollably and came back to the office for coffee sometime after three. He was a small balding man in his late thirties and on leaving he said,

"I really have enjoyed meeting you boys and I think you are just what we are looking for as lawyers for our clients. I think I will be able to send you four or five cases a week if you can handle it and I am really excited about what we can do"

Having assured him we could handle this new influx of work we said our goodbyes with him laughing and winking as he got into his car. We never heard from him again. There had been one or two lunches like this as well as the 'just meeting you' type, which we were now beginning to discourage.

It was around this time that an insurance agent friend said he wanted to arrange a lunch with an insurance broker he knew called Norman Scaggs and, reluctantly we agreed. As the day arrived we thought about inventing an excuse, but we decided to go through with it. Norman was a tall man with a full beard and very softly spoken. We went through the usual routine of small talk and anecdote which went down reasonably well. When he said that he liked us and could send us three or four accident cases a week, it was all we could do not to ask if they would be delivered by Santa's elves, but we remained polite. The next day Norman rang me and gave me instructions on three new car accident cases. Another lesson learned;

never judge the person in front of you on the basis of your experience of someone else. Norman was as good as his word and we built up a very good working relationship and friendship over the next few years. It was a big moment for me because it was the birth of a proper litigation practice with a regular supply of cases, which enabled me to build up a reputation within the town and also in court. The supply of work was welcome but wasn't enough to allow us to really develop and expand. I had my eye on WA Smith, a longstanding broker which was the biggest in the town and one with a very large client base. Then one of my friends, John Edelsten from the Leeds Permanent Building Society, arranged a meeting for me with Phil Smith, who ran WA Smith. The restrictions in those days meant I wasn't allowed to pitch for work from him, or explain that we could relieve him of stress and benefit his clients. I had to dance around it and ask him what he did about car accidents involving his clients. He told me that, in keeping with most brokers they handled the claims themselves, but that it was an awful lot of work for no reward and they were often out of their depth. When someone was injured, they would tell them to instruct a solicitor. He eventually asked if I could help him, which allowed me to say yes and explain that I was developing a scheme which could take all of his accident work under one umbrella. Phil remains one of the most pleasant and honest people I have dealt with and all he wanted was a good service for his clients. The big fish was landed and we were flying. Or so I thought.

I had developed an idea for car accident clients whilst working for Mincoffs. I was instructed by a bus driver who had been involved in an accident which wasn't his fault. He only had third party insurance and didn't realise that with third party, his own insurers were not involved and that it was left to the other driver's insurers to investigate the matter before paying anything. The point was that he drove the first bus on a morning and other than a taxi, which he couldn't afford he had no way of getting into work. It was his case that led me to approaching a garage client of mine and hiring my bus driver a car on credit, to be paid for at the end of the case. Although the garage owner was very sceptical he did it. Thus my bus driver was able to get into work every day and when the third party insurers admitted liability, the car was repaired and they paid the hire bill in full. My garage client was so impressed that he asked if we could do it again, but I said it was a one off. Now that I was in my own practice with a regular supply of car accident work, I saw that we could set up a scheme to provide hire cars on credit for third party repairs. This practice is commonplace now but at the time nobody was doing it.

The first thing I did was check the professional regulations and one of them at the time stated that a solicitor couldn't have an arrangement with an insurance broker. I had no arrangement with Norman who was just recommending clients to us. However, my plan was that WA Smith would be my client, we would handle their claims and Smith's would introduce the new service as a benefit to their clients. I couldn't see anything wrong with that but I rang the Law Society to check. I spoke to someone in the professional standards department and explained exactly what I had in mind. She confirmed there was no breach of regulation and it was fine as long as I didn't restrict the right of Smith's clients to go elsewhere. I worked with Phil on the wording of the arrangement emphasising in bold type that clients were free to use their own solicitor if they chose to do so. Over the months I set up a credit facility with a repairing garage and my friend Malcolm Burgess purchased a fleet of new Ford Fiestas to supply hire cars from his garage. These were really exciting times; I knew I could make it work and the influx of business was moving us up into a higher league.

Once we were under way and people understood it, we started to make swift progress. Smith's was indeed a large practice and having perfected the paperwork the cases started to come in on a daily basis. They were delivered by Phil's father who was in his seventies, and caused our increasing numbers of staff to stop what they were doing for what became a daily spectacle. Mr Smith Senior would pull up outside our office and stop without indicating, causing cars to slam on their brakes, and drivers to sound their horns. He would then open his car door into traffic causing the same reaction, come into our office with a handful of new cases, nod to the receptionist and keeping his head low say,
"These are for Mr McArdle"
He would then walk quickly out of the office, open his door into traffic and pull out without indicating to the familiar sound of tooting car horns. It's fair to say there was a good chance that Mr Smith Senior had caused most of the accidents he was passing on to us.

To begin with the claims were settled without difficulty and Phil Smith and his clients were delighted. He had been relieved of the burden of dealing with unproductive work and his clients were enjoying a new first class service. As I had predicted, Phil got all the credit. Occasionally, clients would bring him a bottle of wine.
"Typical. I come up with the idea, do all of the work and you get the praise and the bloody booze!" I used to complain to him. I was delighted

because it was a win win situation and there was no way Phil would have continued if his clients weren't happy. After a time however the insurers became unhappy. They were not used to ordinary people having access to cars and the task of third party repairs being made easy. Insurers were used to controlling claims and sending people to garages that they had arrangements with, whilst the poor innocent victim of the accident had to use the bus or walk. Some insurers adopted a fairly standard insurance position of electing not to pay on the basis that they just didn't like the scheme. I had anticipated this and told each one opposed to it that I would issue proceedings. Another ploy by the insurers was to say they wouldn't pay our costs, but the small claims court limit was £100 at the time which meant that for every claim over that figure, they were obliged to pay the solicitor's costs. It was to become another area of conflict, but on a much larger scale.

It followed a similar pattern to the dispute with the local solicitors in that the less antagonistic insurers quickly came to an understanding with us, small though we were, but three large companies decided to see if I was bluffing and refused to pay. I simply issued proceedings without warning, which meant they had a furious client ringing them asking why they hadn't settled the claim and what the hell did they pay premiums for. This went on for a few months and I was issuing several sets of proceedings every day to the bemusement of the local court. Some even went to court hearings, but I had unearthed legal authorities to support my position. Handling the cases myself, I won. Two of the insurers had seen enough, withdrawing their objection and agreeing to pay reasonable claims and costs. The third however, ironically the inaptly named Co Operative Insurance, stood firm. Mr Nesbitt, their local office manager came to see me and couldn't disguise his contempt. He was a thin man in his late thirties with very dark hair and unblinking eyes. He went through his prepared speech about how I was single-handedly putting up the cost of insurance premiums and how he was protecting them. I am not sure what he expected me to say, but I told him that my interest was exclusively for my clients and I imagined his bosses were more interested in profits rather than the size of premiums. I went on to say that he either accepted the position or set himself up for a lot of unsuccessful and expensive court appearances.

In the event, he didn't accept the position and took to writing me three page letters on most claims which in the main, set out why my client didn't NEED a car and could easily catch a bus. Where he confused himself was in always saying a claimant must mitigate their loss or make that loss as small as possible in the circumstances. I told him every time that a claimant was only required to show that a loss was reasonable, not that it was necessary, and that if a claimant had gone to the trouble of buying a car it was reasonable to have a temporary replacement if that car was taken away through no fault of the claimant. This particular argument went on for more than a year on all of our cases with the Co Op before Mr. Nesbitt conceded. I was developing a reputation of someone to avoid when one of the Co Operative's claims representatives came to see me and found he got along pretty well with me. Two or three meetings later he confided that he had been apprehensive when he first met me, saying, *'everybody in our office knows who you are and my boss hates your guts!'*

Phil Smith attended a dinner somewhere in the south of England and found himself sitting beside a stranger to his right who introduced himself as a senior manager in The Bradford Pennine Insurance Company.
"Hello Phil, where are you from then?"
"Hartlepool" replied Phil
"HARTLEPOOL? I hate Hartlepool"
"Oh why is that then?" asked Phil, "What don't you like about the town?"
"Never been there and never will, but there is a firm of solicitors there who make my life a fucking misery. It's so bad I even watch the football scores on a Saturday night and hope Hartlepool have lost"
I had also attracted the attention of a district judge called Brougham (pronounced Broom) who used to be a partner in a local firm representing insurance companies, before he was appointed a deputy district judge. He was a small man with something of an attitude. He could be quite funny though and initially we shared a laugh or two in the many times I appeared before him. I was in court most days and encountered most of the judges, and Brougham clearly had a short fuse. Most of the younger lawyers were intimidated by him and the older ones would have preferred somebody else dealing with their cases. Outbursts of irritation were common and on one occasion the chief clerk at the court asked me if I had heard that there was a movement amongst lawyers to complain about him. I hadn't, but I wouldn't have been surprised. I'm not sure what Brougham's view of me or our relationship was, but on one application he asked me to stay behind when the application was completed. He said he didn't like all the claims I was issuing, so I explained the background and in particular the car hire element. He told me he wasn't keen on that either, but I explained the legal authorities I had found and said I would do what I felt was right for my

clients and not every judge would share his opinion, which he seemed to accept.

In the event he hadn't accepted it and our relationship deteriorated rapidly. On another application he again asked me to wait behind and again he raised the subject. I repeated my position and he told me that other solicitors had raised concerns with him. I asked him on what basis would it be proper to talk to a member of the judiciary about a solicitor on matters that he might be deciding and asked him to name these lawyers. He refused and I said I wondered if they were the same lawyers who had met to discuss closing us down to avoid competition. Voices were now being raised and the conversation deteriorated as he became more aggressive and so did I. It ended with me saying that if he had any concerns he could complain to the Law Society and I in turn had recourse to The Lord Chancellors Office (effectively his employer). I gathered up my file and swiftly opened the door to see all faces in the lawyers' narrow waiting area staring at me, some with open mouths. They had overheard the heated debate and their stress levels had soared. I always regret not saying to them, *'Well, he is in a really good mood now!'* Overall, having appeared before many judges I have to say that the standard is generally high and the vast majority care about what they do, and try to reach a fair result. Some however, see the opportunity to exercise power and perhaps seek vicarious revenge for their own treatment as too much of a temptation to resist. I am not saying this was the case with Brougham, but he wasn't a man I liked.

Eccentrics amongst the judiciary were very common, perhaps more so than now when a politically incorrect statement will go viral on social media within hours. One such example was a young woman in her early twenties, who happened to be my client. I called her to the witness box and she gave her evidence well before the defendant was called to the witness box. He was a man in his forties who gave his evidence competently, but under cross examination from me started to wilt. I could see that after twenty minutes or so he had lost his fight and I never forgot the final few questions and answers.

"So I put it to you that you overtook a line of parked vehicles without checking that it was safe to overtake?"

"Yes," admitted the defendant

"If you had checked and seen my client, you wouldn't have attempted to overtake would you?"

"No I wouldn't"

"So you didn't see my client at all did you?" I demanded

"No"

"So this accident was entirely your fault, was it not?"

"Yes, it was," said the defendant quietly. I had no further questions and my opponent, a very experienced advocate made a final speech where he did his best, but accepted an admission had been made. As I sat to write down the terms of my victory the judge summed up saying,

"I know the defendant said it was entirely his fault, but I think this GIRL was driving like she owned the road and I find she was 60% responsible for the accident."

I could hardly believe my ears, but even 40% of our claim was worth more than 60% of the defendant's claim so we had still won. I stood and applied for costs, prompting an exchange,

"I apply for an order for costs, Your Honour on behalf of the plaintiff,"

"How can the plaintiff receive costs when she was mainly responsible?"

"Because of the size of the respective claims and those are the rules of the court," I explained

"That can't be right, can it?" he said turning to my opponent

"Sadly, Mr McArdle is correct," my opponent confirmed

"Very well costs to the plaintiff, but it does not sound right to me"

I urged my client to appeal and said that the judge may as well have said that she should be at home learning how to cook and sew for when she finds a husband, but the bruising had been too much and she was happy to be ahead on points.

I was mixing a caseload of all types of work, building up the litigation department and making all of the court appearances myself. This was an unhealthy mix and caught me out more than once. I had a fairly complex three party matter due for a hearing in open court, but found myself with little time to prepare as I had so many other things to do. I had discovered that if I prepared too soon on a court hearing where I was the advocate, I peaked too soon and became frustrated at not being able to do the case there and then. As I was preparing the cases anyway I tended to read them thoroughly on the morning of the hearing and then I was energised to go. On this particular day other tasks got in the way and I just grabbed the file as I shot off to court, thinking that I would read it quickly there. Having changed into my tabs and gown I sat in the front bench to read the papers and to my horror realised that I had brought the wrong file. Too late to do anything about it and too serious to admit, I bluffed my way through it, occasionally apparently looking up some piece of information in the file for the benefit of the judge. It was evident that I was too busy. I was enjoying a run of success with advocacy, but I knew something had to give if I was to build up the practice. I could deal with many cases in the office but only one at court. I had to find one or two barristers that I could trust to do the advocacy so that I could spend more time in the office.

Other insurance brokers were joining my accident scheme and with the natural increase in work, young as we were, we were developing a reputation as accident experts. There were approaches from new clients every day and I remember two in particular. The first was a very overweight man in his late twenties who came into my room, sat down and as was the Hartlepool way, told me half a story imagining that I knew the rest.

Man "Yeah, I was with Davey and we hit the other car like, so you need to get the money off them"
Me "Do you mean you have had a car accident?"
Man "Aye, is Davey not here?" as there was only the two of us in the room it seemed fairly obvious that Davey had failed to join us.
Me "Tell me what happened"
Man "Why, Davey was driving like and we came round the bend and the car was there like and we hit it"
Me "The car was there? Do you mean you ran into another car on the same side of the road?" At that point the door opened and in walked Davey who was as thin as his friend was fat, winked at me and nodded at his friend.
Man "Aye the other car had crashed into a car and we crashed into him"
Me "So do you mean that the other car had been involved in an accident before you came round the bend and was stationery?"
Man "Aye"
Me "So it could be said that Davey should have seen it and stopped?"
Man "No you don't understand. He had crashed, which he shouldn't have done and if he hadn't, we wouldn't have hit him"
Me "No I'm sorry, he may well have been at fault for his accident, but he was there to be seen and you should have stopped. If Davey was driving it looks like this accident was his fault, but you can claim from his insurers as you were a passenger," at which the portly man stood up and said,
"Come on Davey, let's go and find a solicitor who isn't completely SHITE," he said as he and the wordless Davey left; you can't win them all!

The second was a more amiable client. Reception buzzed me to tell me there was a lady asking to see me about her husband, but she didn't have an appointment. I said that was fine and to send her in. She was a charming lady in her seventies and she told me that her husband had been hit by a car whilst he was crossing the road. He wasn't seriously injured, but had been badly bruised. All they were worried about were his spectacles which had been broken and would cost £60 to replace. Nothing to worry about madam we will get you much more than the cost of the replacement spectacles. Leave everything to me. Over the next few months I organised a medical report, contacted the insurance company and started negotiations. The insurers offered £1,000 (about £4,000 today) and I got both clients in and told them to reject. The offer went to £1,500 and finally after another six months or so to £2,250 (about £9,000 today). I was satisfied that I had shaken the last penny out of the insurers. I was feeling very smug with myself and looking forward to telling them the great news. They were both suitably impressed and there was lots of sighing and even a little tear. As they were leaving the lady turned to me at the door and said,

"Do you know Mr McArdle this is more money than we have ever had in our lives?" My already swollen head was now growing to a size that might give me difficulty leaving the building as I bathed in the knowledge of the result and the change in their lives. Without any malice whatever or making any real point to me she took a step towards the door, hesitated and said,

"Mind you, £1,000 was more than we have ever had in our lives and we have been worried sick these last six months," and then she was gone. I knew something important had just happened although I didn't know what it was, but my swollen head was rapidly deflating. I was to use this story many times over the years, in particular to law students and young lawyers after which I would pose the question 'what was the correct settlement in that case?' The answer was that I didn't know and that was the lesson I had learnt. Instead of just two dimensionally going after a result that I thought correct, I should add the third dimension of the affect the case would have on the client, which would vary from person to person. Get to know the client, find out how they feel about what you are doing and look to lessen the strain. I felt I was a better lawyer after that case or more accurately, after that remark.

I never looked at somebody on the basis of how much money we could make out of a case and that never changed. In the vast majority of litigation cases the clients paid nothing as the costs were recovered from the insurers on the other side, but my resolve was tested early on. We had quite a good flow of domestic property work, but had little commercial work. That changed when Norman Scaggs introduced me to a client who bought commercial property. Subsequently, we were instructed in a number of commercial property transactions, one being the purchase of a hotel which was the biggest property deal we had handled and the biggest fee payer. Having completed the transaction, the client rang me. He explained that he was buying another hotel and asked me to accompany him the following Tuesday to a meeting with the planning department. I checked my diary and said that I couldn't as I was in court that day. He told me he needed me at the meeting and asked me to get someone else to do the court case, which I refused. He asked how much money I was making from the court case, indicating that I would make much more from his transaction. I told him that the other case was every bit as important to the person I was representing and that the fee was irrelevant. He then said that if that was the case, he would have to get another lawyer and I replied that was up to him, concluding the conversation. I went into Malcolm's room to announce we had just lost our biggest client, but I never had a second's doubt that I had done the right thing. Not only morally, but I never wanted any client to think I was on the end of a piece of string or that they were a priority over every other client. A few days later the hotelier rang me to check my availability for rearranging a meeting, giving me a selection of dates. I was free on one of them and neither of us mentioned his threat again. Every day was a new adventure with no indication of what the day may bring in terms of new cases and new experiences and as much as I enjoyed the fact that we were doing well and were clearly moving up a financial ladder, it was still about the cases for me.

Phil Davison was a client I first acted for at Reeds. He was completely bald, slightly built, of uncertain age but was clearly a leader. In the case I handled at Reeds, Davison came in with three fellow Hartlepool dock workers and all four spoke at once. When I managed to calm them down they explained to me that there were two types of dock workers, red and black book holders. The black book holders were the Registered Dockers and they effectively decided who did what. The red book holders were subordinate to them and pretty much did all of the work. Their passage to black book status was blocked by some mediaeval practice that allowed relatives of the black book holders to overtake them. I just knew that this was wrong and agreed to take on the case. Having done so, things escalated with threats of violence, sackings and goodness knows what else. I adopted an approach of suing both the employer and the union for allowing the situation and, in a very acrimonious atmosphere, received an offer that all red book holders (from memory about 60 or so) would be offered black book status except my clients. To the collective red book group's credit, they refused and the offer was revised to everyone except Phil. Once again this was refused, leading to total success. This led to me being hated and loved in equal measure by factions at the docks.

Phil was a very decent and likeable man who hadn't forgotten the case and came to offer his support once we opened in Hartlepool. Consequently I was to act in a number of dock related matters. One was a particularly tragic case where a lorry driver drove onto the dock area and reversed his truck into position using his rear view mirrors. His fatal mistake was to rely on the mirrors alone which showed only a view either side of his lorry. He didn't know that he was reversing into an area, directly behind him, that was cut into the dock side. In other words, he was several yards closer to the dock side than he thought and his vehicle fell backwards into the deep water, submerging the lorry and drowning him in what must have been an appalling death. The case was fully contested by the port authority, but we won damages for his widow in a high court hearing by successfully arguing that barriers should have been present to prevent the accident. Nothing can replace the loss of a loved one, but financial compensation can remove the strain of the loss of earning capacity, especially where children are involved. I desperately wanted to succeed with that one.

Cases didn't need to be so dramatic to bring me in contact with human suffering, where the difference a little care and consideration can make is palpable. I took on a straight forward accident matter and when the medical report was ready my client's wife rang to say her husband, only in his forties, now had an unrelated cancer and was too ill to leave the house. I saw him at home the next day and he was lying on their sofa in the living room with that familiar colour of an advanced cancer patient. I read him his report, but his interest was limited because of his illness. He was watching an old black and white television which didn't even have remote control so that he had to ask his wife or children to change channel or painfully do it himself. Solicitors were not allowed to advance funds, but I had an idea which I mentioned to his wife outside as I was leaving. I spoke to a local supplier and after some heavy persuasion a brand new large colour television with the latest remote control was delivered to his home on my guarantee that it would be paid for when the case was settled. Two days later I called to see him and a grey, gloom filled room had been transformed by the delivery. The man was visibly excited by the facility to change channels from his sofa, seeing everything in glorious colour and the children were smiling and sensing a change in atmosphere in their parents.

The disaster would still strike but at least some pleasure had been supplied. I walked out of that house six inches taller than when I had walked in. My mother cried when I told her the story.

Hartlepool wasn't a place you would associate with celebrities, but I was to meet the ultimate celebrity because of my location. I had a call from a business colleague one day asking me if I would like to have lunch with Prince Charles. The friend wasn't someone likely to wind me up so I asked him what he meant. He told me that the Prince of Wales had a special interest in Hartlepool and was part of a process to reinvigorate the town. He was attending a lunch with a small number of Hartlepool business people and was then meeting up with some national figures to show them around. I said I would be happy to attend. The day came and I arrived at the designated meeting place and saw people I knew who were as surprised as me to be there. As we all milled around there was a gathering crowd of people outside with their flags and cameras, waiting to catch a glimpse of Royalty. An equerry, dressed as though he had just come off the set of 'The Charge of the Light Brigade' with full sized ceremonial sword and an accent that would cut glass, explained to us what would happen. He was very pleasant and said the Prince would like to meet us all individually and would we mind standing in a line on a table-to-table basis after we had eaten. We all agreed.

Whilst we were waiting, I spotted what I thought were special branch officers and decided to have a chat with them to see what security existed. This was during the time when the IRA was active and Prince Charles was a prime target, as had been his uncle Lord Mountbatten who had been murdered by the IRA. I was as philosophical about being there as I am about flying; the chances are small and if your number is up there is not much you can do about it, but it was different for Prince Charles who was a daily target. They were indeed special branch and quite friendly. They were armed discretely and told me frankly that they had advised him not to come as they had no way of guaranteeing security and his safety. They were less concerned about the venue having checked it and researched us before they came, but Prince Charles always insisted that he met the people and would go over to the crowds and talk to them everywhere he went. At the time, Charles was portrayed in the press as something of an eccentric toff with little or no understanding of life. Here was a glimpse of the truth; he was a man of real courage who risked his life every day to meet people and engage in direct contact with the business community to create development. This was amplified when he arrived in his car and a bus pulled in nearby which carried the people he had in tow. Alan Sugar and Richard Branson were amongst those business titans sitting on the bus which led me to say to a friend of mine,

"Well there you go, who else but a member of the Royal Family could get all of those guys to sit on a bus and go to Hartlepool" I certainly saw him in a very different light and even more so when I was asked to go up to meet him. We all had small name badges on our lapels and when the man in front of me moved away I was beckoned forward by the equerry. Prince Charles was leaning against the back of a chair and without appearing to look at my lapel he shook my hand and said,

"Hello Mr McArdle, what do you think of the possibilities for development of Hartlepool and what needs to be done to help the process?" I was in the middle of replying when someone brought him a plate of food and he said, "I am sorry, do you mind if I eat while we chat as I haven't had anything since breakfast?" It was a short conversation but I thought him very slick in his dealing with people. He was also tanned and a much more attractive figure live than when appearing in photographs in the press. The most important thing was I believed his interest in the town to be genuine and he was using his status and celebrity to try and achieve something significant in this and many other towns. An eccentric, out of touch toff he certainly wasn't. Whether he played a part or not, the town did benefit enormously in the years that followed with large areas being redeveloped.

We were now well known, the cases were coming thick and fast and we had moved out of our rented premises and bought bigger and higher profile premises on York Road, the main street in Hartlepool. We were taking on additional staff and had also decided to find a site for our second office. As usual this wouldn't be without drama and obstacle, but we were used to that. Soon however, my career and my love of football were to merge into an interesting situation.

CHAPTER 17: Football

In the summer of 1984 I received a call from our accountant Malcolm Lancaster. He had joined the board at Hartlepool United and told me the club was in a lot of trouble, which I knew anyway because it appeared regularly in the local press. He asked if I would go to that evening's board meeting to give them some advice and I agreed. The board comprised of nine directors, all in their thirties or forties and all giving their time free to help the club. Malcolm introduced me to everyone, including John Smart the chairman and well known Tyneside businessman. I listened whilst they explained the problem and the advice they'd received from a large firm of solicitors in Newcastle. I knew the advice was wrong and explained their actual position and what I thought they should do. They had no money and were massively fire fighting, but were determined to survive.

I went home to my then wife and said I knew what was going to happen next; Malcolm Lancaster would ring me and invite me to join the board, but there was no way I would be that daft. Malcolm duly rang and made the offer, which I politely refused although I did say I would advise them from time to time to help out. A week and three phone calls later and I accepted the offer, establishing that I was indeed daft, but I had three conditions; I wouldn't put money in to the club, I would do it for six months only and I didn't want a vote at meetings. My role was advisory only because I didn't want to get involved in club politics. In the event, I was there for two years or so during a roller coaster of a ride for the club.

Once appointed, I realised how bad things were. Former directors, chairmen and the Inland Revenue were trying to liquidate the club, whilst various others were suing for money. I took on all of the litigation free of charge and had to keep reminding myself of my love of the game. One former owner had started high court proceedings and seemed determined to end the club's existence. I had dealt with him some years before when, as a quarry owner, he had served notice on his tenant who was renting the quarry for storing scrap cars. When the tenant failed to move, he used bulldozers to bury the poor man's entire stock of vehicles and we successfully sued him for the damage caused.

With all of the claims it was a question of day to day management and either a very solid defence or coming to a workable accommodation for long term repayment. It was like brushing away the tide on a daily basis. A major problem was that the club no longer had a bank account; the club's reputation with the local banks really was that bad! Malcolm and I overcame the problem by setting up a new company and a new trading account for commercial activities. The club employed a commercial manager and we started to make profit. That manager was the former Burnley goalkeeper Alan Stevenson who did a brilliant job. He was bright, engaging and full of ideas. He set up sportsman dinners, competitions and raffles to raise what for us was a significant amount of money, which kept things going. One day Alan rang me with an unusual edge to his usual calm and enthusiastic voice and said,

"John, I've been arrested for selling lottery tickets illegally" He had indeed been arrested, but all that was required was to amend licences which we did, although I may have wickedly led him to believe there was an outside chance of prison and deportation to Australia! The other thing I remember about Alan is him once saying to me,

"Do you remember the save of the century by Gordon Banks for England in the 1970 world cup?"

"Yes" I replied

"Well, I have at least emulated it if not bettered it. Unfortunately it was for Hartlepool reserves last Tuesday night and only three people and a dog saw it ......gutted!" Calls to the office from the club secretary were also frequent, but my favourite was a somewhat hysterical one.

"JOHN. The bailiffs are here and they have taken the goalposts"

"What? But have they left the crossbars?" was my quip. The story appeared on the TV news that night (not my crossbar remark) and in the newspapers the following day, but like all things it was sorted. Good thing too, otherwise Malcolm and I would have had to use coats for goalposts the following Saturday.

I had only been at the club for a few hours when I made my television debut. The cameras came into a meeting and I took it upon myself to answer a question no one else wanted to, and therefore inadvertently took over a job. Every time the club was asked to make a statement publicly, I was asked to do it and I appeared on both radio and television several times. Although some of my lawyer friends thought I had turned into a diva, I never sought the publicity but found that it didn't cause me any anxiety to do it. I was also trying to sort out the company law matters when my then assistant Phil Mitchell informed me there hadn't been an annual general meeting for six years. As the title suggests the meeting should take place every year, so we hurriedly pulled together the information, called a meeting and whizzed through six years in five minutes as I presented to a full room of people who didn't seem to know what was happening. We started to make real progress in sorting out the litigation and the legalities whilst Malcolm Lancaster and Alan Stephenson sorted out the finance. I attended most of the home matches and made Malcolm laugh one day when I told him that he had transformed my football watching. I used to think that a wayward shot or clearance out of the ground was poor play whereas now I thought there goes sixty quid, the cost of the ball.

The manager at the time was Billy Horner, a softly spoken but very knowledgeable football man. At one board meeting he asked what we were going to do about our centre forward, who refused to travel to away games because he had an aversion to leaving Hartlepool. I said I had heard of many people who had an aversion to entering the town but never of leaving it. It was however, no joke. Our professional footballer had tried, but insisted that the coach driver stop on the outskirts of the town to let him off. I asked Billy to show me the contract, said the player was in breach of it and had to be sacked. Money was still tight and we couldn't afford to pay someone who was only available for half of the fixtures. The player was duly sacked. To my amazement, the Professional Footballers Association (PFA) took up the case and served notice of a dispute upon us. I simply couldn't understand on what basis, but after some correspondence we agreed to an independent tribunal hearing which took place at Maine Road, the then home of Manchester City. I agreed to deal with it on behalf of the club, but several of the directors came with me for a day out. When I arrived at the club car park a number of kids ran to my car with autograph books as I suppose I was still young enough to be a player, but I had to disappoint them and tell them I was only a lawyer.

Once inside I met my opposing advocate, Brendon Batson the former West Bromwich Albion player who was the PFA representative. He was easy to get along with and very charming, and I told him I thought their action was without foundation. The tribunal was made up of a law professor who was the chairman, Graham Kelly the secretary of the Football League and Gordon Taylor the chief executive of the PFA, who was therefore Batson's boss. This was strange to say the least, but with such a clear case I didn't consider it to be too much of a problem. Not for the first time or last, my confidence was misplaced. Witnesses were called and Taylor could hardly contain his distaste of me sacking one of his members. I could tell that things weren't going well and we faced the real prospect of losing as I was already a goal down to Taylor and the other two seemed to be wavering. It was to the astonishment of my co-directors that I then launched an attack on Taylor. Standing up during Batson's examination of a witness I said to the chairman,

"I must object, not only to the tone of these proceedings, but the makeup of the tribunal itself. Mr Taylor has shown himself throughout the matter today to be biased and incapable of disguising it. He sits in judgement over a work colleague in my fellow advocate, clearly wants to support the member of his organisation regardless of the facts and should be barred from these proceedings" Taylor exploded with rage, which was entirely beneficial to me as I just pointed at him and said,

"There we are. Do you need any further evidence than that?" The chairman who was a very well educated and quietly spoken man asked if we could adjourn for a few minutes and I walked back to our room with my co directors.

One said, "John, what the fuck are you doing? We'll get slaughtered" I explained that we were going to lose anyway and if we lost now, I could get the decision set aside by a judge as I had raised the subject of bias. They were unconvinced and shortly afterwards we were called back in. I was expecting a staunch defence of my allegation as I was playing for an adjournment when the chairman said,

"Mr McArdle, Mr Taylor accepts that his behaviour was less than neutral and wishes to apologise to you for that (Taylor looked keener to challenge me to a duel than apologise). We can adjourn the matter or try and find a solution. Are you happy to discuss the possibility of a compromise?" I replied that I couldn't see any compromise that involved the club in expense, but he asked,

"If the insurers are prepared to treat the matter as a medical condition and meet all payments, would that be acceptable?"

Telephone calls then took place, leading to the insurer paying up the player's contract and we left with the matter sorted and both sides winning. I did wonder why the PFA hadn't suggested that in the first place and was a little surprised the insurers agreed, but all I really cared about was that the club was not out of pocket. Neither the club nor I had anything against the player although I did ask Billy Horner, in future, to avoid signing a centre half that refused to head the ball or a goalkeeper who couldn't wear gloves!

I turned up at a Hartlepool board meeting one night and the ground was in darkness as I made my way to the boardroom. There was a new face in the ante room who introduced himself as Mr Smart's solicitor. When I asked him what he was doing there, he told me he was looking after Mr Smart's interests and had no answer when I said that's what I thought I was doing. Once inside I asked John to explain himself and he told us that press friends had told him of a move to oust him and he just wanted protection. I told him that I was insulted that he would think he needed independent legal advice when I was there and, given that was how he felt I resigned with immediate effect. A little dramatic perhaps, but I walked to my car and started to drive back home with the Newcastle based Metro radio playing. No more than five minutes into the journey they went to the news desk and the sports reporter said, *'Also breaking news tonight; the legal director of Hartlepool United has resigned and stormed out of a board meeting.'* How did they know? Why would anyone care? Am I hallucinating? In any event I look back at my time at Hartlepool United very fondly and feel that it was purely the energy and determination of local businessmen that kept the club afloat. I still look at for their results every Saturday.

One final Hartlepool United memory involved the now premiership club Middlesbrough who in 1986 faced financial ruin and was locked out of its ground at Ayresome Park. After much financial wrangling the club managed to survive, but only on the basis that it could fulfil its first fixture of the season. Hartlepool came to the rescue and let Middlesbrough play at its ground. As a gesture of gratitude the directors of Middlesbrough gave the directors of Hartlepool a match at Ayresome Park, a ground that had hosted world cup fixtures in 1966 and had the biggest playing surface in the country. We had ten directors who all played and our team was made up with our physiotherapist who was in his fifties. Middlesbrough had only four directors and made up their team with reserve players. I played right wing against Middlesbrough's reserve left back, who was happy to give me a twenty yard start, catch me and take the ball off me without breaking sweat. At half time the score was 2-2 as one of our directors, Alan Bamford, was a decent player and had scored twice. In the second half Middlesbrough brought on their young manager Willie Maddren (former England under 23 player) who scored 6 goals and we lost 8-2! At the end of the match our chairman John Smart was so tired that he had his shower lying on the tiles in the communal shower. Maybe they should have just sent us a bottle of wine!

Around the same time that I resigned from Hartlepool, I became more involved with my own club, Sunderland. The crowds at Roker Park were dwindling, despite the fact that for once the club was reasonably comfortable in the top tier of football under a somewhat dour manager called Alan Durban. The average crowd had fallen to around 15,000 and this brought a published comment from Chairman Sir Tom Cowie, that Newcastle fans were more loyal than those of Sunderland. As you might imagine his comment caused outrage. This was tantamount to the chairman of the Pakistan cricket board saying that he thought the Indian team supporters were superior to his own. It was an ill thought out comment to say the least. Two solicitor friends of mine, Graham Sylvester and John Hall met with me and I suggested we write an open letter by response, hoping that the newspapers might publish it. I still had Doug Wetherall's telephone number from my Newcastle United case, who was still the sports correspondent for the Daily Mail, so I called him and he suggested I send the letter to him. The letter was a balanced attempt to have Sir Tom re think his aloof, dismissive approach and consider greater investment whilst utilising the fans' support rather than alienating it. Doug liked it so much that he put it on the back page and other newspapers also gave it coverage.

Two things happened as a result of the publication of the letter. Firstly I was contacted by two members of Durham County Council who had also published a story about how they, as Sunderland fans, had united against the chairman of the club despite their political differences of one being a Labour councillor and the other being a Conservative councillor. They were holding a meeting in Chester Le Street and asked me to speak from the top table. The second event was a call from Sir Tom Cowie's PA asking me to meet him. John Hall couldn't make it, but Graham Sylvester and I went to Sir Tom's office at his motor business headquarters in Sunderland. We couldn't find it at first and I stopped the car so that Graham could ask directions from a local who was standing at a bus shelter. Graham opened his window and, bearing in mind he is from London, leaned out and said in a cultured voice trying to fake a Sunderland accent,
"Excuse me bonnie lad, can you tell me where Cowie's head office is?" After the man gave directions and I drove away, I looked at Graham and said laughing,
"Excuse me bonnie lad? Why not ask him where his whippet is or if he has his pitman's lamp on him! Great accent; he'll go home tonight and tell his wife that some daft cockney stopped to ask him directions today!" We duly arrived, and were introduced to a very engaging, friendly and relaxed Sir Tom. He was doing his best to appease us when in walked his co-director and bane of his life Barry Batey. I vaguely knew Batey, an estate agent in

Sunderland, having met him on a few occasions. Cowie disguised his dislike of Batey and introduced us, which led to the rough diamond Batey barking out,

"How come they get this special press conference, eh?"

"Well, we are not the press and this is not a conference. We are here at the invitation of your chairman," I replied. Batey continued his aggressive approach until I said,

"Look Barry, I'm addressing a meeting in Chester Le Street next week when I will be referring to this meeting. What do you want me to say? That I met the directors and they couldn't give a shit about your views and although they invited me in for a chat, it was to tell me to mind my own business?" The urbane Cowie turned to Batey and said,

"Barry, I have invited these gentlemen in as I have always thought it a good idea to say something, even if it is just goodnight!" This had the desired effect and led to a positive discussion. Batey, to my surprise, came to the Chester-le-Street meeting and after I had addressed a packed house of a few hundred supporters, he stood up and spoke to, what was for him a hostile crowd. Some time afterwards Sir Tom resigned, selling his shares to Bob Murray the new chairman and majority shareholder. Doug Wetherall rang me and said he had mentioned me to Murray who wanted to meet me. I went to Roker Park and waited in the directors' room. I thought of the 11 year old me standing outside the ground hoping for autographs or saving up to buy a black and white picture of a player, yet here I was sitting in the engine room of the club. When Bob Murray walked in the spell broke and I went into professional mode or "show time "as I would tell myself before a court appearance.

Bob was a very different character to Cowie. Quietly spoken, a little unsure of himself and, it seemed to me averse to confrontation. This troubled me a little, in that Barry Batey was still there and I imagined the aggravation Bob would face. I talked to him about it and over the next couple of years a very public battle between them was played out. Murray won and stayed in contact with me, inviting me for games and coming to see me at the office. I always offered my support and assured him that I didn't want anything in exchange. I would happily act for the club for free and help him when he needed it, and didn't need to be rewarded with a position. On one particular match day, I was one of two guests and we were both made to feel we were being groomed for directorships. The other man duly became one but when my turn came I had decided against it. I had a young family and the idea of being so committed, especially at weekends, didn't appeal.

It was a genuine conflict as I would have been very proud to represent the club and had some ideas that I would have liked to implement as part of a team of directors. I wasn't formally offered the position, but the club secretary contacted me and said that Bob was offering me shares in the club which was then a private company. Once I was a shareholder, the next move may have been an appointment. I thought long and hard about it, but wrote to Bob declining the offer and telling him that I didn't agree with the direction the club was going in and I didn't want to become the new Barry Batey. I wished him every success. The club became a public company a few years later and if I had bought the offered shares they would have increased in value to the tune of 40 times their purchase price (shrewd as ever!). Murray put all of his effort into the building of a new stadium which was an enormous success but was unable to translate that to the team. In 2006 he sold his interests in the club to a consortium of businessmen and left with a mixed reaction. I always found him a genuinely nice caring man who loved the club, but I felt he needed people around him to provide the talents he lacked. He also needed to want that to happen.

So my career had brought me close to the sport that had dominated my childhood and gave me an insight into the running of it. It is now a game overrun with cash and subject to enormous corruption from the very top, all of the way down. I have been involved in cases and in conversations which indicate to me that bribery and cash payments in the transfer of players are common and drain the game. What a pity. It was time for me to concentrate on my own business again, and on looking for more offices.

CHAPTER 18: Growth and recruitment

Malcolm Donnelly and I had looked at a couple of places for a second office, but settled on Darlington for no particular reason. Malcolm Burgess lived in the town and I met him for a walk through it to see if there was a potential office that took our fancy. We passed a property in Outram Street with a 'For Sale' sign outside and I stopped and looked at it. It had a shop front, looked a little like the first office we rented in Hartlepool and I felt it was perfect. I rang the estate agent who told me the price and I made him an offer. I informed him who we were and that we could proceed immediately. There was a moment's delay, and then he said the property was sold subject to contract. It didn't ring true, so I asked Malcolm Burgess if he could find out who the owner was. Malcolm spoke to the owner, who confirmed it wasn't sold and that he hadn't been told of our interest. Call me paranoid, but here was another attempt, it seemed, to strangle the growth of our fledgling business. As they were estate agents it seemed strange, but perhaps they had been told we were trouble and perhaps we were. Anyway, we did the deal with the owner in 1983. The property needed quite a bit of work including a new shop front, damp proof course and new toilets as well as decoration throughout and we eventually opened in 1984.

Although the building was small, we now had our second office. We had employed a receptionist and a typist, and transferred our trainee solicitor to Darlington, with Malcolm Donnelly and me taking turns to spend some part of the day there. Malcolm lost interest in it fairly soon and began to refer to it as the 'Darlington problem', but I knew if we were going to grow we needed a presence in more than one town, so finding a way to develop the new office was essential. Geoff Cardwell was an obvious choice as he was not only a very good friend of mine but a very good lawyer. The only problem was that he was undergoing a schedule of qualification with his employers, Tyne and Wear Council in Jesmond, and he lived in Sunderland. We took him out for lunch, told him of our plans and asked if he fancied joining us. He was keen, but committed to his College of Law finals in the coming months. We said we would wait and he could work part time for us during holidays as a way of supplementing his income. Problem solved, but the increase in the number of cases was giving me a real headache. I knew I was taking on too much and started to count down the weeks until Geoff's arrival.

One of the reasons I was so overrun was that we had taken on our biggest broker to date and the numbers of car accident claims had more than doubled overnight. Phil Smith had recommended me to Arnott Insurance Brokers who had offices in Middlesbrough and Sunderland, and had a client base of maybe 25,000. I had met Ian Fletcher first and then his co director Derrick Arnott both of whom loved the idea of the scheme and I assured them we could handle the enormous influx of work. This was my usual response; secure the work and then solve how to deliver it. The number of new cases was as high as we anticipated and the excitement of a big leap up the development ladder more than made up for the huge increase in work for the firm and me personally. I frantically tried to develop systems in a pre computer based operation and started to recruit staff. Geoff Cardwell joined us full time and held surgeries at Arnott's offices, bringing armfuls of work back each time. Even at my young age, I should have expected a setback; smooth running didn't exist or at least it didn't for me. It came when a lawyer friend told me that I had made such waves in the insurance world, that his firm had been approached to find a way to stop us using any method possible. I don't think they intended mafia style executions, but any loophole or irregularity was to be explored. His firm refused to help, but clearly someone accepted the challenge because we received a letter from the Law Society detailing a complaint that we were breaching the rules on arrangements with third parties. As I mentioned, I had spoken to the Law Society and sought their advice before setting up the original scheme, particularly on the subject of not breaching any regulation. They had confirmed that the scheme was acceptable and our agreements with insurance brokers didn't breach the current regulations. I rang them to remind them of the advice they'd given me and, to my amazement they acknowledged the advice, but said they were mistaken. I was to stop the scheme they had approved. When writing this now, I find it hard to believe that I took this in my stride. This was dreadful news and quite why I felt I would find a solution, or that there even was one, I'm really not sure. Put it down to wishful thinking.

I studied the regulations line by line until I could almost recite them. What I had sought to say was that this wasn't an arrangement, but that the firm was being employed by the broker who was the client. Having reread the rules, I saw a path. An arrangement could exist with a third party or organisation as long as that organisation wasn't set up for the purpose of legal advice and that the advice was just part of its function. So we could have an arrangement with a club or association, but not a broker.

Some years earlier Derrick Arnott had formed The Northern Motorists Association (NORMA) for the benefit of Arnott clients, with the idea of getting discounts on a number of motor based services. The organisation had made it onto the television screens, which he was very proud of. He was somewhat less proud of the fact that it hadn't worked and had fallen into disuse. However, using NORMA as the conduit for my accident scheme seemed to be the way of overcoming the regulation, but l decided, having lost faith in the advisory powers of the Law Society, to obtain a specialist barrister's opinion. That opinion confirmed my view and the barrister drafted the necessary documents to enliven NORMA. We were up and running without any delay and the insurance sponsored nuclear attack upon us had failed.

Funnily enough, Derrick Arnott wrote a book after he retired and made mention of the accident scheme as though it was his idea. More of that later, but I'm afraid his recollections of events is inaccurate. Like most insurance brokers of the time they handled the claims themselves, but it was an awful lot of work for no reward and they were often out of their depth, which was why they came to me. Although he was very interested, he had nothing to do with the setting up of the scheme (l still have the documents that prove that), other than providing the clients and his office space for surgeries. He was to benefit in the years ahead because of the scheme, but would eventually find himself marginalised and finally out of office because of a relationship with an individual that would cost us both dearly, but again much more of that later.

One day my surveyor friend Alan Cowie rang me and asked me if l knew that the property next door to our Darlington office was for sale, adding that he was surprised we weren't buying it. l told him that l had looked at it before but we didn't need it. As soon as l put the phone down l realised that l was talking nonsense and asked the estate agents for the keys to look again. Shortly after that we bought the property and knocked through. We now had a major office with much more accommodation and l decided to use it as my main office, visiting the Hartlepool office one day a week. Conveniently, we had sold our family home near Hartlepool and were renting in Darlington whilst looking around for a suitable house. l wanted a change of environment and moving to Darlington both professionally and personally seemed like a good idea. My secretary in Hartlepool was Joanne Richardson who had joined us straight from school. She was indispensable to me and thankfully she agreed to travel from her home in Hartlepool every day, along with Diane Risebury who would organise the bigger office. When all the refurbishment work was done we transferred files and although I returned to Hartlepool once or occasionally twice a week to see clients, my main efforts were in building up the new office in Darlington and expanding.

I found the expansion very exciting and maybe that hid the fact that I was taking on more and more. Despite Geoff and more staff joining us, I still had the largest caseload and the most time consuming cases, on top of the administration and the development plans. None of it seemed like work to me and I was living my fantasy of being in control of my own destiny and flexing my legal and business muscles. I worked nonstop from getting into the office to going home. Gone were the days when, on a whim Malcolm and I could drive down to the golf club for a game of snooker at 10 o'clock in the morning, or go to the pub at lunchtime for a meal and game of darts. If we were not careful we might even have to grow up! Despite all of the excitement of the business side of things, doing the job with a passion to succeed for the client was still the most important thing to me. As busy as I was, I always gave full attention to the client in front of me and never took telephone calls during an appointment or found myself thinking about other cases. However, through tiredness I occasionally found that my powers of concentration slipped a little. At the end of a long day I would say goodbye to my penultimate client and as they left, slump onto my desk before buzzing reception and asking them to send the last one up. The drained, almost slumbering beast would spring into life when the door opened; it was 'show time' again. I recall one such day when my last client was a very pleasant middle aged lady who, on being asked how I could help, began her story. After a few minutes, I realised that I hadn't been listening, so I tuned in hoping to pick up the threads. I was normally able to do it, but on this occasion.... nothing.

"I'm sorry there is a bit I am not following," I said with authority.

"Oh, which bit?" she said sympathetically.

"I wasn't sure where you said you were .....when the incident happened?"

"Which incident do you mean?" she enquired.

"Well for the avoidance of doubt, why don't you start again from the beginning and I will take some notes?" I said. A masterstroke, I felt!

"Oh yes no problem" she replied cheerfully. I took out my pen and opened my notebook as she started and thought how clever I had been to escape the embarrassment of having to explain that unfortunately, because of the timing of the appointment, she had drawn a short straw and that whatever

138

brainpower I possessed had been expended some time ago and I might even need directions to get home. A few other thoughts flashed through my mind before a red light came on and I realised I hadn't been listening to the story for a second time and was once again lost as to what precisely I was supposed to be advising her about. What should I say this time? *'Sorry I don't speak English and I can't follow your story'.* Maybe *'could you to write it down and I'll read it when I am awake?'* would work. Instead I said, "Oh look at that. I was following that so much I forgot to write the notes; better make sure we get all of this down, so you started by saying?" It seemed to work although she probably went home and told her husband that the solicitor was alright, but seemed to have been drinking or maybe he was high on medication. Often by the time I got home I had wound down so much on the journey back, that a question as to what I might like for dinner was too much as all of my decision making powers had deserted me. In the years ahead my wife Gillian would often say to friends that there was no point in asking me anything as, *'John leaves his brain in the office'.* Some people in the office might disagree. An essential ingredient of growth in any business is the recruitment of staff and I certainly had a mixed experience in that regard. As my mother used to say, "There is nothing stranger than folk".

CHAPTER 19: You need staff

In many ways, because I had already been working for nine years I was an old 25 years of age when we set up the practice. However, the fact remains that I was very young to be in the position I was. I was very confident and never worried about my lack of experience, probably due to a lack of knowledge of the things I should have been worried about. Without doubt, I put more thought into the opening of our fifth office than I had into the setting up of the business in the first place.

I immediately had to get used to being an employer and I always saw that as a responsibility not a benefit. I had no problem with the role, but I knew that the decisions were mine to make and that others would be affected by them; decisions such as whether to offer a job to someone and, equally importantly whether to reject an applicant. I added a middle-aged woman to our small team who had worked for me at Mincoffs in Newcastle, as I thought the addition of someone older would be a wise decision. This turned out to be a mistake as she didn't settle into the role, became unpredictable within the small office and as I learned later, bullied our new office junior.

That office junior was a pocket battleship called Diane Barnard (now Risebury) who I found impressive on interview. She was sixteen years old, short, attractive and shy, but she looked me in the eye when answering every question I asked her. I recognised something special in her and knew she would add something significant to our team. I was right about that one; Diane went on to be our receptionist, then bookkeeper, then office manager and another couple of roles. When I retired completely in 2015 she was still there and quite the most popular member of staff we ever had. I mentioned in my retirement speech how much I valued her and recalled one occasion when I learned that a client had been difficult in reception, creating a fuss and making a complaint. I went to see Diane and asked her if it was true.

She replied, "Yes he did, but I didn't tell you because you would have come down full of hell and made the situation worse. I handled it."

"Fair enough" I said, walking back upstairs seeing her point.

I hated people being nice to the partners of the firm or to people they deemed to be important, but unpleasant to staff or people they deemed unimportant. Even if they were friends or acquaintances, I would tackle it. The staff knew that I would not tolerate rudeness to them. Diane thought that was a good thing, but that I might be oversensitive about it and saw it as her job to protect me from too many interruptions and to sometimes protect the clients from me. In doing so she would be very economical with the truth and was simply the best benevolent liar I have ever met. All of her lies were delivered with compassion and created to defuse situations. Clients would take one look at her innocent, angelic and sincere face and no matter what she said they would assume she was telling the truth.

"So even though Mr McArdle has been dealing with my case this morning, he cannot take my calls because he has a throat infection" ... must be true. "So Mr Donnelly is out at court all day and that person singing in his room is a workman decorating"... must be true. She was a great asset to the practice.

I was also fortunate with Joanne Archbold, another teenager who worked as our junior and then became my secretary. She was very quiet and shy, but massively efficient. Some years into the job she was playing badminton, heard a crack like a rifle shot and realised that her Achilles tendon had snapped. She was taken to hospital, encased in plaster and signed off on sick leave for a number of weeks. Typically of her, she telephoned a few days later asking if I could set up some equipment at her house so that she could do my typing. She was worried about the work not being done properly and she was bored. Not many people would do that. I didn't need a second invitation and set up the equipment and a delivery and collection service almost immediately.

Unfortunately, not all appointments were as successful. During interviews I always recalled Mr Flynn's very good advice of appearing interested, asking questions and looking the part. He told me that a friend of his who interviewed many people said he always noted the state of cleanliness of fingernails and shoes, as well as how the person was sitting during interview. The correct way was to sit with a straight back, uncrossed legs and unfolded arms. Sadly this advice had not been extended to some of the people I interviewed.

Applying for the job of an office junior, an eighteen year old male from Hartlepool came into my room with his hands in his pockets, his head slumped forwards and sat down without being invited. He kept his hands in his pockets, thrust his legs forward and sat with his backside halfway down the seat and his shoulders just above the top of the chair. As tempted as I was to say *'thank you very much I have seen enough, goodbye'* I asked him a few questions and got a few mumbled answers. The question I remember best was,

"What do you see yourself doing in five years time?"

"I would hope to have progressed" he replied.

"To what?" I enquired.

"Dunno. To whatever you progress to I suppose" he said, hands never leaving his pockets. He didn't get the job.

A nineteen year old girl from Hartlepool applied for a post of junior typist and came for her interview wearing a very short skirt and, being as kind as I can be, was a little too heavy to be wearing it comfortably. Not that she was in any way embarrassed by the large expanse of flesh on display, which I suspect she wrongly thought was an advantage to her. She was also too familiar and too confident.

"Hello, I am John McArdle and this is my business partner Malcolm Donnelly" I said

"Hiya Malcolm, you alright?" she replied, almost winking at him.

"Fine thanks, do you live in the town?" Malcolm asked.

"Yeah I live in Grosvenor Street, where do youse two live?"

At one point Malcolm made a remark which I cannot remember after all of these years, but it was a light hearted comment to which she replied whilst looking at me and winking,

"He's a queer one isn't he? We'll have to watch him won't we, eh?" Unsurprisingly, she didn't get the job and when Malcolm returned from court later that day, he told me that he had seen her cocking her leg over the central reservation barrier on the dual carriageway whilst crossing the road, and yes she was still wearing that short skirt!

Then there was the twenty four year old male who applied to be an assistant solicitor. Having qualified at another firm, he gave a surprisingly uninspiring interview. He was a pale, thin and very quietly spoken person and it was difficult to imagine what kind of work he could do that would instil any confidence at all in a client. I did most of the talking for him during the interview, but then I asked him if he had any questions for us.

"Ah..ah....do you pay expenses for the interview?"

"No" was my reply. No job offer there either.

Others were successful at interview and it was whilst they were in the job that disaster struck. One such employee had been working for us for a few weeks when I received a call from the fraud squad. He was our trainee legal executive who had arrived after leaving his job in a bank, which he had found unfulfilling. During his interview he had mentioned that his unusual middle name was because he was a distant relation of Freddie Mercury of Queen, the hottest band of their time; perhaps I should have been suspicious then.

When the fraud squad sergeant arrived at our office he informed Malcolm and me that far from leaving the bank of his own accord, the lad had been fired for dishonesty. The sergeant explained that pound coins had been stolen in fairly large quantities and the bank, upon becoming suspicious had moved him to another branch where the same thing had happened again. During his employment with us the fraud squad had gathered enough information to arrest him and were going to do so from our office, as long as we didn't object. We didn't, but to avoid upsetting the other staff we asked if they could arrest him after everyone had gone home. When I asked the sergeant how confident he was of our employee's guilt, he said, "Mr McArdle, I have been a police officer for 30 years and I can tell you he is guilty, no doubt about it." We asked the young lad to stay back after work and he was duly arrested and driven away looking ashen.

Following his arrest we were both in shock and tried to imagine how you could possibly get hundreds of pound coins out of a bank at the end of a day. We speculated that filling your trouser pockets would not work, as your trousers would end up around your ankles, whilst putting them into a very long container down your trousers would make you walk like a robot or a man with two broken legs. Unbelievably, the next day we received a call from the same fraud squad sergeant to say that he had been released without charge adding, "I'm sure he is innocent Mr McArdle."
"Hang on a minute, yesterday you told me you were sure he was guilty," I reminded him.
"Yes, but I have spoken to him now and I'm sure he is innocent."
At this point Geoff Cardwell had joined the partnership and the three of us discussed this unexpected development between us. Their view, which was quite correct as it turned out, was that having lied to us anyway he should be sacked. I should have listened to them, but I wanted to give him a chance and argued that he was unlikely to put on his CV that he was under investigation for theft in his previous job. I eventually persuaded them, against their better judgement and they agreed to let him stay. I surprised him with the news of a second chance, but sometime later £50 went missing from someone's drawer. The obvious candidate was him and, although there was no real evidence against him, Malcolm and Geoff both gave me that 'hope you know what you are doing' look.

Then another matter arose concerning an obscene birthday card he sent to one of girls. She didn't want to tell me, but I found out about it from one of her colleagues. I asked her to bring it to me and inside a standard card he had drawn a childlike drawing of a man with an enormous penis. Underneath he had written *I bet your dad has a big cock like this.* I asked the girl if she knew why he had done it or if there had been some conversation that made it relevant, but she said not. Whilst she didn't understand the card, she didn't feel upset enough to make a complaint. I could not leave it, sent her back to her desk and requested he come to my office where I showed him the card and asked him if he had sent it. He looked at it for a second or two and said he couldn't remember. "Can't remember? DID YOU OR DIDN'T YOU?" I demanded, fixing him with a stare.

"Yes" he spluttered.

"If you do anything like that again we will dismiss you and frankly I am worried about what might be going on in your head"

Needless to say, I kept a close eye on him and subsequently became suspicious when I asked him about some legal executive exams he had been sitting, financed by us. He gave a less than satisfactory answer which caused me to start an investigation, particularly as he had just sent in a sick note for the third week running. I found the invoices for the courses and noticed a similarity. I realised that he had taken last year's receipt, photocopied it with the date covered, written in the new date and photocopied it again to present it for payment. In doing that, it looked like a photocopy of a genuine receipt. He had in effect stolen the value of a course he had not attended and taken the time off on study leave for examinations he didn't sit.

I told Geoff what I had discovered and informed him I was driving out to his home where I was likely to strangle him. Geoff said he was coming with me, partly to ensure the boy's safety. When we arrived at his parents' house, his father said he was asleep in bed.

"You better wake him," I ordered

Having returned from the room upstairs his father said, "I've tried, but I can't wake him up"

"Let me have a go, I am sure I will be able to manage it and if you don't let me I am coming back with the police" I said

"Let me try again" his father replied.

At no stage had this man asked us who we were and upon returning again he said, "Can I tell you the truth? He isn't here; he's at the leisure centre".

Geoff and I turned on our heels and speed walked to the leisure centre in Thornaby which attracted more than its fair share of hostile looking youths and men who, since we were dressed in blue suits and overcoats probably assumed we were CID looking for an arrest. Benefitting from this assumption, we walked all through the leisure centre, including the gents changing rooms without a word of protest from anyone. Failed search over, we walked back to the house to find our employee sitting with his parents. I immediately went for him, asking why he was not at work if he was fit enough for the leisure centre. He mumbled some reply and then I moved on.

"Can you tell me what happened in your recent exams?"

"I passed one of them but have to re sit another," he almost whispered

"Which one did you pass?" I said staring like an assassin.

"I'm not sure" he replied meekly.

"Not sure? You're not sure which one you passed?" I exclaimed before adding, "Which course did you do"

"The correspondence course" he replied

"This one?" I asked holding up the doctored receipt

"Yes, that one"

"You liar, you have copied last year's receipt and claimed for a course you did not do and then you took time off for examinations you did not sit," I said raising the temperature and my voice. He said nothing so I went on, "I am going to ask you once more and you had better stop lying to me. Did you or did you not forge the receipt for this course?"

"Yes" he said obviously bewildered as to how we had found out.

I exploded and told him what an ungrateful little shit he was and that he could expect a call from the police before telling Geoff he better get me out of there before I did strangle him. The police were informed and he was duly convicted, having pleaded guilty to the theft of the course fees. He was never charged with the theft of the coins from the bank or the £50, where he remains hot favourite.

Strange as that situation was, we soon found ourselves in a worse one. We had taken on a bright typist come receptionist who wanted to be a lawyer and agreed to facilitate her ambition with training and professional exam support. She settled into the team very well and over a few years progressed to handling some smaller cases herself, as well as being full time executive support on other cases. One day Geoff could not find a file and more surprisingly nor could our queen of the filing room, Barbara Robson. Very occasionally files went missing, but Barbara always managed to trace them. She saw it as her vocation to be able to trace every one of the thousands of files, both active and inactive within the office. This file however was different and as the urgency of its location intensified, staff volunteered to stay after work to find it. Every cabinet in the office was emptied to see if the file had become entangled in another one, or had fallen down the back of the cabinet itself, but despite our efforts the file remained missing.

I was still hopeful that the ever resourceful Barbara would find it in the attic, or cellar or in the turn ups of somebody's trousers, but nothing. My concern increased when another file went missing, quickly followed by two more. I knew then that someone was behind it and, much like a murder mystery I went through the list of suspects in my head. My main suspicion fell upon the trainee who we shall call Mary (not her real name), as she was broadly the common denominator, although motive was absent. She had taken a week's holiday leave and had recently moved from her parent's home to live with her boyfriend, but we didn't have her number there. Geoff agreed to ring her father who he knew from acting for him and said he was looking for a file. He gave the name of the first file and said he just wondered if Mary had been working on it at home before she moved. The father said he would look and came back saying that the file was not there, but gave the name of another file that was; we were not even aware of that one's disappearance. There was still the possibility of an innocent explanation, but I was more suspicious than ever. Any doubt that I had was removed the following day when I received this letter from Mary.

Dear John,

As you know I am currently on holiday, but I became aware that yesterday you arranged for Geoff Cardwell to ring my father and enquire about a missing file and to ask if it was at their house. It is clear to me that you think that I am somehow responsible for the recent missing files. I cannot imagine why you would think I would remove files from the office when I have spent so much time with other members of staff searching for them.

I am very grateful for the opportunity you have given me at the firm and for the personal training and guidance from you in particular. However, trust is an important part of any employer/employee relationship and as a result of your totally unfounded suspicion of me on the files issue I feel that trust has broken down. I am therefore tendering my resignation with immediate effect.

Yours sincerely

Geoff was in another office that day and I rang him and said, "It is definitely her and I am off to her house now to get the files back" He replied in his usual sensible way of asking me to exercise caution, adding his usual warning that one day I'll get myself sliced in two by a Samurai sword as I bludgeon my way into conflict. I arrived at Mary's address a few minutes later and banged on the door, which was opened by her boyfriend. I asked to see her and upon being told she was not there, just walked in and said, "Right, I have come for the files and if you give them to me now we can avoid a lot of trouble"

"What files?" he enquired, apparently in all innocence.

I was by now searching his house without his permission and looking behind chairs, tables and under the stairs. As I reached the sofa beside the window I said, "Those files," pointing at a pile of ten or so files behind the sofa. He was silent as I moved to count them. I grabbed the files, brushed past him and drove back to the office. Whilst going through them, I noticed that the original file was not amongst them and rang Geoff to tell him I was going back, which increased his vision of the sword attack.

Once again I hammered on the door and this time when the boyfriend opened up I saw Mary standing in the living room sobbing. I approached them both and said that I realised Mary's actions were signs of stress, not dishonesty or malice, but that she had to return all of the files to me. The tears increased as Mary, held up by her boyfriend insisted that I had all of the files. I told her that I did not as I could identity at least one that was still missing. She finally conceded and asked her partner to go and get the files. To my amazement and horror he walked slowly upstairs and came back down a few seconds later with two plastic carrier bags holding another twenty or so files to add to those I already had. As I was leaving, I turned to Mary and said that I did not accept her resignation as obviously this was health related, and she should come in and see me when she felt better. In fact she never did and she moved on. She did however stay in contact with Geoff and sent clients to the office from time to time.

What she intended to do with the files was not clear, but as she had resigned I imagine she would have destroyed them which would have been disastrous for us; remember these were the days before computers and electronic back up. There really was no motive or logical explanation other than an inability to cope and a reluctance to admit it. Geoff and I worked through the files to see what had happened and in her stressed state, Mary had been typing letters to clients, insurers and solicitors but never sending them, instead leaving carbon letters in the file to make it look like work was being done. This meant real chaos for us because we could not rely on the files for accuracy. We made the decision to contact all parties on all of the files in which she had been involved. In that contact we explained the position and asked our opponents for copies of their most recent correspondence so that we could be sure as to the position. Amazingly not one opponent tried to take advantage, including those with whom we had a peppery relationship and after much effort, order was restored. I think most companies could see that such a thing could happen to them, but it was generous of them all to be so understanding.

There were other employees who came and went, and then there were those who pretended an expertise they didn't have. There was one other thief who upon being questioned by the police about a cheque she made out to herself, denied all knowledge until the police officer found our cheque book in her handbag. However, by and large the employees that I worked with were a pleasure to be with and many of them became friends.

At my retirement dinner I looked around the room and saw many who had never worked anywhere else, many who had worked at the practice for more than twenty years and two partners that had undertaken their training contract with us. My secretary of 18 years, Rachel Woods had worked for me since leaving school and at that same dinner I explained that my previous three secretaries had all been called Joanne, so she had to get used to me calling her Joanne for the first year. She, along with so many others, had found some reason to stay. Not bad, not bad at all. We must have managed to do some things right.

Picking up where I left off before this chapter, we were now entering the 1990's and the firm was well established and increasingly profitable. The Darlington office was the largest office in both space and turnover and Hartlepool was doing well, but I was aware that Malcolm Donnelly was becoming increasingly unhappy and distant. He once said to Geoff that he preferred it when there was just the two of us and we were much smaller, which was an unfortunate thing to say to the third partner, but Geoff didn't take offence. Over a period of time I tried a number of things to engage

Malcolm with the firm's development, but eventually we decided to go our separate ways. Malcolm started his own firm on the ground floor of our Hartlepool office and we kept the first floor until we found alternative premises in the town. We peacefully divided up our joint assets and remained friends, which was a great relief to me.

Having bought our new Hartlepool office, I set my sights on an office in Sunderland as the next part of the development. That part was to be exciting and devastating in equal measure for a reason I could never have predicted.

CHAPTER 20: A career in property

In the years between 1985 and 1992 my life had changed considerably. On a personal front my daughter was born in 1986 (my son was born in 1982) and we all lived in a beautiful Georgian house in Middleton St George. I had always admired another house in the village, which had become the house of my dreams, and then it became available. The year was 1990 and the property was Brake House, which is a Victorian house in its own grounds and surrounded by a high wall which gave it an air of mystery. In the years that I had lived in the village the wall, some of the building and the many trees were all that I could see, but I knew I would like it.

The house was owned by the bestselling author Philippa Gregory, who I had met a few times at dinner parties and the rumour was that she was leaving because of her media work in London. I rang her and asked if I could come and see her, and she agreed to meet. As I walked up the curving sparsely gravelled drive I saw the house and its somewhat neglected grounds for the first time. By the time I had reached the door I was totally smitten and knew that I must buy it if I could. Philippa confirmed the rumour, showed me around the house and the grounds, and told me the valuation she had been given by the estate agent. The place needed a lot of work, especially the gardens but I agreed the price she asked and the deal was done. I wanted it so that my two young children could play in complete safety with their friends and could enjoy it for as much of their childhood as possible.

The practice had begun to thrive on the back of my relationship with the insurance brokers, to the extent that we had three offices in Darlington, Hartlepool and Sunderland, and covered the rest of the North East from those bases. I was looking to complete the set with an office in Newcastle and had the continued support of the bank which seemed prepared to go with anything I found. To add to this mix, Malcolm Burgess and I had accidentally embarked on a property development business. I say accidentally because we'd seen a property for sale in the Lake District and we talked about buying it for the use of both families. This was in 1987 and so off we went to our first property auction. In the car we agreed that we wouldn't go above £40,000 and although I knew the format of a property auction, I had no experience of it. Thanks to the BBC programme "Homes Under the Hammer" everyone now knows that you are obliged to buy on a successful bid, must have the finance sorted out in advance and the deposit immediately available.

On the day, I looked around a full room which emptied a little before our property came up. The auctioneer asked for bids at £25,000 then £20,000 before finally getting one at £18,000 and the action started. The bids went up to £31,000 before losing steam and I came in at that price, which as a new bidder seemed to do the trick and it looked as though we had bought under budget. A young woman with a toddler in a pushchair was fiddling about with her child and handbag, and actually facing away from the auctioneer, so I hadn't paid her much attention until she raised her hand, still looking away, and bid £32,000. The next few seconds (and I mean seconds) brought in a new male bidder and saw me exceed our limit with my final bid of £44,000 before the partly concentrating mother bought the property for £80,000, leaving Malcolm and me open mouthed and shell-shocked. On the drive back, we had a laugh at how we had been mugged and how easy it was to get carried away at these auctions before Malcolm said that whilst we were out we may as well look at property he had seen in a village outside Darlington. His intention was that we could buy, renovate and sell for a profit. We stopped at what were two small properties, one of which was fire damaged and Malcolm said that we could acquire both and use a builder he knew if I could raise the finance. I said yes and over the coming months we obtained planning permission and rebuilt the properties making a handsome profit. We had the bug then and all because we failed to buy that holiday property in the Lake District.

Over the next few years we bought and sold a few properties, but the most significant purchase was a piece of land near Darlington which we bought in order to relocate Malcolm's car hire and repairing garage business. Having bought it with the profit we made on the sale of the first deal we found ourselves transported into a different league. Property developers and large companies contacted us about the site, including the main buyer for Sainsbury's. He was a very charming and interesting character and said,

"It's a funny town Darlington. I mean it is quite prosperous. You could lift it up and move it to the South and it would fit in. It seems almost out of place here in the North East"

Managing not to be offended by this somewhat patronising remark, I let him go on and he added,

"Well, Mr McArdle you have a terrific site here and when the new road is built it will be very valuable. I would build a supermarket here, but somehow I suspect we will build in the centre of the town. Sainsbury's are big on socio-economic studies before coming to a decision, whereas old man Morrison (Morrison's supermarket chain) comes out to every site, licks his finger, sticks it in the air and just decides to buy there and then."

He was right. Sainsbury's did buy a site in the middle of the town and Morrison's built a huge store at Morton Palms, near our site. However, the interest didn't stop and we were approached by Petrofina, a large oil company which is now part of the Total Group. We met a lively middle aged Scotsman who talked incessantly about the deals he was involved in and peppered every story with chuckles and a wink. Although difficult to follow, he appeared to be expressing an interest in buying a quarter of our land at the front for a petrol servicing station and when I pinned him down , he said he would pay £500,000 for it. I tried not to faint, scream or wet myself before replying with a measured nod. When I put on my lawyers hat and offered him exclusivity at £550,000 he agreed and even sent a fax to that effect. It was subject to a number of conditions, including the new road. It was fortunate that we didn't spend the money because after a few weeks we lost all contact with him. As for the new road, well that came 20 years later!

This high octane, but no delivery interest was beginning to irritate both of us when Malcolm was approached by a mutual friend, David Penman. He suggested joining forces and applying for the Nissan franchise in Darlington. We had the land, David had the expertise as he already ran a motor franchise, and we could jointly build and run it. All Nissan dealerships in the country were available at the time as an object lesson in not picking a fight you are likely to lose. A very colourful businessman called Octav Botnar had the sole distribution rights over Nissan cars in Britain, owning all the Nissan dealerships in the country which totalled more than 200. In 1991 he was in dispute with Nissan and apparently expected them to back down. They didn't and terminated his agreement and all of his dealerships, allowing us to apply to the new Nissan UK company to build a garage and sell their products in Darlington. We met their representative who told us we would need to build a garage to their specification and gave us a timescale to do it. Malcolm and I decided that rather than wait for someone else, we would develop the site ourselves starting with this project. David, Malcolm and I formed a company called PMB Ltd (bet you can guess how we came up with that!), entered into a deal with Nissan and started down the planning permission route. Now you may think there is a theme of nothing in my life being straightforward and you would be correct. It was about to continue as the application went in and I entered the world of planning law and local politics.

I went to meet the then chief planning officer, Laurie Mulrine who I was advised, was very difficult and that I would get nowhere if I got on the wrong side of him. At our first meeting Malcolm and I were accompanied by our architect and a full set of plans, which showed our site and our proposed garage building. Mr Mulrine, a slim shortish man in his forties, met us with a less than friendly air and managed to avoid smiling throughout. I explained what we wanted to do and asked him what he thought. He looked at our carefully drawn plans and told us that he would prefer the building to be moved to the right hand side of the plot, pointing with his right index finger to the spot of his preference. I asked him to confirm that if we did that, he would be happy to approve the scheme. He agreed with a nod. I shook his hand and agreed to have the plans redrawn. As I left I said to our architect, John Taylor, that Mulrine didn't seem too bad and that the meeting had gone well. John was a very good architect, an affable and unflappable professional who duly went off and redrew the plans, putting the garage in the position pointed out by Mr Mulrine. I suspect, by the look on his face, he knew that it wasn't going to be that easy. We all met up again three weeks later with the new plans and the garage virtually on the spot where Mulrine left his fingerprint. Having opened the plans I waited for him to say how pleased he was with it, but he looked for a few seconds and then put his finger a few inches to the left of where we had originally planned the garage before saying,

"I would prefer it there"

"Do you mean you want us to build the garage where you are pointing?" I asked. "We don't own that land, you are pointing outside our boundary"

"I know, but you could buy it couldn't you?"

"Sorry, I am a little confused. Are you suggesting we buy more land from an owner who might not want to sell when we have more than enough land already?" I mused still being polite.

"Yes, but you have them over a barrel, don't you?" he replied expressionless. Giving myself time to think I adopted the courtroom technique that was very familiar to me; I was deciding if anything was salvageable and how hot my response should be. Should I still be conciliatory or should I flex a muscle or two.

"I don't want to be difficult here, but you may remember that we had a previous meeting and redrew the plans placing the garage exactly where you said you wanted it. I cannot agree to apply for permission on land we don't own, so I'm afraid I am going to have to ask you to say whether or not you would object to the existing plan" A few seconds delay and a fair bit of rising tension, and he replied,

"OK, but I can tell you I won't be buying a car from this site"

"Well as disappointing as that news is, we will have to live with it. However, you are saying that you will support this application?"

"With conditions which I will write to you about" was his surly response.

We left in a mixture of bewilderment and amusement, but my long experience was that victories such as these often lead to further declarations of hostilities and Mr Mulrine didn't disappoint; his conditions were onerous. They involved us carrying out a large range of site tests, borehole results and expensive and time consuming methane protection of the building, all of which we did. In all the years the property has been built, there has been no methane warning from any of the alarms, but the place was built as though it was in Chernobyl. If there is ever a nuclear attack, I am confident that the building will withstand it.

Mulrine kept coming up with requests for further information and the delays were putting us close to our Nissan deadline. I wasn't prepared to miss the deadline, so I wrote to Mulrine and said we had complied with all that we could and that he knew things were time sensitive, so for those reasons we were opening as planned. I waited for a negative response and intended to resist any further delay, by injunction if necessary. There was no immediate response and we completed the building, opened for business and duly traded for a few weeks. Strangely, Mulrine's response was to go out on two different occasions at night and file a criminal summons on us for illuminating a totem pole sign on the site without planning permission. The only problem for him was that we did have planning permission, granted by his department. The summons was dismissed with costs to be paid by the Council. In 1996 plans were submitted for a second garage and again we were met with barely concealed animosity. After a few meetings which seemed to get more and more difficult, I asked for a word alone with him and said,

"Mr Mulrine, it is clear that we don't get on and that is unfortunate, but does not need to get in the way of the business we have to do together, which is not often. If we don't find a way to work together then my experience as a litigation lawyer is that these disputes will be settled in another room, where neither of us have control over the outcome, but the consequences of which will be significant for at least one of us and possibly both. I suggest we start again and try and find a more accommodating path"

Although he stared at me unblinking throughout, he nodded his agreement. Sadly, he couldn't bring himself to do so. I had a call from the Franchise

Manager at Citroen for whom we were building the second garage, who told me Mulrine had telephoned him and told him he did not believe we had the money to complete the building and were not co-operating fully with his department. I asked if he was prepared to make a signed statement to that effect and he said he would be delighted to, making some very unflattering and unprintable observations about Mulrine. This was an incredible development. I knew there was no way I could work with Mulrine or even reason with him so, not out of malice but simple practicality, I brought an action in defamation against him and his employers. To begin with the action was defended, but I knew they would lose as we did have the funds to complete and the records showed that we had tried to co-operate. I also employed a planning consultant who was amazed at our experience and pointed out that the planning department actually had a statutory obligation to help us, not hinder us, as we were creating employment in the town. Eventually the Council paid compensation and costs to us in a settlement preventing the need for a trial. I met with Mr Mulrine's new boss who apologised for my experiences. He assured me there would be no repetition in the future, which indeed there wasn't. In a re-organisation of the department Mr Mulrine left his employment, either voluntarily or otherwise and our paths never crossed again.

A postscript to all of this was a couple of years later when I was having a dead tree removed at home. I had approached the council for permission, which was duly granted. Whilst the tree was being removed someone must have telephoned the council to complain because, upon my return from work, there was a handwritten letter waiting for me which read,

Dear Householder,

You appear to be removing a tree from a conservation area without permission which is a criminal offence and can lead to severe penalties. You should stop this activity immediately and contact the Council Offices for the further guidance.

Yours faithfully

The letter was signed by Mulrine's assistant who I had always found to be very pleasant, but it was clear to me that he hadn't realised that permission was granted and that the house belonged to me. When I rang him he answered with a touch of trepidation in his voice, as he must have thought I was ringing about the garage site which had been the source of so much acrimony and ultimate embarrassment to his department.

"I thought everything was sorted on the site now, but what can I do for you?"

"No, it is not about the site Adrian, it's about a letter sent to Brake House" I replied.

"Brake House?" he asked confused.

"Yes, a letter to stop work on a tree" I answered.

"Work on a tree?" confusion was growing.

"Yes, a handwritten letter delivered today threatening possible execution" I light-heartedly added. It was penny dropping moment!

"Ah yes, are you acting for the owner?" he said as though that was bad enough.

"No Adrian, worse than that. I am the owner and I think you will find we have permission from your arborist to take the dead tree down!" Seconds delay whilst the penny hit the ground and no doubt unpleasant memories flood in!

"Oh my God John, I am really sorry. What can I say?"

"No problem Adrian, genuine mistake. Got to laugh though, haven't you?" I responded.

"I'll try" he ended.

So here I was in the summer of 1992. I had successfully battled attempts to stop me qualifying, stop the firm from existing, then stop it trading, followed by an attempt to prevent the garage site being developed. My accident scheme had now been formed into a separate business and everything was growing at a fast pace. I was 39 years old, living in my forever home with my wife and two beautiful children, enjoying the trappings of success and maybe even thinking that my biggest challenges were behind me. How wrong I was. I was weeks away from a challenge I couldn't have seen coming and one which would jeopardise everything I had and that of a great many people around me.

CHAPTER 21: Disaster strikes

There are two moments in the summer of 1992 that appeared almost insignificant at the time, but they have stayed as clear in my mind today as they were there back then, because they preceded the crisis that was about to strike.

The first was when I found myself a victim of my own success, in that I had no time to myself at all. I had given up my Saturday afternoon suffering at Roker Park and the frustration of supporting Sunderland, as it infringed too much on my time with my family. As busy as I was, I always got home in time to get the children ready for bed and read them a story, and to ensure we had family time I never worked in the evenings or at weekends, but the price was a crazy work schedule during the week. The businesses took up a huge amount of time and energy, and my determination that they wouldn't interfere with family time meant that I worked at an unsustainable pace. I had an enormous caseload as a practicing litigator and even during the short drive between offices a dozen or so messages would be left for me. These were the days before mobile phones and returning calls had to be fitted in between dealing with the work at the office I was visiting and seeing clients. I was overloading myself and these really were adrenalin filled days.

I knew I needed some down time and driving between offices one day, I decided that a long lunch at Durham County Cricket's ground in Chester Le Street, where Durham was playing Yorkshire, would do me good. However, such were the demands on my time that I couldn't. Angered by this and aware of the need to relax, I decided to go to the morning session the next day. I told no one, including my wife, so that I wouldn't be disturbed as I sat in the sunshine watching the cricket and recharging my batteries. If someone had come up to me then and asked what unused capacity I had left, I would have said none. If they had asked how I would cope with the breakdown of my marriage, loss of 90% of the work I had built up over 14 years and a possible custody battle for the children, I would have said shoot me now.

The second moment happened at my then brother-in-law's wedding in Cumbria. My then wife enjoyed something of the 'Princess Diana' status in her family and was sitting amongst them in the glow of it; she was married to a lawyer, drove a Mercedes, lived in a beautiful house, had a busy social life and of course, had two lovely children. Like me she came from a working class background and the lifestyle must have been a pleasant surprise for her family to witness and enjoy. My nine year old son Simon was a pageboy in full uniform and my five year old daughter Nicola was a bridesmaid. They had a wonderful day and stayed up through the evening, before boarding the private bus taking us back to my parents-in-law's house. As we boarded the bus Simon approached the bus driver and started a long conversation with him; he behaved no differently whether talking to a principal at the wedding, to someone serving the drinks or the guy driving the bus. I was very proud of him and the absence of edge or signs of the privileged life that Simon was leading. The picture was complete when Nicola, now running on empty got onto the bus and pushing past the person in front of her yelled,

"Where's Daddy?"

Seeing me about to sit down she summoned up her last piece of energy, jumped onto my knee, threw her arms around my neck and fell into a deep sleep, the like of which is reserved for children in their place of safety. As I gently moved her into a cradling position on my lap, I surveyed the scene and thought to myself that I had it all and that nobody could possibly wish for more. What I didn't know was that my wife had already embarked upon an affair which would not only end our marriage and destroy the security that the children had enjoyed, but perhaps had chosen the worst possible person to have an affair with. The world that we had known was coming to an end in a spectacular fashion and this time I couldn't do anything to stop it. All I could do was minimise the damage.

I have thought long and hard about what I should and should not say about these times. My conclusion is that the details are too personal and therefore I will keep them to a minimum. However, this is a genuine honest attempt at a book about my career and the people I have met, so it is impossible to do that justice without some context. My ex wife may have a very different interpretation of events and it is not my intention to cause her embarrassment or re open wounds, but certain aspects are just factual and that is what I will try and stick to. The person with whom she had the affair was Brooks Mileson who was then involved in the uninsured loss business which was jointly running my accident scheme. The history of his involvement is very relevant. We encounter beneficial people in our lives by accident and so it is with those who turn out to be malevolent.

I first encountered Mileson in the 1980's when he telephoned my office in response to a letter blaming his company for a car accident. He tried to argue the matter before telling me he was just trying to help me, which led me to say something that he was to dine out on for years,

'Mr Mileson, if I ever find myself in need of your help I will know it is time for me to find another career. Either, forward the letter to your insurer or I will sue your company. It is a matter of complete indifference to me.' A few years later I was at a dinner where Mike Graham, then a friend of the practice, introduced Mileson to me and he remembered the incident. It wasn't unusual to meet somebody I had sued and quite often they became clients, which is what happened here. Mileson rang me later in the week and asked me to act for him and his two small companies, one a building firm and the other a builders' merchant. I had taken an initial dislike to him, although I had moderated that view at the dinner. In any event, we never chose clients on likability.

It transpired that Mike Graham had also introduced Mileson to Derrick Arnott, which resulted in them forming a property development company to buy, develop and sell properties in a buoyant market. As a result, Mileson managed to engineer his way in to Arnotts and find out how it was funded, as well gaining access to my accident scheme. Much later he wanted Derrick and me to form a separate company and to split the shares three ways. Initially I declined, but he was insistent. As he confirmed later, that insistence was to make sure I was invested in a business as opposed to being free to do it with someone else. I was aware of that, but based on previous experience my major concern was my legal firm and the regulations. I thought it over and after taking the views of my partners and independent Counsel, I agreed. Mileson, up to my last conversation with him before him reinvented himself, was a fairly nondescript individual. He was about forty, had dark hair, moustache and was about six feet tall and a little overweight. He had a certain local charm about him and could be entertaining, but he always had an edge and many people seemed to dislike him. He lived modestly, but was clearly ambitious and often would sit silently in business meetings eyeing up the other attendees. Geoff Cardwell said he reminded him of a preying mantis. His growing involvement in Arnotts meant more interaction with me and our firm. Shortly before my discovery of his affair with my wife, he suggested I gave up law and join him on a fifty/fifty basis to *'make some real money'* and also as he put it, *'to stop collecting lame ducks'.* This was a reference to everyone else with whom I was connected. There was never any possibility of that. Even though we got on pretty well at that time, I turned down individual property deals he offered me, as I had no wish to be more involved with him than I was. I had seen something of his real character, although I had no idea how bad it would turn out to be.

When the new accident business was formed we bought premises called Morton House near Chester Le Street which was an old manor house in 12 acres of land. It became the base of the operation and Arnotts head office. I held a claims surgery there once a week and whilst there, took the opportunity to ensure the scheme was working properly, often encountering Mileson. He had something of a split personality; excruciatingly friendly to those he was trying to charm and cold indifference to those he either controlled or had no interest in. At Morton House with him one day, he telephoned one of the Arnotts managers and, without any pleasantries, demanded he come to his room straight away. I actually thought the man was in the same building, but when I realised he was in Middlesbrough, a car journey of more than 30 miles away, I got up to leave. He asked me what the problem was and I told him it was him and the way he spoke to his staff. These exchanges were mostly fairly light hearted from my point of view, but there were times when they were not.

Mileson's insistence that he wanted my private line number at work was met with a brick wall. He wanted access to me whenever he chose, without going through reception, and I always refused. I never accepted interruption when seeing a client. In fact, the only person who had the number was my then wife. As the businesses grew, so did his desire for direct contact. He also knew that I didn't welcome work calls at home, so when Mike Graham invited me out for lunch with him and Mileson I was fairly sure I knew why. As I was leaving the office to join them for lunch, I told Malcolm Burgess that I thought it was to push for greater access and he just laughed saying they should know better. It was exactly the reason and after a few pleasantries Graham gave me his pitch about them needing direct access to me at all times, as I was vital to their very important operation. I answered their points about contact, saying that I always got back to them on the same day, but I would not have client appointments interrupted. I added that I didn't welcome calls at home, because that was family time as they well knew. Graham, who was doing all the talking, threatened to take the work away if I didn't capitulate and I calmly invited them to do so saying I felt I was unlikely to starve. This was shades of the hotelier of years before but, as I knew them better, I also calmly told them they could do with slightly less self importance and if they felt they could have better representation elsewhere I would pass on their papers. A little later Mileson told Malcolm about the meeting and said I had wiped the floor with them and not given them the 'lickings of a dog'!

A few years later, with the uninsured loss company going well, Mileson managed to place himself in a position of power with Arnott Insurance Brokers and was in the process of marginalising Derrick Arnott who seemed oblivious to it. I tried to warn Derrick to be careful and although I was not privy to what was going on in that part of the business, I knew that increased power to Mileson was dangerous. Mileson then made some changes which saw him become managing director of Arnotts, whilst also being a director of the uninsured loss company. I advised him that, as he owed a fiduciary duty to both I thought he now had a conflict of interest. He seemed fine with that, but a couple of days later asked me if I was coming in as usual on Wednesday. I was and when I arrived he said,
"When you said the other day that I have a conflict of interest, I just wanted to say that I think you are wrong; that you insult me, that you are conceited, arrogant, pompous and generally....a...a.. shithead" I'm afraid I laughed and replied,
"Wow, has that taken you three days to compose? What a pity you couldn't think of that when we were having the conversation. Conceited and arrogant; well yes but Colchester United standard compared to your Manchester United standard of coming into companies when you don't fully understand how they work, changing them to suit yourself and putting yourself in control. Pompous maybe, but I will always speak out especially when I am charged with advising those companies. It ill-fits you to be so thin skinned. Shithead? Ok, I'll give you that one" He had nothing left. It had taken all of his energy to come up with that assault and, given the large scale dishonesty that I was later to discover it is still remarkable to me that he seemed genuinely insulted. I am not sure what he expected from me in response, but he was unable to argue and ran out of steam.

His dependence on me for legal protection and for a form of validation was breeding a huge resentment in him that incidents such as these only fuelled. My great sin was that I believed that I could handle him and although I had no idea how dishonest and devious he was, I knew enough to realise he was at least unsavoury and I should have disassociated myself from him. It seemed too difficult to do because of mutual friends and contacts like Derrick Arnott and Mike Graham, plus the growth in all of the businesses couldn't be denied. I felt I had moved a safe distance by not getting involved in his property deals and equally importantly not letting him get involved in any of mine. There is great vanity in persuading yourself of a situation and as I have said many times to people, there is no deception like self deception. I even sensed a personal danger in his flirting with my wife. I wasn't then and am not now a jealous person and flirting caused me no discomfort, but Mileson told me one day that Derrick Arnott's wife had made a move on him. I am not saying this happened, just that he told me that it had and when I related the story to my wife, I warned her to be careful as he would like nothing better than to be relating a similar story about her. Geoff's preying mantis image was to be proved correct. Mileson bided his time and at the height of potential for all of the companies, he took a risk that was to cause enormous consequences and, in the process would move him from non smoker to a 100 cigarette a day habit, see him become an illegal drug user, have a lifetime on anti-depressants and grow a pony tail.

We had started to have an annual summer barbecue at Morton House where staff of all of the companies including the law firm would enjoy drinks, food, outdoor games and a chance to meet up. I won't go into details, but this is where he made his move. It will always be my opinion that he had in mind nothing but an attraction to the infliction of damage and a desire to test his power and influence. In the years both up to and following his marriage to my wife, he was involved in many other incidents with other women. He had affairs with wives of staff members, friends that my ex-wife had cultivated, in fact anyone he could impress. I have always had an instinct for people having affairs and have often said that I can smell it. To have that instinct about my own wife was a complete shock, but all the signs that I had recognised in others were beginning to show. It was only a matter of weeks from his first move to me confronting my wife and her tearfully admitting the situation. Those conversations and the details will remain private, but when I confronted him his only concern was that I didn't tell his wife. I told him that I wouldn't, as it was enough that she was married to him without me making it worse and I called him some things that I cannot print here. I was trapped. The businesses were intertwined and every day I was faced with the huge number of people who would be affected by a war. The most important of all were my two children who knew nothing but a happy life and a happy home.

I carried this burden for a few weeks. It was all I could think about and I confided in only a very few people. It was frankly a relief when the separation came a few weeks later, the news was public and my pretence came to an end. All of a sudden I was subject of all the local gossip and the spotlight was on me. We had a cleaner at home at the time, who was a mature student earning some extra money. When I told her the news she said that my wife had told her earlier on in the day. She told me she was shocked and couldn't get her head around it as we seemed so happy and seemed to have everything. I told her I would like her to work some extra hours if that was ok and she said she would do anything to help. She then asked me when I would be moving out and I said I was staying and would be keeping the house.

"Oh are you going to be living in separate parts?" she asked

"No, she is leaving" I replied but this caused her to almost freeze

"You are asking her to go and moving someone else in?" she said, startled

"Nobody is moving in; she is having the affair and is moving out"

"WHAT?" she screeched, "No, you can't mean it," she said feebly

"I'm afraid so" The next day she asked if she could have a word and apologised for the previous day.

"I still can't believe it," she said "she spoke to me only a few weeks ago and told me that as much as she loved the children, you were her life and her rock, and that if anything happened to you she would have no life at all. If anything she was terrified you might find somebody else"

"Seems to have changed her mind," I said trying to make light of it.

After suffering for a few weeks, trying to make the marriage work and living a lie, the enormity of the situation hit me. We had returned from a family holiday in Florida and I had a telephone conversation whilst she was at her parents' house, which proved to me that the marriage was over. That night I went out with one of the partners, Phil Mitchell for a drink and felt remarkably calm as I discussed it with him. As I went home to an empty house, I wondered if I could be over the worst and if I would just carry on. The children were staying with their mother and her parents on a pre-planned additional holiday in the Lake District and I went to bed in a reflective mood. I got up the next morning and had breakfast before driving the five miles or so to work. The anaesthetic of the previous night seemed to be wearing off as I walked into the office. I felt as though my head was connected to somebody else's body, but decided to just power through as I had done so many times before in different situations. I started to work on some cases and noticed that my hands were shaking. The voice in the dictating machine seemed to belong to someone else and I realised that the events were catching up with me. Trying in vain to regroup I realised two things; I couldn't continue to work that day and I couldn't afford to have the staff see me weak as there was going to be a huge fight ahead and they had to believe that I was going to win it. I just knew Mileson would try and strangle the business that they all relied on.

Geoff Cardwell was on holiday at home that day. I rang him, told him what had happened and said I was going home to pack and then was off to a hotel somewhere to pull myself together. He knew the problem, but I was now telling him the marriage was over. I got home and within an hour or so Geoff and Phil arrived to persuade me to go to my brother's house in Letchworth. Their concern for me was both touching and genuine, and showed the value of your business partners being friends, not just colleagues. I followed the advice and took the long lonely drive. Brian and Alison had just had twin boys and the irony of a very happy house wasn't lost on me, but it was just what I needed. I loved the boys that we had all waited so long for and Brian and Alison were brilliant with me. Measured, supportive and non judgemental they talked and talked it through. They were not critical of my wife at this stage as their concern was to save the marriage if possible and to protect the children.

The next day the mists began to clear and in the afternoon I rang my parents-in-law's home, spoke to my wife and said I was driving up to the Lake District to clear the air. This is a journey of 240 miles and Alison begged me to stay, at least until Brian got back from work, but I had to go and sort it out. Tears were forming in her eyes as I kissed her and said not to worry and that I would be fine. She ran into the house and grabbed some biscuits and water for the journey and I was off. For the first hour or so of the journey I adopted a very positive spin and felt that I could save the marriage and the innocence of the children. That was emotion at work, but inevitably reality kicked in on the long journey and although I remained positive I realised the task was probably too great. I did my best when I met my wife and once again I'll keep that conversation private, but the marriage was over. My parents-in-law, who had at first been ashamed of their daughter's actions and were very supportive of me, had changed sides which made me anxious to get the children home. The next morning I drove them home with the agreement that we would tell them together.

In all of the things I have done and all of the things I have seen, the worst was seeing my children so upset when we told them we were separating. They had no way of seeing it coming and were so young. I shall never forget it or lose that image of the different moments of realisation on both of their faces.

A very difficult domestic few days followed, but l was a new man. l had lost quite a bit of weight in the weeks before without anyone seeming to notice, but they did now. At home l reassured the kids that we wouldn't be moving house and they wouldn't be moving schools. l told them that they would be living with me, but that their Mum still loved them very much and they could see her whenever they wanted. l said my mother was coming to live with us for a few weeks whilst we found a nanny and that they would help choose the nanny. They loved my mother very much and had been used to staying with her often, so the blow was cushioned. l came home earlier every night and started something that was to last until my son went to university aged 20, which we called 'Your 10 minutes'. This was me sitting on each of their beds in turn encouraging them to talk about anything they wanted to, with a promise that l would answer any question about anything. As an act of security we had started a club between the three of us which met at the bottom bunk of some bunk beds every night and we invented secret signs and codes as a game. This added a little excitement for them to add to the feeling of security and as they got a little older it developed into a separate discussion. The idea was that in a very relaxed atmosphere, they could feel comfortable in discussing any worries they had and feel open to ask me anything. It worked really well and was therapeutic for me too, as l loved my children so much and the closeness with them was as good for me as it was for them. l had always been close to them, but this was something deeper.

It was of course an incredibly difficult time. My well ordered but very busy life had been thrown into total chaos. Each day seemed to bring a new challenge and l must have been importing adrenalin to get through some of them. In those early days l was approaching my life like l did my case load, one situation at a time. My ability to concentrate on one case at a time was invaluable to me in dealing with the stress of the end of my marriage, the care of my children and the running of the businesses.

l found myself doing the family shopping, which l had never done before and after my mother returned home also the cooking, initially with a little help from friends and then from our new nanny who would prepare the odd evening meal. After a few weeks Simon said,
"Hey Dad, l think you've done really well. No offence, but when Mum left l imagined burnt beans on toast for tea, but it hasn't been like that at all"
l think the staff had a little more faith in me than my son, but nevertheless l collected them all together as soon as the split became known and as best as

I can remember said,

"I wanted to speak to you all to tell you what is happening, so that you know and don't need to guess. I also wanted to apologise to you that my personal life is going to cause you some uncertainty and concern about your jobs. My marriage has come to an end and my wife will be going to live with Brooks Mileson. I really don't know what effect this will have on the firm; you all know he is involved with businesses that impact on our firm, but I make you two promises. The first is that I will not start a war and will do everything I can to avoid it. The second is that if he starts a war, I will win it, as he neither has the intelligence nor the strength to succeed. I haven't changed and I haven't weakened, and anyone who wants a fight can have one. Please try not to worry." I can honestly say that I meant every word. I was ready to do whatever deals were required or to fight any fight. It was just as well because the war did indeed come.

CHAPTER 22: Brooks Mileson

I was remarkably calm and my concentration on the children meant that I didn't dwell on any other problem for too long. The firm had enough work for at least a year and it was still coming in from NORMA whilst Mileson pretended to be seeking a peaceful solution. The separation was at the end of October 1992 and on Christmas Eve, Mileson had his new solicitors in Newcastle serve some papers on me at home. These papers were claims for approximately £200,000 worth of building costs which he said I owed his building firm. The true cost was more like £40,000, being the sum owed at the end of the building of the garage at PMB's site, but this was subject to a counterclaim as his building team had, in fact built it forty meters from the spot it was supposed to be on and contrary to the planning permission we had. This ridiculously exaggerated claim was clearly a form of attack, but like so much of what was to follow it was ill-conceived. I instructed a solicitor friend called Tony Mallon to act for me. Tony was aggressive by nature and wouldn't be fazed by any aggression shown to him.

Matters heated up when both Mike Graham and Derrick Arnott lined up behind Mileson. They used the same firm of lawyers to say that I had defamed Mileson by calling him a liar, a cheat and not a person to be trusted. I was now being attacked by former friends. Derrick Arnott has written a book in which he refers to these times and says he had no choice but to support his managing director. I think he was wrong and should have adopted a neutral approach, but instead he ignored my earlier warning to be careful of Mileson and seemed to see salvation in giving him support. It was no surprise to me that a few years later Arnott was himself out of his own businesses at the hands of the man he chose to support. Mileson thought that Arnott was a fool and regularly told me so. On one occasion he said that Arnott had composed a letter to his own wife setting out the problems he thought they had in their marriage and some solutions he had in mind. Mileson thought that was funny enough, but he said Arnott had photocopied the letter and left the original in the photocopier which had been brought to him. He returned the letter to the copier, but not before he had retained a copy for entertainment purposes.

Mileson seemed to be setting up a number of different businesses with different shareholdings and I was sure that he was hatching a plot to oust Arnott, hence my earlier warning. A story he once told me about his first job rather sets the scene for the man he was to become. He worked for

a company where a middle aged man took him under his wing. He was like a father to Mileson and taught him everything about the job. When Mileson was still very young, the man suffered a heart attack and was off work for a few months. Mileson held the fort during his mentor's illness until he was invited to a meeting with the MD who told him they were very impressed with his work, but that his mentor had recovered and was ready to return to work. The boss was keen to reward Mileson for his efforts and asked him what he would like and also how he felt about the return of his father figure. I expected Mileson to say that he was pleased his mentor had recovered, that he would support him fully and wanted him restored to his former position. Instead, and to my utter amazement, he replied that he did not want him back and that he could do his job better for less money. Wide eyed, I asked what the boss said and with incredulity he replied,
"He sacked me"
"Good for him" I replied laughing at the morality which was completely lost on Mileson. The story betrayed his real character which was almost psychopathic in destroying anyone who helped him or any base that he was trying to spring from. Mike Graham is described in Arnott's book in very unflattering terms and I won't add to them. I will say that his betrayal of me was surprising and looked to be an attempt to suck up to a man he was afraid of. He had reason to be, too. A few months before these events, whilst on a business trip Mileson told me he had decided to get rid of Graham. When I asked why he said, *'Because he is fucking useless, he can't do anything'* I realised this was a potentially explosive position as I considered Mike a friend and as he was not employed by a company I was involved in, I couldn't veto it. I spoke to Graham and whilst not letting on that he was in danger, suggested he develop a second string to his bow. I also tried to persuade Mileson of the consequences of rocking a boat and eventually he changed his mind. Graham's betrayal of me was a bitter pill to swallow at a difficult time.

In the January of 1993, Mileson's new lawyers called for a meeting and we duly all met up at Tony Mallon's office. Three lawyers from the Newcastle firm arrived with Mileson. I was determined to let Tony do the talking and he dealt with issues relating to the now three sets of high court proceedings (soon to be five) that had been started against me. Mileson confided in a mutual friend that, in his opinion attacking me was the best form of defence to the attacks he fully expected from me. Questioning the wisdom of launching attacks against me, Mileson told the mutual friend that he thought I was no longer the man I had been and was weakened by events.

After dealing with procedural matters, one of the lawyers said they had some proposals for Mr McArdle and produced an offer letter to buy my shares in the uninsured loss company, which were in my wife's name. The offer was £300,000 and it came without admission that the shares were mine. Curious in that they also were acting for my wife who was now claiming title to the shares. The company had recently been valued at £1.5 million and therefore my shares were worth £500,000, but I was not interested in selling in any event. Following a discussion on this and other matters they turned their attention to my defamation of their client and told Tony that if I did not withdraw my remarks and undertake not to repeat them, they would serve high court papers seeking substantial damages from me. Tony began to answer but I interrupted saying,

"I will deal with this Tony. If you are referring to me calling Mr Mileson a liar, a cheat and not a man to be trusted then I do not withdraw them and in fact I am happy to repeat them here today in front of him. Mr Mileson is a liar, a cheat and not a man to be trusted and I am prepared to give evidence to the court to prove it on any proceedings you bring"

One of the partners started to reply which caused Tony to stand up and walk towards his door saying,

"Okay you lot, I've heard enough get out" Taken aback, they began shuffling their papers somewhat red faced and chivvied along by Tony adding, "Come on, come on. Get a move on. Out you go"

As one of them passed Tony he said,

"We will be issuing proceedings for defamation against Mr McArdle and reporting your conduct to the Law Society"

"Oh, for fuck's sake!!!" was Tony's only response. After they left we had been talking for a few minutes when Tony was called to reception and on his return said that Mileson wanted to speak to me alone. Contrary to his advice I agreed. Mileson came in and said he might sort something out about future work to the firm, but he wanted some assurances about the future. He said he was worried about me stabbing him in the back and I replied that was his style and any attack from me would be face to face. In any event, I told him I would give him my word that we would keep our dispute between the two of us and make sure nobody else was involved, including all of the businesses and staff. He said no to that, as he obviously drew comfort from the fact that he saw hostages standing between us. No claim in defamation was ever brought against me.

My shares in the uninsured loss company were now in my wife's name and under Mileson's control, giving him a two thirds stake and total control over the company. He evidently planned to starve my firm of work whilst the actions brought against me, as well as divorce proceedings and financial orders, would either bankrupt me or financially weaken me so much that I couldn't fight back.

Somewhat ironically, a few days after the separation my wife told me that Brooks was not interested in money or power. Not only was he not interested in the shares in her name, but he was willing to give me his shares as well, so that I had two thirds. I told her that I accepted his offer. She told me that she knew I didn't believe him or trust him, but that was because I didn't know him.

"Okay, ring him now and tell him," I said

She said she knew I was testing him, but she was so confident that she rang him in front of me and said,

"Hello Brooks, John is here and I've told him that you will not claim his shares and will give him your shares as well. He says he wants to take you up on your offer" After a short delay I asked what he said. Still holding the telephone she said,

"He's laughing"

"I bet he is" I replied calmly. Hard to imagine that was ever taken seriously and in the years that followed he ended up with all of the shares by getting rid of Arnott. Sadly, he also saddled the company with enormous debts. A former colleague said of him that a rat had been placed in charge of the cheese store and guess what......he was eating all of the cheese. Following the meeting at Tony's office I went to London to meet my barrister who we had appointed to prepare for the war that I thought was inevitable. The barrister asked why I thought Mileson would seek to starve the firm of work, as that would damage his interests not to mention my wife's financial claims. He thought it the least likely scenario, but I replied that I had underestimated his capacity for destruction previously and would not do so again. A few weeks later the work stopped abruptly and anyone who had doubted it was now convinced.

My wife had moved to another firm of solicitors who were even more aggressive than those before and I was faced with divorce proceedings seeking substantial sums, including a settlement for the house the children and I were living in, plus a settlement for the previous house which remained unsold and held under a mortgage. I was also facing the firm's loss of eighty five to ninety per cent of new work; the new PMB garage being subject to high court action from Mileson's building company, personal high court actions against me and also more high court actions by Mileson claiming negligence against the firm. Then there was the possibility of a custody application for the children at a time when in matrimonial cases eighty nine per cent of children were living with their mothers. In addition, my wife caused constant aggravation on matters of contact. The children were living with me and my wife decided that she would not make arrangements with me to see them, but instead directly with the children themselves who were only ten and six. I refused to allow that for reasons of safety and said she could write to me if she wouldn't ring, especially as she wouldn't speak to the nanny either. At least I had a workforce and partners who seemed to have faith in me, but they must have worried that I might blow a gasket.

Even as I write this now, I wonder how I managed to stay sane, never mind avoid the gasket blowing, but the truth is I did stay very upbeat and was always confident that I would survive. I prepared for an application for custody (which never came) by keeping a diary of daily events which was a factual account of the children's routine and I kept their lives as normal as possible. They stayed in the same house, went to the same school and went to the local health club for swimming and play as usual. Friends and family were fantastically supportive and the young nanny was perfect for them. After a few months another person entered their lives. She was to become the love of my life and as it turned out a surrogate mother to them, but more of her later.

I stabilised the court actions against me and some years later had them all struck out in the high court. The real challenge was replacing the work. Mileson made a mistake in his delay in stopping the work, which had allowed me to stockpile more of it and prepare a contingency plan. The delay was probably due to him trying to persuade his then allies that he was a reasonable man, but his seizing of complete control of NORMA and Arnotts made the views of others less relevant. He had a knack of persuading people to commit to him and once they had done so, he had control of them making it difficult for them to disentangle. My contingency plan was to set up a new company and to effectively compete with the company running my accident scheme. The rules on solicitors practice involvement had eased and I set up a company called A & B Assistance which performed the same function as NORMA. I did this with the help of Malcolm Burgess who had been sacked as a provider of hire cars, presumably on the basis of being my friend. Mileson replaced him with himself as a hire car company. When Derrick Arnott was ousted, Arnott's brother in law was also sacked and the remainder of the car hire business went to you know who. Well, he might as well shaft everybody.

A & B was a success from the beginning. A number of insurance brokers switched from NORMA, particularly those who had no love for Arnotts, and new ones were recruited. Malcolm and I had recruited Jan Thomson from NORMA as she dealt with us more than she did with anyone else, including Mileson. She was a married woman in her forties who was very feisty, but she knew the business inside out and was brilliant with the brokers. She had an encyclopaedic memory of who worked at each broker's office and knew the names of their children, boyfriends, girlfriends, etc. She also believed that Mileson had not expected the opportunity he got and never intended to do anymore than damage me, but was now determined to take full advantage of it at everyone's expense.

Jim Phillips, a friend since college days joined us and along with Geoff, Phil and I we arranged evening events, meetings, in fact whatever it required to present and explain what we did. These were very uncertain times and the involvement of Jim Phillips was particularly important. Before the advent of all my problems, we had offered him a full partnership which would have more than doubled his earnings and reduced his administration burden, but he turned it down after giving himself a week or two to think about it. His reason was that he didn't feel he could add enough value to the business to justify the terms. Now that we were facing a crisis and possible failure he was prepared to risk what he had built up to join the fight; not many people would be prepared to make either of those decisions. I used to tease him in the years that followed by saying it just showed that he had very poor judgement! In reality it proved what a decent man he is. Jim was and is an immensely likeable and popular figure, especially in Sunderland where he is well known and with his help and charm, we were able to recruit quickly. Over the next eighteen months or so all of the effort bore fruit. We were so successful that not only was all the lost work replaced, but increased and the firm expanded as opposed to collapsing, as had been Mileson's plan.

Another source of work manifested itself in a very surprising way. Mileson had developed a habit of telling everyone who would listen that I was a complete monster who was totally ruthless and capable of anything. When he fell out with these people, as he almost always did, they came looking for me in the hope that they could unleash 'the beast' on him. I always explained that I could only act if there was no conflict of interest and, contrary to what they may have been told and as with anyone else, I would only act if I felt they were likely to win. There were a number of people who needed representation, others that needed some advice and some who just wanted to get something off their chests. Here is a selection of those I can write about:

A former director in one of Mileson's companies explained he was part of a group of former Mileson acquaintances who met regularly to exchange tales and express their hatred of him. He said he hoped he didn't cause me offence, but his group was quietly pleased that Mileson had crossed me, as they were hopeful he would now get his comeuppance. He said that if I let it be known that I was seeking revenge against Mileson, I would have a mile long line of people outside my office wanting to help. I assured him I wasn't doing that, but he told me of his of experiences anyway. One included noticing that a corporate client of Mileson's had overpaid by £17,000 because they had overlooked an interim payment. When he told him, Mileson simply asked if the client knew they had overpaid. He replied that they did not and Mileson replied, 'Good, the money is ours then'.

I pointed out that this was theft and he agreed, but said this sort of thing was commonplace with Mileson. I suggested he could go to the police or even go to the victim, but he said he ought to have done it at the time and that he had a family to think about. Instead, he had left the company as soon as he could.

A former employee whose job it was to organise the work on building contracts had a story to tell. He had noticed that there was considerable over ordering of building materials on a number of jobs. The excess would then be removed and presumably transferred elsewhere. He went to see Mileson and had a conversation about it.

"Brooks, I think you should know that there seems to be some dishonesty on your working sites. I've taken some details and it seems that somebody is deliberately over ordering on all your sites and then stealing the excess, which must be causing a loss to your clients"

"Do you know that for sure?" asked Mileson

"I'm absolutely sure" he replied handing over lists of items. "I have the details of the over ordering on all of these contracts"

"Well that is amazing. You will have to leave this with me and I will find out what's going on, but I want to thank you for bringing it to my attention, I am very impressed"

The employee was made redundant a few weeks later and somewhat naively, didn't tie the two incidents together. He went to see Mileson for a second conversation,

"Brooks, I wonder if you can give me some advice on running my own business as I am thinking of becoming self employed"

"Self employed? Why? Are you leaving us?" Mileson asked

"Yes, I've been made redundant" the employee responded.

"What? I don't know anything about this. I will have to look into it" Believing him, the employee retold the story to someone in the office, who said,

"Don't be stupid. Brooks knows you've been finished because he told them to get rid of you when you complained about the contracts. It's him who asks for the excess materials and it is him who uses it" This man was still shocked about the theft and, feeling that something had to be done, was prepared to give evidence if necessary. I am not sure what he decided to do.

Another company director told me of a scam where a genuine theft or break in would become a profit making opportunity, and it was a story also told to me by an unrelated employee. When accounting for the loss a number of bogus invoices would be raised for equipment that didn't exist. They would be presented as hire invoices for tools and commercial equipment, for which the insurer duly paid out. This was of course fraud and/or theft, but also conspiracy as presumably other companies were involved in providing the invoices. I was given details of actual claims and, with permission spoke to the insurers on one identified claim who confirmed the presentation of the invoices I was told about. I don't know what the insurers did about it, but the director estimated there were about thirty or forty fraudulent claims over the years.

Many more people came to see me and of course I can't say that all the stories were accurate. What I can say is that a number of these people had never met each other and their experiences sounded similar to mine in Mileson's potential manipulation of having an affair with my wife and simultaneously trying to persuade me to join his business and give up my own. These meetings were helpful to my partners and me, as they removed any doubt as to the kind of character we were up against and reinforced my belief that the battles had to be fought and won, with no place for complacency.

As I knew he would, despite the risks, he tried to choke the firm of work and launched several attacks in the hope that he would destroy the entity that had given him so much assistance and protection over the years, whilst in the process affecting other people and businesses that had done him no harm. Waiting for the next attack was not a healthy option. His new lawyers in Newcastle now had all of the accident work that I had created and were acting in the cases brought against me and others related to me. In addition, they were involved in several complaints about me and the firm made to the Law Society by Mileson. All of these complaints were dismissed. When they hired a private investigator to serve papers on me, he made an appointment to see me in the office, pretending to be a client and served me there. I immediately made a complaint to The Law Society about their conduct and the complaint was upheld.

Tony Mallon advised me that any information given to me by others of a criminal nature should be passed on to the police or the Inland Revenue as to fail to do so would be contrary to our duty as solicitors and may be misread as attempting to withhold information for personal benefit. When permission was given by those seeking advice, the information was passed on to the appropriate authorities and victims. The truth is that I never went out looking for information. It came looking for me. In the years that followed contact became very infrequent with all attacks repelled and the high court cases against us struck out. The firm was doing well and I considered the matters between us closed. I did however watch in some disbelief as Brooks Mileson reinvented himself again as a multi-millionaire.

I still had people coming to see me who were intimidated or irritated by him and my advice was always that he should neither be underestimated nor overestimated. He was not however a multi-millionaire. A wealthy businessman instructed me to research Mileson's companies at Companies House and I then sat down with him and created the picture for him. Mileson now had a large number of companies with large turnovers, but with huge debts. My assessment was that the whole group was probably insolvent. Some years later I was to meet a former managing director who told me that my assessment was correct and that the group came close to closure on several occasions, only to be saved by either an unexpected event or the reluctance of the bank to crystallise their losses. Notwithstanding this, Mileson developed an interest in football that he had certainly kept secret from me in the years I had known him and, having failed to acquire an interest in Carlisle United (he lived in Carlisle) he bought a little Scottish club called Gretna, which set him on his way to his biggest and ultimately fatal deception.

Gretna was historically a lower league football club on the border of England and Scotland. They finally joined the Scottish league in 2002 and what appeared to be a fairy tale soon developed. They had an average crowd of a couple of hundred supporters, but as a result of a 'multi-millionaire owner' they bought players and rose through the leagues, winning promotion to The Scottish premiership and eventually playing in the Scottish cup final. This brought national publicity to Mileson who appeared on football programmes on the BBC, where he implied he had been approached by large English premiership clubs wanting his millions. In some newspapers he was quoted as being worth more than £100 million and earning more than David Beckham. It was of course all an illusion.

I was to meet another discarded associate who confirmed not only the financial mess, but the source of the money going into Gretna. One of the companies Mileson now controlled was a medical legal business, which provided medical reports for accident victims and charged for doing so. A doctor might charge £400 for providing a report and the medical legal company may charge £150 on top of that for organising it. Mileson acquired the company with his usual modus operandi of taking in the owners and then forcing them out. What Mileson realised is that surgeons are not very good accountants. The source told me that one of the surgeons had sent in a list of outstanding medical reports and totalled it at £210,000, but that in fact the list was wrong and the total outstanding was nearer £250,000. He was instructed to agree the lower figure and to pay it at £10,000 per month with the balance being kept. In other words the company would recover all of the money due to the doctor but keep the money he was unaware of, thus stealing £40,000 from that particular surgeon alone. I obtained the man's permission and rang the surgeon who was from Oxford. He verified the figures I had been given and the arrangement entered into. He also confirmed he was a poor bookkeeper and I told him what the position really was, suggesting he should go and see his own lawyer for advice. I told him of my background and from where I had obtained the information. I don't know what he did about it. In the conversation with the former associate he told me that thousands of pounds every week was sent from the medical legal company to Gretna, money that should have been sent to the doctors who had completed medical reports on patients. So there you have it; the mystery of the funding of Gretna solved.

Gretna collapsed publicly and spectacularly and ended up as another entity destroyed by involvement with Mileson. Even today there are those who believe it was only ill-health that led to the club's demise, but being an innocent recipient of stolen funds was always going to be a house built on sand. His world was falling about his ears and despite the sale of the valuable companies for £46 million; the combined debts and the continued mad spending of other people's money could only have a bad outcome. Mileson died in November 2008. He was found floating in his own garden pond and everything quickly unravelled. His house was repossessed by the bank for non payment of the mortgage and he was posthumously bankrupted with debts of £9 million. In other words, far from being wealthy he had spent £9 million he didn't have. As they say "you could not make it up".

CHAPTER 23: A new life

It's funny how things happen and, in the middle of all of this mayhem I was to meet an enormously important person, namely my life partner. After my separation I thought about my personal future and decided that, for five years or so I wouldn't embark on anything serious; I would concentrate on the welfare of my young children and protect the businesses. However, I knew it was important to get my life back on track and in the very little free time I had, I did go out with a few women. The first one was very soon after the separation when Phil Mitchell spoke to an attractive brunette in a night club in Hartlepool saying, *'I know this sounds like a line, but a friend of mine is recently separated and doesn't get out much as he is looking after his kids, but I am sure he would find you very attractive. Do you mind if I give him your number?'* She didn't mind and we went out. She, along with the others I saw (I met the others myself and was not employing Phil as a pimp!) was generally very nervous, which was a bit of a surprise as I thought that women in their thirties would be a little more relaxed. However, at the firm's office Christmas lunch at the Parkhead Hotel near Bishop Auckland I met a very confident woman.

The owners of the Parkhead Hotel were clients and had asked me to have a word with a member of staff who needed advice. Having arrived and seen to the seating for everyone, I was introduced to Gillian Cartwright; a slim, very attractive woman who shook my hand, told me she was divorcing and would I check some documents for her. I said I would and asked her to ring the office in the New Year and make an appointment for a chat. When she breezed in to the office for that appointment she produced her documents and I went through them with her. I have on many occasions reminded her that she was one of very few clients who came around to my side of the desk and stood at my shoulder, although she refrained from sitting on my knee. She has always maintained it was to make sure I was looking at the right page. I told her that I thought she was selling herself short in the divorce and shouldn't sign the agreement, but she said that she was happy with it and wanted it over. If we had acted for her I wouldn't have asked her out, as there are rules about that. A lawyer should be aware that he or she will meet vulnerable people and should bear that in mind before forming any personal relationships, even at the end of a case. There did not however, seem to be much vulnerability about the confident Mrs Cartwright.

Having given her a few days to think matters over, I rang her to ask if she had decided to sign the document and not take matters any further and she confirmed that she had. I said that as we were near neighbours we might go out for a drink one night and she said she would like that, so we named a date. I picked her up at her cottage, a mile or so from where I lived and we drove to Durham City for a drink. She has never let me forget that I didn't take her out for dinner that first night, but I have always explained that she might have been a complete lunatic and it's easier to curtail a drink date than a dinner date. Also, it tends to spoil things if you spray food over each other in conversation! Anyway there was nothing to be concerned about as we got on well immediately and here was a woman who appeared confident, engaging and attractive. In fact, I was to learn that the nerves were being hidden as she had changed four or five times before my arrival. Add a convincing actress to the list!

I had neither the time nor inclination for a serious relationship at that point, but meeting up with her was always a highlight of the week. I was honest about my situation; there was still a risk of an application for custody of the children and Tony Mallon had advised that I shouldn't introduce any new women to them. I had no intention of doing that anyway, but one Saturday night I was cooking a meal for the kids when Simon came into the kitchen and stood fiddling with some crockery.

"Dad, can I ask you a question?"

"Of course you can, what is it?" I replied

"Do you think you will ever get married again?"

"Oh I don't know, I can't say I've thought about. Why do you ask?" I said trying to think what it meant.

"No reason, I just wondered," he said fiddling with and nearly dropping a plate.

"Are you worried that somebody else might come and live here?" I speculated.

"A little bit maybe" he answered.

"Well, all I can say is that nobody will be coming here to live unless you and Nicola want her to come" I made clear.

"So you mean if you had a girlfriend and me and Nic didn't like her, you would get rid of her?" he questioned.

"Absolutely" I answered, stirring the food.

"Cool" he responded walking off to the living room suitably reassured.

Gillian was certainly something different from the other women I had seen. Although born in Portsmouth she had lived in Cyprus and Germany as a child as her father was in the army. She had been educated at a boarding school in Germany and, in her early twenties and having done a number of jobs, she decided to become an air stewardess with Gulf Air, living in Bahrain. The Middle East was very different then and it was an unusual and brave move. She was a 'Trolley Dolly' for five years, often attending the royal flights before becoming the accounts manager for Qantas and running their Bahrain office. Her book would be much more interesting than mine as she has a million stories of those days and the lives they led. One of my favourites was of her doing a flight for a particular Arab royal family on which a fat young prince kept clicking his fingers as if summoning a slave saying,

"Pepsi, Pepsi". After the fourth command for a Pepsi, Gillian signalled him to come forward to the galley and when he did she closed the curtain and slapped him across the head saying,

"If you click your fingers at me once more you will get another one" Whenever that particular Arab royal family is on television, I always look for a portly ruler with a twitch and an aversion to Pepsi Cola!

My great fortune was that she had come back to England before her marriage breakdown and following the separation was living in the North East. We had been going out for a few months and she asked me if I was seeing other people. I answered that I was not in a position to give proper attention to a relationship and off the top of my head said, *'After the kids and work I have about 15 per cent left and if that's enough for you then I am happy to agree that I won't see anyone else'.* It wasn't much of an offer, but it was all I had and it was honest. Gillian accepted that and was never demanding at all. She knew my position and that I was only free on a Friday night when my wife picked up the kids from school and returned them to me on Saturday. For Friday night and until the Saturday deadline I was single again. Unlike Cinderella I had to be home by 5.00pm when I turned back into the single parent, but it was a job that I loved. Sometimes the children would bring back a tale of woe or aggravation, and after a few more months the overnight contact was stopped by their mother. Gillian never made an issue of not meeting the children, but they were beginning to.

I always answered the children's questions, telling them as much of the truth as I could. They knew I was seeing someone regularly now and kept asking when they could meet her. I just put them off politely. One Sunday Gillian rang me saying she had some plants for the garden and would leave them at the bottom of the drive, so as not to disturb the children.

"Sod this," I said, "I haven't done anything wrong, just come over for tea now and meet the kids". At first she said no as it might cause trouble for me, but to be frank I had so much trouble anyway that one more piece wouldn't make any difference. I told the children and they were really excited and wanted her to come that minute, but I said she would be around in about an hour. Cleverly she brought two of her cats and the kids were smitten with them and her. I have given a lot of advice to people on this subject over the years, which is if you have children then you should never introduce your new partner unless they want you to do so. If they are young, they should be reassured that they are still your priority and that you will sacrifice the relationship with the new person in your life if it doesn't work for them. I did this instinctively and meant everything I said to the children, but as the years went by they saw Gillian as much as their choice as mine and, although they have had their problems with me, they have never had a problem with her.

Gillian began to stay over a little more often and came out with us to restaurants and on day trips. When the children got up the next morning they were always disappointed if she wasn't there. In fact Simon had developed an enormous crush on Gillian as well as seeing her in a maternal role, whereas Nicola just loved having a woman come out with us. She loved my mother and Rachel the nanny, but when we went out with Gillian she was her own special female adult. I had been taking Nicola into the male changing room at the health club, getting her ready for swimming and washing her hair afterwards which she loved, but not as much as walking hand in hand with Gillian into the female changing room.

As with much of my life, just when things start to balance out something happens. This time it was Rachel the nanny telling me that she was pregnant and that she and her partner were moving back to Wales. There was nothing I could do to change her mind about staying and I knew the children would be devastated. Gillian to my surprise, offered to do the job and reduce her hours at the Parkhead Hotel. She had never had children and was giving up her chance of having any of her own to take on someone else's. When I was sure that she was sure, I spoke to the children upstairs; a conversation which I have never forgotten.
"So kids, I have some bad news. Rachel will be leaving us soon as she is going to have a baby and is moving away" Pause, as children get a little tearful.
"We have to have a new nanny and like before, you can help choose the person. Is there anybody you can think of?" I asked.

After a few seconds of bemused expressions Simon said,

"Well I can think of somebody, but it's impossible because she has a job"

"Who's that then?"

"Gillian, but I know we can't have her"

"Well, what if I told you she is prepared to give it a try and change her hours at work?" Elation from the little ones! The other conversation I haven't forgotten was some time later. Gillian was staying more than she was leaving and, sitting together on the same bed they both said they wished Gillian would never go home.

I said, "Why don't we ask Gillian to come and live with us?" Much jumping on the bed and *let's ask her now* from the children before I added,

"Now just hang on a minute, if we ask Gillian to come and live with us that means we love her"

"We do, we do" came the reply.

"Yes, but if we love her that is forever not just for now"

"It is, it is forever" more jumping.

"Well if Gillian lives here, then if she asks you to do something that is just like me asking and you can't say it's not her place to tell you what to do"

"We won't, we won't" even more jumping on the bed.

"If Gillian comes to live with us, she's not a guest and wouldn't sleep in the guest room, would she? She would sleep in my room and then it would become our room, wouldn't it?" I said cleverly dealing with the subject of sleeping together when the kids were in residence and not just when they weren't.

"Yes, yes"

"Well I think it would be nice if you asked her. She's downstairs" I said which was met with squeals of delight and off they ran before Nicola aged seven turned back and said to me,

"Did you say that Gillian would sleep in your bed?"

"Yes"

Nicola looked at me, paused and then with a smile said,

"Sexy, sexy" and gave me a nudge! As an afterthought she asked if she would still be able to come into my bed at night if she wanted to and I said of course she would, which indeed she did often particularly when wetting the bed. No point in messing up her own bed.

The children were very keen over the next year or so for us to get married and on the 29th June 1995 we did. Nicola was Gillian's sole bridesmaid and Simon was my best man. Simon asked me if a best man made a speech and I told him they usually did, but he didn't need to. He told me that if he was going to do the job, he would do it properly and aged 12 he stood up to the microphone and delivered an excellent speech which was very funny. One line that brought the house down was,

"Nic and I are so pleased they got married because when Dad was on his own there was a long line of women wanting to go out with him ...well according to Dad anyway" He also called Gillian mum for the first time which caused many aahh's. Simon is a successful lawyer in his own right now, with his own wife and daughter and still calls Gillian mum. One line that I can just about remember from my own speech was,

"When Gillian and I first got together she told me that just before she came back to England she had been on a private yacht in the Middle East where they were drinking champagne out of glass slippers. Realising I had to impress her, I took her to Seaburn beach in Sunderland on a cold February day and bought her a bag of chips on the seafront, telling her that if she stopped crying I might buy her an ice cream. Hey, I know how to treat a lady!"

It was not easy for Gillian coming into our lives at that time but she brought order, style and total commitment with her. She completed our little family and as I write this we have celebrated our 22nd wedding anniversary and are rarely apart. The stability she brought to the children was shown every day; she never once let them come home to an empty house and she set up routines for meals, home work and free time. I was always easy to fool but not her. Upon being told they had no homework she would search their bags and find it. She was never late in collecting them or delivering them anywhere they wanted to go and when Simon went to university, she made up his bed in his halls of residence and arranged his room. She is the love of my life and another example of good things happening when you least expect them. Just as well as there was another earthquake rumbling underneath my feet.

CHAPTER 24: Back to the day job

My life was far from trouble free but I was married again, the children were more settled and the attacks from Mileson had been repelled, plus the firm was thriving. Malcolm Burgess and I found a new office in Jesmond, just outside of Newcastle and expanded the uninsured loss business as well as the legal practice. I felt that I could now concentrate a little more on my day job of being a lawyer and the cases continued to come thick and fast.

In the days before conditional fees or 'no win no fee' arrangements there was nothing in place to help people who found themselves in need of a lawyer, unless they qualified for legal aid. If you had an accident which was not your fault or had a dispute with someone, you could only receive legal aid if you passed a complex financial test and even then the assistance was often limited and required a large contribution. In the majority of cases, people didn't qualify and faced great uncertainty if they needed a lawyer for any form of litigation. In the early 1990's a legal expense product was becoming available which meant that people could insure against certain legal possibilities such as accidents, medical negligence and dismissal from work, but it was very early days for these products. We operated in predominantly working class areas where money was very tight and spending it on legal cases was often impossible. Early regulations did not help either because we were not allowed to fund actions or assist with loans. Before the advent of legal expense products, or for those who did not have them, there were severe risks for people bringing litigation.

I acted for a very brave Hartlepool lady who worked in a care home. She had injured her back as a result of being asked to lift heavy and uncooperative patients and, after a period of absence she had been sacked. She would have lost an industrial tribunal, as her dismissal would have been deemed fair because of her condition. Our only option was a civil action for damages for negligence of the employers in asking her to lift when it was unsafe. To my surprise, both the insurers and the employers were very aggressively defensive and refused to pay anything, so we started court action in the high court. I would say that in the vast majority of cases when such action was taken, the insurers knew that we meant business and discussions led to settlement. Not this one. This lady's case went to a hearing. She wanted to know the position and I remember discussing the costs of the other side, the cost of our barrister and other expenses which excluding our fees came to around £50,000 in total. She said that her house was worth £50,000 and if she lost, she would just sell it. This was genuinely a case of someone putting their house on a bet, however calculated that bet was.

As the day of the hearing approached I still thought that a call would come but when it didn't, I went through the defendants witness statements and the documents they had disclosed and discovered several discrepancies in their evidence. I discussed these with the barrister who was presenting the case and on the morning of the trial we were met with the same refusal to budge. My client was terrified, but a righteous determination which I was to see many times in people settled over her. She gave her evidence convincingly and as I had hoped, the care home manager did not. We were able to establish that one of the days when our client was supposed to have asked for help in lifting in accordance with her training, she was in fact there on her own and on another day when she was 'trained on lifting', she was off work on sick leave.

The judge began the summing up at the end, which is always a nervous time because however well things have gone the judgement can always go against you. In a long summation he talked of the normal risk of lifting and of the office register which showed that training had been organised for the plaintiff but then ended,
"However, I take into account the evidence of the defendants on the question of training and the variation between the documents and that evidence. On the whole I found the plaintiff to be an impressive witness who was placed in a position of risk and that such risk was a breach of her employer's duty to her. I accordingly find that the plaintiff is entitled to damages which I assess at £55,000. The defendants will also be responsible for the plaintiff's costs, such costs to be assessed if not agreed" She had won what was for her a life changing sum of money and had risked her house in doing it.

Catastrophic cases are always difficult as they deal with real human suffering and as they take so long to conclude, a real bond is created with the individual and the family. One such case involved a young man in his late twenties who was involved in a very serious road accident in Hartlepool whilst on his way to work. The growing computer industry was his trade and he was married to an attractive, intelligent and charming wife. They had bought a nice house on mortgage and like in so many of these cases were settling into a very happy routine when it was all taken away. We will call him Tony (not his real name). I was told of this accident as we represented his insurance broker and I could see from the list of injuries that Tony was in bad shape. His physical injuries were bad enough, consisting of multiple bone fractures, but it was his head injury that was most concerning. His wife came to see me and explained in more detail the problems that Tony had and that he was still in intensive care, with no guarantee of survival. It was far too early to talk about the case we would build, but it is always reassuring to a spouse in this situation to have someone to talk to who they know will sort out any financial difficulties.

Several weeks later Tony was released from hospital and I arranged to go and see him at his home. His wife said that his mental function had been reduced and that she had to teach him to speak and to remember things. They would watch a television programme for ten minutes and then she would switch it off and see how much of it Tony could remember and how many words he could say. She then told me Tony had been rehearsing his opening sentence to me and that she would now go and get him. I stood in their sitting room for what seemed an age until the door opened slowly and this young man, bent over with disability shuffled towards me with the assistance of his wife. His hand extended to shake mine, he said very slowly, leaving a large gap between each word, *'Hello Mr McArdle it is a pleasure to meet you and a pity it could not be under better circumstances'* This is exactly what he said to me. It is a sentence I have never forgotten and a position I used over the next few years as a barometer of his improvement. As he started to improve, Tony would to write to me and in those letters he told me of the hate he bore in his heart for the other driver who had done this to him and how he dreamed of harming that man. After the first letter which was filled with profanity he rang to apologise to me for sending it. I said he should always write to me when he had those feelings, assuring him that I would read them personally and then file them, but that he must not ring and apologise, as that was unnecessary. Getting the emotion on the page and off his mind was very helpful to him. The letters continued for a few months and then stopped. They stopped because it had done the trick and he had realised that the other driver had just made a mistake; Tony was beginning to come to terms with his situation.

Over the next couple of years most of Tony's physical symptoms healed and he recovered most of his cognitive skills. However, it is that final one or two percent of cognitive function that allows us to hold down a job and to function normally. Our medical team explained to me that Tony could be shown how to operate his computer and undertake some of his old job reasonably satisfactorily, but he would have to be shown it again tomorrow and the next day and so on. This meant that he could not work in the area for which he was trained and it made his claim very valuable. The insurers took a different view however and after a slow start, they offered to settle his claim for just £100,000 (£210,000 now). The family came to see me and I strongly advised them to refuse the offer, which they did. There followed a lot of activity on the case, but no further offers which made the family very nervous as the months rolled by, but they said they trusted me and we finally received a hearing date. I had by that time instructed an excellent QC called Robin Stewart who I had known for years and I engaged him for the hearing. A few weeks before the trial the offer was increased to £500,000 (£1,050,000 today) and I arranged a conference for the family and the full legal team. I again strongly advised against acceptance and Robin Stewart agreed, but as with most barristers was much more circumspect in doing so. Once again the family agreed to accept the advice. A couple of weeks later Tony's father came to see me, telling me he was not sleeping and that the money offered was a fortune to turn down. He was aware of how much his son relied upon him and his mother and that they would not always be there because of the age factor; I was advising them to turn down an amount of money which would secure his son's future. I told him I was aware of that but also aware of his son's suffering and the family needs. I was sure the case was worth more and we should not weaken in the face of the upcoming hearing.

On the day of the hearing I was still confident, but with that touch of apprehension that I like as it kept me sharp. I calmed Tony down and settled the family before going off to have a look at the list. To my delight I noticed that the QC appointed by the insurers had accepted two briefs that day, which meant he obviously expected one or both to settle. He certainly could not advocate on both. Having told Stewart the news I waited for the expected knock on the door and request for a chat. The barristers and particularly the QC's like to have the chat between them, but my approach is that it is my case and I am the link with the family. Stewart came in after a few minutes and said that the opposition would go to £650,000, but before the family could answer I said that we had not come all this way and done all of the preparation for that. Tell them we will take £850,000 and let him charm you into accepting £800,000. Stewart nodded and left the room to return in twenty minutes to say,
"Well done, you have a deal at £800,000"
The family were too shocked to react and we all walked into court where the settlement was explained to the judge and enshrined into a court order.

As the judge got up to leave I turned to Tony and his family and explained that the case was over. The costs would be paid separately so Tony would receive the full £800,000 (£1,680,000 today). There was a moment's pause before Tony's father took me by the hand, looked me firmly in the eye and said,

"John, there is my hand and my heart".

I must admit that it was all I could do to force back a tear when he said that, but a long journey came to an end. In the years that followed Tony came to visit me often at the office to discuss his personal life and sent me Christmas cards and postcards from his holidays. His marriage, like so many others in this situation didn't survived, but Tony reminded me often of what I used to say to him when he was low and thought that no woman would be interested in him.

"Wait until I get you the money Tony you will be beating the women off with a stick!" When he reminded me of this after the case I told him I was thinking of marrying him myself! He did indeed find somebody who knew nothing of the money when they started going out together and they settled as a couple and had a child.

Cases were very varied, but another that has always stuck in my mind concerned a lovely couple in their late thirties/early forties who had bought a commercial garage near Darlington with a house attached. They had paid £270,000 for it, putting their life savings into it as well as taking on a substantial mortgage. All was going well until the petrol company's agent turned up one day to say that the commercial loan was due for renewal, but gave assurances that it was nothing to worry about and was standard procedure. Subsequently, a valuer turned up and took away the leases before reporting back to the petrol company. A couple of weeks later the agent returned and told the owners that there was a bit of a problem.

"Oh, was the valuation less than we paid?" asked the male owner.

"Yes, it was lower than we expected" he replied.

"Sorry to hear that, how much does he think it's worth then?"

"Nothing" was the shocking response.

The couple had been struggling with this news for a couple of years and had engaged another solicitor, but were subsequently referred to me by one of their friends. I got their files, read through them and could see what had happened. The house, retail garage and petrol site were all leasehold on long leases, with commercial rents payable on the leaseholds. If they had been long leases with only a ground rent of a hundred pounds or so, then they may have had a value similar to that of a freehold, but because there was a commercial rent payable that was not the case and they were without value. When they bought the property, this fact appeared to have eluded my client's bank, the bank's valuer and the solicitor representing them. Worse than that, the lawyer who said he would sort it out for them had made it worse by renegotiating the terms of the lease to apparently improve things, but had in fact now made their property worth minus £100,000. I was not telling them something they didn't know, but I explained it in a way that set out our path to sue two sets of lawyers, a valuer and quite possibly the bank. I explained that it would be a long haul, but I was very confident we would succeed and I started the process.

One Christmas, Gillian and I were out at a works party and I saw my two clients sitting in a corner looking glum. This was a surprise because they had remained upbeat throughout their ordeal and I had grown to like them very much and considered them as friends. I went over to speak to them and they told me the bank was threatening to foreclose and they were considering bankruptcy. I urged them not to do that and said that they would lose all of their potential damages if they did. I also said I would speak to their bank manager. The next working day I rang the manager and explained about the action I was taking and that I was confident of winning before he said,

"That's all very well Mr McArdle, but there is no certainty and the bank is entitled to be paid the money it is owed. We have been patient long enough and that patience has run out"

"I think the issue of whether the bank is entitled to be paid is a moot point as you also failed to notice the obvious flaw in the purchase and it was you who appointed the valuer," I rejoined.

"I hope you are not seriously suggesting that the bank is responsible for this mess," he said righteously.

"What I am saying is, at the moment you are fortunate not to be part of these proceedings, but if you take any enforcement action on the loan I will apply to have your action stayed by the court and add the bank to the list of defendants in the claim that I'm bringing" I delivered calmly.

"ARE YOU THREATENING ME, MR McARDLE?" he bellowed.

"I certainly am" I replied, still calm. I reported the conversation to a slightly alarmed couple and told them my money was on him backing off, but that I was not bluffing. A week later a slightly giggly client rang to tell me that the manager had telephoned to say that the bank was not taking any action, but that he strongly disapproved of their solicitors methods. I told them I was sure I would still manage a good night's sleep! After two hard fought cases over three or four years, the clients recovered all of their losses and more, and were able to move out of the garage and into another business. They remained friends.

What comes with this kind of work is a realisation that you cannot control everything or always win. If you have won some cases for a group of people they often expect that just by instructing your firm they are bound to win again, but I never felt that or that I have some magical formula. There are some cases which I remember for their failures, as well as the successes. An early case in Hartlepool concerned a man who said he was forced off the road by an oncoming vehicle. He was found in his upturned car and was rendered paraplegic by the accident. As no other car was traced, the matter was passed to the Motor Insurers Bureau which deals with cases of untraced drivers and, try as I might, I could not persuade them to accept the claim by believing there was another car involved. The police were not helpful, as the officer who investigated the incident clearly did not believe my client. I took the matter to the final appeal, but lost and had to go and tell the man in his wheelchair that I could not move him out of his little flat and he now faced a life on benefits.

One other case which has never left me had similarities to Tony's case, but with a very different outcome. This again concerned a young male driver involved in an accident which was not his fault. He encountered a cow on the road and in swerving to avoid it was seriously and incurably injured. I assembled a really good legal team with one of the country's best QC's, but in our view a very poor decision by the judge robbed the man of compensation. I feel we did everything we could, but I was as disappointed as the family with the outcome. I would say to any aspiring young lawyer that you have to accept failure as well as success and not to let either influence your decisions or your representation of the next client. You can use the experience you have had, but should not try and avoid disappointment by only accepting clear winners. That said I always hated losing, but I never lost because I didn't care or could not be bothered to do what needed to be done. I might have hated losing, but I was also not afraid of losing.

CHAPTER 25: My mother

Before I move on to the next nightmare, let me reflect on a person who helped me through the last one.

My mother coming to live with us in the troubled times of 1992 was very important to the stability of the house. When you lose a parent as a child, the remaining parent becomes a much more important figure as they take on both roles. In my case, the death of my father when I was 12 years old shortly followed by my brother leaving for university, caused me to grow up faster than I otherwise would have done. I felt the need to become the man of the house and to offer some protection to my mother, not that she ever asked for it nor did she ever make me feel I had any added responsibility. I just felt it.

My mother, Mary McDonald was born on the 6th of August 1919 a year after 'the war to end all wars'. She was born into a family of a steelworker father, a hardworking housewife mother and eventually three other siblings. Her education was limited as it tended to be in those days for families such as hers, and upon leaving school she became a shop assistant. She had a good circle of friends and remained living with her family well into her twenties. Living in a catholic community her life was fairly insular and no doubt but for the advent of war, she would have been married earlier than she was. Prior to the outbreak of the Second World War she had dated some local boys, one of which was my father, but there was nothing serious. Along with some of her friends she joined the women's land army and for the first time saw something of the rest of the country, at one point being billeted in Southend. During these years she developed a love of the cinema and would go to the 'pictures' at least once a week to see the latest Cary Grant or Clark Gable films. She always said that they went to see the film stars rather than the film itself. She also had a love of reading and would often get through a book in two or three days.

After the war she met up with my father again who had returned to Consett from his terrible ordeal in a Japanese prisoner of war camp. They started dating again and in 1946 they were married. They lived for a time with her parents until my Dad, now a police officer, was sent to Newcastle upon Tyne. My brother was born in 1948 and I followed in 1953 to complete our family. I grew up in a happy home where roles seemed fairly clear. My mother looked after the house and the children; my father went to work and earned the money. He gave his wages to my mother and had what he described as pocket money for himself. He worked shifts as a policeman, so was at home at irregular times and it always seemed odd to see him going out to work as I was going to bed. My mother was the constant figure and I can still smell the aroma of her Sunday roast beef and vegetables, and the odour of Monday's washing. Mary was what she described as a plain cook in that curries and pasta were not for her; however she had a repertoire of several excellent meals. She also made cakes, scones and biscuits in a very unfussy but delicious way. It was only when I was older and encountered mothers who could not cook well that I realised how good my mother really was at it. I still miss her coconut cake that she always baked for me when I visited her in my adult life.

As I was growing up, we lived in either police houses or council houses and although my father never earned a large wage, he was always in work and we got by. I encountered poor families in the Catholic schools I went to and I knew we weren't one of them. I also knew that we weren't well off either, although my Dad did buy a car which was unusual in those days. It was a luxury back then, and he had to borrow the money from my mother's parents. I have a picture of the street we lived in and there are just two cars parked in it. It would be wall to wall cars now.

So there was Mary, living an unremarkable life as a happily married wife and a mother of two boys that were something of a handful. In 1965 she was given the devastating news that her husband had cancer and was dying. I mentioned in an earlier chapter that she took the decision not to tell me, but the pain and the fear must have been intense for her. The future was now very uncertain and she was only in her mid forties. She managed the rest of my father's time by doing normal things and crying when nobody was there. My brother had gone to see our doctor to confirm the dreadful news and he too carried an enormous burden at eighteen years of age. Having arranged for me to stay with friends for my father's funeral, she had the emotion of an absolutely full church and the moving spectacle of a police guard of honour to say goodbye to her life partner, who she would never replace.

Mary realised she would have to work and had faced that problem whilst my father was bedridden. She managed to get a job in a local factory and, having not worked for twenty years she was very nervous about the prospect. She was very mild mannered and knew that many women working there were likely to eat her for breakfast. As a non-drinking, nonswearing, well behaved practicing Catholic the odds were against her. It speaks volumes for her likability that the other women moderated their behaviour and were really disappointed when she got her next job and left them.

Her next job was as the manageress of a dry cleaner in our village, which was a much better job. I mentioned earlier about her arrangement for me to sit in the back of the shop after school amongst the dry cleaning, having a cup of coffee and a chocolate biscuit rather than be a latch key kid. She still had this job when I was working and, as I was still living with her, she had ample opportunity to have this much repeated conversation with me.
Mother "There was a woman who came in today and told me her life story"
Me "Oh really, did she have a problem?"
Mother "Yes, she did and she told me all about it"
Me "I bet she did. Does she know your son works in a solicitor's office?"
Mother "That's a terrible thing to say, she was just talking to me and not asking for anything" Then a few days later,
Mother "Do you remember that woman who came in the other day?"
Me "Oh yes"
Mother "Well Mr Smarty Pants, she did want me to ask you something"
It never mattered how often these things happened, my mother always had an open ear and always found the best in people. Nobody was ever fat, they were big boned; nobody was ever ugly they were God's children; nobody was ever all bad, they just probably had a bad childhood. In later years when I had my own practice she would ring me and tell me of some care worker, friend's child, workman, milkman, bus conductor, neighbour or complete stranger who needed help and say,
"I hope you don't mind, but I said you would speak to them"
When I did speak to them they would tell me what a wonderful lady my mother was and that she had said,
"That sounds terrible, but my lad will be able to sort that out for you"
In the years following my father's death she rebuilt her life, formed a large group of friends and always said yes to a social occasion or a holiday. She travelled abroad almost every year and several times went to visit relatives in the USA. Indeed it was due to Mary that the American connection has been preserved. She started writing to her cousins in California which bloomed into return trips for both sides on many occasions.

When my first wife was pregnant with my son Simon, I wanted Mary to be the first to know. We drove from the doctor's surgery to West Cornforth and picked her up from her new job as manageress of the local cake shop. My wife knew Mary very well, but nevertheless I warned her that Mary was likely to keep her emotions in check and was not given to outbursts of excitement. When Mary was told that her first grandchild was on the way she leapt out of her chair and started bouncing up and down on the spot, having let out an ear piercing scream. She then hugged both of us, screamed again and started bouncing up and down even higher. What do I know?

The delight was total and when Simon was born I took to him to his Gran's once a week, so that my wife could have a break and my mother could enjoy her grandchild. A huge bond was forged and when Simon passed his driving test, his long promised treat was to drive to Consett and take his Gran out for lunch. Mary loved all four of her grandchildren (my daughter and my brother's twin boys joined Simon) and she was able to pour her love on them, released from any responsibility which is that rare privileged position of a grandparent. When I broke the news to Mary of the breakdown of my marriage she fell into coping mode and came to live with me and the children, much to their delight. She was by then in her seventies and, suffering from macular degeneration, was partially sighted. The crisis gave her a new lease of life and her support of me and the children was as valuable as it was total. I was in the supermarket with her one day and she was sending me backwards and forwards for food that she was going to cook.

Mary "Go and get some broccoli, nice and green and fresh"

Me on returning with broccoli "There you go"

Mary "That's no use, it's not green enough and doesn't look fresh"

Me "I thought you said you were partially sighted. They'll never give you a dog now," I teased her.

Mary had a school friend called Rose Grimes who worked for a time in the USA, returning to look after her parents and then other members of her family. So committed to them was she that Rose never married, but was like a mother to her nieces and nephews. I'm not sure how it started, but it became a tradition that my mother and I called on Rose on Christmas Eve, accompanied by the children when they came along. Rose began to suffer ill health and had mobility problems which led to her being taken into care just before Christmas one year. My mother and I decided to visit her on Christmas Day which delighted her, but she broke down in tears telling of her hatred of the place. Rose never complained so it must have been bad, but in truth it was the loss of independence that was the worst thing.

Possibly influenced by that stalwart Christmas TV film 'The Great Escape', I promised to get her out of there.

Over the next couple of weeks we got her to be able to make her own tea and having passed one or two other tests, we managed to spring her back to her little house. I invited Rose for a meal, went to collect her and drove the 30 mile journey home with her talking the whole time in her excitement. My mother positioned herself beside her friend at the table, cutting up Rose's meat when nobody was looking as unbeknown to me Rose, who was now mainly in a wheelchair, had lost some feeling in her fingers. The care Mary showed throughout that day really moved me and after I had taken them home I felt compelled to ring her. Although I knew I would struggle to say it (I am even struggling to write it) I ended our conversation with,

"I just wanted to say that the way you were with Rose today was one of the kindest and nicest things I have ever seen. She is so lucky to have you as a friend and I wanted you to know I am very proud of you and love you very much" I just about spluttered it out and didn't wait for a reply as I imagined we were both in tears.

In 2000 Mary's health started to deteriorate. Her eyesight was very much worse and she had other issues. She had moved back to Consett in 1986 and had a wonderful house which gave her access to open countryside and a nice walk to the shops. This was now too much for her and her sister Theresa rang me one day to say that Mary would never tell me, but she needed to move nearer the centre of town and the church. Gillian and I started the search and found a lovely property owned by a charming young couple. In conversation with them they described the sort of house they were looking for which sounded just like my mother's house. We arranged a visit and Gillian and her mother spent all day cleaning and polishing the property into showroom condition. The couple loved it, we arranged a partial property exchange and the move was complete. She lived in the property for a few months before having to undertake major surgery and a long convalescence in hospital. She was discharged just before Christmas and I collected her to bring her back to our house for Christmas. I took her to see her family in Consett and we had a particularly hilarious time when her brother Tommy, who also suffered from macular degeneration, decided to show her how to clean a hearing aid with a tiny pin. The sight of these two trying to locate a tiny hole in a hearing aid with a tiny pin led to my beloved Aunty Joan (Tommy's wife) saying,

"Look at that, talk about the blind leading the blind" and we all fell about laughing.

Sadly, there was not much more to laugh about as Mary died in March of 2001. I gave her a last gift of a black granite headstone with both of my parent's names on it as they were finally reunited in a double grave after 35 years apart. My uncle Thomas had once said to me that when he died there would only be a handful of people at the funeral because he lived in London, but that when my mother died the church would be full. He was right. The church was so full that people had to stand at the back and amongst them was the couple with whom she had exchanged houses. Mary was not someone you forgot. She was the kindest and nicest person I have known. Courage is doing something when you are scared and she may well have often found herself scared or lonely, but I never knew her to put herself first. She was funny, often by accident and loved to laugh. In later life she even liked the odd drink, particularly if she was with her boys and Brian and I had some great times with her at family occasions or New Year's Eve. Although she never got over it, she was never defined by the loss of the husband she loved, but sought consolation in her family, friends and church.

One final story about the church; I had long since stopped going, but to please Mary I was married in a Catholic church. The priest had asked me to sign a statement that I would bring up any children we had as Catholics. I had refused and Mary was horrified. I told her that I had agreed to consider the children's upbringing and changed the wording on the form to reflect that. The priest asked permission of the bishop and permission was duly granted. A few years later I faced the same issue at Simon's christening. It was a different priest and this time there was no agreement. I had spoken to the priest on a few occasions and surprisingly he asked me just to sign the statement even if I didn't mean it. I was not prepared to do that and said I tried very hard never to lie and telling lies to God didn't seem like a good idea. He rang me later to say the bishop had not given consent (probably fed up with my amendments to his forms) and I rang Mary to give her the bad news. Sometime later and after she had spoken to the priest, I saw her. She was beaming and gave me a surprise hug.

"What's that for?" I enquired.

"I apologised to the priest about you, but he said there was nothing to apologise for and that I shouldn't worry about you not going to church, as it was clear to him that you lived a Christian life and that was better than some people who go to church all of the time" she replied. So there you are. God's agent had given me a pass and Mary felt a weight had been removed.

There was only one consolation in my mother's death. She was spared witnessing the rest of 2001, which was to turn into a complete nightmare for me and once again put me in the face of ruin.

CHAPTER 26: Not again

Our close friends John and Joan Fidler invited us to Bahrain for a holiday in the late summer of 2001 and I was really looking forward to it. The loss of Mary at the beginning of the year had been followed by my daughter deciding that she wanted to live with her mother and Mileson after nine years with us.

This dark year had picked up somewhat when I got a call from a garage proprietor asking if I would be interested in selling the PMB garage business. I had never intended to be in sole charge of the business, but having stepped in when I realised PMB was in trouble, that was the position I was in. I had taken on personal guarantees to secure finance and everyone's jobs and Geoff Cardwell suggested my mother may have prompted this enquiry from a position of influence 'Upstairs'! As it turned out it was not the original enquirer, but another one that eventually negotiated the purchase of the business with me retaining the land and buildings as their landlord on a handsome rent. It is worth clarifying at this point that PMB and the site it stood on were held as two different companies.

Gillian and I had a fantastic holiday in Bahrain where our friends entertained us lavishly in their huge house and on their small boat. One of the boat trips saw ours and other boats moored off a sandbank in the middle of the ocean. The British Military Attaché was sitting in a deckchair up to his waist in the water reading the Daily Telegraph, whilst ex-pats on the other boats exchanged champagne and smoked salmon sandwiches with us. Looking up at me he said,
"Yes it's a dirty job John, but somebody has to do it!" The American base was nearby and the US air force was getting ready for a second Gulf War bombing campaign. What I didn't know in this idyllic setting was that I would be returning home to face my own second war less than ten years after the last one.

When I sold the PMB garage business I appointed an agent to move into PMB and oversee the transfer of the business to the new owners. I confided in him that I had suspicions of dishonesty and asked him to pay special attention to the parts and accounts departments. The reason for my suspicion was that my financial exposure was growing on a regular basis. He worked there for a couple of weeks and, on the day of the sale, rang me saying he didn't believe there had been any incidents of theft. My bank manager and friend Tim Sanderson kept in touch and we talked at length about why my financial exposure was growing, whilst still considering the possibility of theft. A detailed internal investigation led to the conclusion that the explanation lay with the amount of stock carried in terms of cars and the sums owed by manufacturers and Government schemes such as Motability. I remained concerned, but PMB's accounts were audited annually and my spreadsheets of information from the accounts department broadly added up and explained the increased borrowing.

Running a retail garage is a complex task. The motor manufacturers have a number of schemes and initiatives going at any one time, as do the many finance houses with which you deal. Cars themselves are often out on loan, hire or with sales staff so that a headcount of vehicles is difficult. Nonetheless, the sale was completed toward the end of 2001 and was supposed to be followed by a gradual calling in of monies due and a payment of sums owed, which would lead to a final balance in the trading company and me as a landlord of the site receiving rent. Shortly after the sale it became clear that there were major problems. Demands quickly came in for repayment of loans, finance on cars or groups of cars and a financial black hole was beginning to emerge. The only questions were; how big was the hole and were we dealing with theft?

When the PMB garage opened in 1992 we interviewed a number of people for prominent positions and one of these was Mary Blair who applied for the job of accounts manager. The role included overseeing the transactions of buying and selling all stock and producing monthly figures. She also provided all of the information for the annual audit. She had worked for the now closed Nissan dealership in Darlington and therefore had all of the necessary experience. She was in her mid-forties and had the deep rasping voice of a heavy smoker, but came across as a kind, caring and hardworking mother who was looking for stability in her life. She was the obvious choice and we gave her the job.

Over the nine years that followed we promoted her, increased her salary and she became the person that the staff trusted and confided in. She was, as I was to say later, everyone's favourite auntie. Mary also sought my advice on a regular basis on her problems within her family and her life, and all of the advice and any representation I gave her was given free of charge. One piece of advice she sought was to do with the setting up of a little shop for her daughter. It was a bridal wear business in leased premises that Mary set up to provide her daughter with an income. She needed some help to begin with, but would tell me how well it was going and that they were thinking of expanding. She duly did expand into premises in Newcastle as well as moving to bigger premises in Darlington. I watched with some trepidation as somebody working in an accounts department whilst running another business is a clear risk. I gently raised the issue with the new managing director Mark Tranmer, who told me that he trusted Mary implicitly, but more reassuringly that she could not be stealing without his knowledge because all cheques had to be signed by two directors. I even sent a friend of mine from the motor trade in to have a look prior to the sale and he reported that all seemed well. However, the evidence post-sale was becoming overwhelming and I telephoned Mary in her new post with my purchasers. I explained that things seemed to be suggesting there was a major problem and her only answer was,

"Not according to my figures"

I told her that I was now investigating and would get to the bottom of it.

The Dealership was being run for the new owners by Bill Robson, who told me there was a problem with the parts department and I went in to find that at least £30,000 of parts were missing or unaccounted for. In addition, I discovered that some of the cars which appeared on the balance sheet as our stock actually belonged to Mitsubishi and with that I called in the police. I had little hard evidence, but I told the detectives that I strongly suspected Mary Blair and the proceeds of her crimes may well have gone into her other business and a new house she had bought. Although I didn't know Bill Robson very well at the time I liked him very much and took the risk of telling him of my suspicions, asking him to keep an eye on Mary and make sure his systems were tight. Every day seemed to bring more bad news as business debts emerged and assets were shown to be massively overvalued. I knew there had to have been dishonesty, but for the moment I couldn't prove it, nor did I know how bad it was. I organised an increased facility with the bank for £200,000, but with the daily drain it was soon gone. Eventually Tim Sanderson told me that matters had been taken out of his hands and RBS, which had taken over Nat West, had referred it to a division of that bank known as special lending services based in Manchester. Tim and I drove down there to meet up with two young bankers, who were very pleasant in the way that two vultures might be pleasant to a dying animal just before tearing the flesh from its bones. I explained the situation and that the borrowing on the whole site including the business stood at about £1.1 million, with the site valued at £1.3 million. I was not asking for any more money, just the opportunity to consolidate that facility into a loan whilst I got to the bottom of what was happening. I also explained that the long awaited new road was finally going to be built and may well double the value of the site, which had further development potential. I had the plans and documents with me and we went through them all. At the end of the meeting, one of the vultures told me they thought the bank would agree to help, but would want a fee and also a small part of the development value.

"How small?"I asked

It wouldn't be anything to worry about, they would work it out and send me their proposals, they said. Three days later they confirmed their offer to lend me the money they had already lent me, for a fee of £10,000 and fifty per cent of the value of the land over £1.2 million. I thought it must be a misprint and rang the author of the letter to ask him if there had been some mistake. He confirmed there had not.

"So if this site is worth £5 million pounds in a few years time, you want a fee of £1,900,000 excluding the £10,000 you want now, for not recalling a loan you have already lent me?" I asked.

He replied, "Well, that's one way of looking at it"

I was shocked, but ended up saying something for use later on.

"You do realise that I have no choice here, don't you?"

The site was to be worth more than the figure I quoted and I was to embark on a fight with RBS later, but for then I was just dealing with crises on a first come first served basis. What really shocked me was quite how stressed I was and the way it consumed my every waking hour. I was shocked because, comparing it with my crisis of ten years before when absolutely everything I had was in jeopardy, this was just about money. I suppose I should have understood the stress as I found that not only had my bank turned against me after years of being their blue eyed boy who could do no wrong, but they had been joined by most if not all of the motor trade establishment who threatened legal action or took it on a daily basis. Even some of the staff at PMB joined in. I suppose I just could not believe I was here again in the centre of a nightmare, so soon after the last one.

Gillian was fantastic throughout and kept telling me that if we had to buy a smaller house we would and even started to describe the little cottage she would refurbish. I told her she was getting too excited about that project and in any event I had not worked hard all of my life to let anyone take the benefits off me. We took to going for walks and on one of them passed the Devonport Hotel in our village when she said,

"Let's go in for a drink"

I said I hadn't brought any money out with me, but she produced a £10 note and said,

"No, but I did and you need a drink"

Slowly I began to get to grips with things and although new problems came up from time to time it seemed the worst was over. The loan repayment was around the same figure as the rent on the site and I had rearranged other payments so that I could manage them on my drawings from the firm, which was still going strong. However, it was a real nightmare and it took up a huge amount of time and energy. One day I was in the office when the detective dealing with the case rang and said,

"Hello John, you were right it was Mary Blair. We have traced the account she was paying the stolen money into and out of and so far, we are up to £550,000 that she has spent and we are still counting"

The two officers came to see me with the evidence and with their plan of action. They said that teams of officers would simultaneously land at Mary's house, her daughter's house and each of her three places of business. They would place criminal administrators in charge and try to recover as much of the stolen money as possible. It was imperative that we did not tell anyone as the raids had to be completely secret to be effective. They stayed in touch and then rang to say the date was in two weeks time. We waited excitedly until the day before the raid when one of the officers rang and said,

"The raids are off for tomorrow, she is in Australia"

It turned out it was just a holiday and a new date was set. A few days before the given date, Gillian and I were shopping in Marks and Spencer in Darlington and as I was loading the shopping into the boot of our car I heard Gillian say,

"Hello Mary, how are you doing?"

Thinking she was joking I looked up and there was the soon to be arrested thief walking confidently past our car. I said,

"Oh hello Mary, how are you?"

Looking straight ahead and without breaking stride she replied, "I'm fine, just keeping my head down".

In the early hours of the Saturday morning, teams of officers pounced on all sites and when Mary answered the door she apparently said,

"I have been expecting you".

She admitted all offences before claiming that she was suffering from amnesia and could remember nothing. She had stolen about £1.1 million pounds from PMB, around £200,000 from Bill Robson's company, as well as having credit card debts with her husband of £200,000. At the time it was the biggest fraud case Teesside police had ever dealt with. She was sentenced to five years imprisonment and all of her assets including her home were seized and sold. She had been stealing for years, starting with a few hundred pounds and then a few thousand leading up to almost £250,000 in her last year. Her primary method was to produce a genuine financial statement from a hire purchase company showing a balance due on a part exchanged car, whereby she produced a cheque for counter signing by other director with an explanation that she would fill in the payee later as it might be to another finance company, or some other funding plan. Once she had that second signature, she would make the cheque out to herself or her nephew and if it was him, he would sign a cheque to her and receive £100 for putting it through his account. He also went to prison.

There are regulations in place to prevent money laundering like this, in that banks are obliged to know their customers and their expected means, and report any suspicious transactions. This nephew was a teenager who opened a bank account, paid hundreds of thousands of pounds in and out it with the commission being the balance to him. Short of calling the account 'My Money Laundering Account' he could not have made it more obvious that he was involved in criminal behaviour, but as far as I know the bank escaped sanction. As we all discovered in 2008 there appears to be one law for banks and one for the rest of us. The police also arrested a number of Mary's family members and we attended a trial of her son-in-law, a former PMB salesman, who had received several thousands of pounds into his bank account. He claimed not to understand why and also claimed that he was just fooled by Mary, plus a variety of other explanations, but despite this he was acquitted at the end of his trial. Juries are often confused by fraud trials and his barrister was very good at adding to it.

The remarkable thing about that trial was the antipathy that Gillian and I faced from the Blair family and friends. Gillian was particularly shocked, as far as from any embarrassment or remorse, there appeared naked aggression directed towards us. Mary and her nephew had admitted the offences and yet here the family was staring at us as though some great injustice had befallen them. Indeed Mary's daughter had told someone we knew that her mother was innocent and that I had made the whole thing up to disguise a failing business. What is it that turns an apparently normal respectable mother and employee into a thief and fraudster on a giant scale? It is a difficult question. When I first began to suspect Mary, Gillian dismissed it as totally implausible. She saw quite a bit of Mary who had told her all about her life, her divorce, her children and the death of her mother. She had confided her innermost thoughts and emotions to Gillian, but there were two comments she made that convinced my wife that it couldn't be her. One was relating to a thief that I had caught in the sales team, when Mary said to Gillian,

"You just can't believe it, can you? Terrible to be stealing at all, but to steal from John, well you'd think he would realise that John would find out and then there would be all hell to pay. He would be the last person you would dare steal from"

The second occasion was when I took over the whole business when it was in trouble and Mary beckoned Gillian into her room, closed the door and said,

"I just want you to know how much I and all the staff appreciate what John is doing. I realise he is sticking his neck out for us all and I am determined to make it a success for him"

To add to this, Mary had come to see me at the office and told me she had a temporary cash flow problem in her business and could not pay her VAT. She said she was really embarrassed to ask me after all I had done for her, but could I make her a short term loan of £30,000. I loaned her the money, interest free and she repaid it after a few weeks no doubt with money she stole from PMB.

During these times Mary was stealing tens of thousands of pounds per month. A person whom I had trusted, had been to my home with her husband for meals, had borrowed money from me interest free and had received free legal services for herself and her family, had put me at risk of financial ruin and risked the futures of all of her work colleagues and friends who had relied upon her. The reason appeared simple greed and a desire for a false image of a successful business woman to present to her family and anyone she came into contact with. Years later I was talking to Bob O'Lone, who had been the business manager during most of Mary's time, but had left as he was not able to make the business the success he was expecting. He told me that he could never forgive Mary for what she did and that whilst he enjoyed his current job, he would always think his big chance was with PMB and what he could have made it and created for himself alongside Malcolm Burgess and me. He felt robbed of that chance by someone who worked alongside him and whom he had considered a friend. Very sadly Bob came to see me a short time later to tell me he had terminal cancer and we hurriedly put his affairs in order. He died shortly after and attending his very full funeral I was to reflect on what a decent, kind and honourable man he was, much loved by his family and friends. He was more of a success than he knew and Mary Blair and those like her were never fit to spend time with him.

It was time for me to regroup once again and embark upon a course to save the Garage site, stem the financial bleed and once I had done that, move into my area of expertise.....litigation against those responsible. At least I had some control over that.

CHAPTER 27: Survival and retribution

Once I knew the worst was over and that I had survived, I started to think about trying to fix the mess. It is no good trying to repair a leak, however big, without first stopping the flow through it. Both Citroen and Mitsubishi were in touch with me over newly found debt, as were their parent companies that organised car finance. Other garages and trade creditors that Mary had concealed were also making their claims. My accountant and friend Trevor Thorne advised me to bring in a specialist insolvency firm to clean up the PMB mess.

I contacted the firm on Tyneside who were very helpful from the beginning and gave me the option of just walking away. I didn't want to do that, however appealing it sounded. I wanted to get to the bottom of it and make sure that as many people as possible were paid in full. I also intended a number of legal actions myself. At the time of greatest stress I drove my son Simon down to Cardiff for him to look at the university there and on the long journey, I told him what was happening and that I was trying to preserve the site for the family. He rather sweetly said that if it was causing me stress I should perhaps think about walking away. As it was with Gillian, it is very reassuring when the people you love put your well being ahead of any gain they might enjoy. Nonetheless I decided on a plan to not only survive, but to turn things around. It would take time and energy, but once again being a litigation lawyer came to my aid.

My plan was daunting in its complexities: I would sell the site for its current value to a new company I would form, thus removing the stigma Mary Blair had given the site; I would liquidate PMB and appoint the insolvency company to deal with it; start an action against Mary Blair to recover as much of her assets as possible; start an action against PMB's auditor for negligence in failing to spot the fraud; fight the motor manufacturers on some of the debts they were claiming; I would lease the Garage premises to the existing tenants from the new company; investigate RBS and consider my position in relation to their dealings with me, either bringing an action or a complaint against them; claim tax relief for some of the losses and finally, I would remain focused on the legal practice and the uninsured loss work to avoid a real disaster.

Once Mary was arrested the Crown Prosecution Service took over the actions against her, but the accountants appointed by the CPS took about a third of the proceeds recovered which was outrageous. I formed a new company and sold the site to it, so that it had none of the taint of Mary's criminality. The ownership of the site was complex as other interests had historically been involved, but when I reached the point of sale and transferred the funds to the liquidator I felt like a boat had been cut free from a burning ship. Rent was now being paid which covered the enormous mortgage and nobody else was involved but me.

The action against the auditor was something that I could easily handle. The barrister who was helping me was Julian Goose. He went on to become a QC and a judge, and was one of the most talented lawyers I ever worked with. Julian said my firm should not act in the case and advised me to instruct another firm. I approached three large firms in Newcastle and Leeds and their advice varied from telling me I would lose, to one saying they may act for me on a no win/no fee basis, but I would have to pay them £10,000 to assess my chances first.... is it any wonder people aren't keen on lawyers? I rang Julian telling him that I was representing myself and would try to remember that old legal adage of 'a lawyer who acts for himself has a fool for a client'. I started the long and familiar legal proceedings and after more than three years the auditor's solicitors settled the case. To begin with it was defended, but I discovered that despite coming to the premises with a team, the auditors did not follow their own procedures which were set out in their appointment letter and very largely relied upon Mary for detail. It was akin to asking the rat if the cheese was in the store as opposed to looking at the cheese. As we neared a final hearing a substantial offer was made, which I rejected. It was followed by another which I also refused. The lawyer on the other side, a very experienced and reasonable man, rang me and asked me to give him a number I found acceptable and he would see if that would end it. It did. The details are subject to a confidentiality clause so I can't disclose them, but in all of the actions put together, I reckon I recovered about seventy five per cent of the money Mary stole.

Much the greater prize was the retention of the site which was growing in value at an alarming rate. My breakthrough with the bank came as a result of the criminal proceedings brought by the CPS. Trial evidence included a number of cheques that were presented without two directors' signatures and therefore were outside of the mandate I had given the bank. I was a mixture of furious and elated as I now had my weapon to use against them. I could barely conceal my fury as I launched my complaint, which led to a meeting with the local bank director. He sat in front of me and I delivered the evidence of the bank's failings, pointing out that it should not have honoured the cheques and should have alerted me to the problem. Instead of doing that, it stood back and when I was wounded, forced me to enter into a contract to take a large piece of the value of the site from me. I was now in full flow and not exhibiting the calm exterior I normally present when I said,

"Let me tell you what percentage of the site you will get.....NONE ....not one percent. I would rather lose it all. You really do not know me at all, but let me assure you that I am not given to bluffing nor am I afraid to lose"

I still remember almost word for word his reply,

"The bank would not litigate with a customer of your standing Mr McArdle; we will accept a nominal sum for the bank's interest in the site"

Somewhat taken aback I asked him what that nominal sum was and he said he could not say at the moment, but it was nothing to be concerned about (does that sound familiar?). This is where I made a mistake that I would not have made for a client. I took my foot off the pedal and assumed the matter resolved without ensuring it was. Going back to that legal adage, I was being the 'fool' in the relationship of solicitor and client.

The real problem was the continuing growth of the site's value and when the building of the long awaited new road started, it was impossible to ignore that it had more than doubled in value. Having never had an acceptable definition of nominal from the bank, it altered its position. No doubt someone up the line looked at the legal document which was now promising to return to them a seven figure sum and wondered why they were simply not collecting it. RBS instructed an expensive firm of solicitors in London who started correspondence with me to recover the bank's investment. All bets were off and I went on the attack with all guns blazing. We were in full blown dispute. Threats of legal proceedings were exchanged and the bank's position was that they legally owned a significant percentage of my site and if I wanted to buy it back I would have to pay for the privilege. Their lawyers came up to the North East to deliver the news to me personally that their client might take £300,000 now and I conveyed the message that they would have to pull that sum from my cold dead hands.

At some point, I played the mediation card. In recent years there has been a rise in mediation services to settle legal disputes. This is where an independent person is appointed by both sides to meet up on a given day and see if a compromise can be achieved. The mediator is often a lawyer and I had done a number of these mediations for clients and found them to work very well. I used to explain to clients the usual success of mediation by using the analogy of going to the cinema as opposed to watching a film at home. If you take the trouble to get ready, go out and pay to see a film, you tend to be in the mood to be entertained and be willing for the film to be good. On the other hand if you watch a film at home, you tend to be easily distracted and almost start the process thinking it unlikely that you will sit through it. In mediation, both sides have come out and paid to see the film. I always did mediations as a sole lawyer, but I was often against legal teams of barristers and solicitors and when they were joined by their clients and their client's insurers, their side of the room could be quite crowded. I would be there with my client or clients and often the process lasted well into the evening.

In this dispute I was both client and lawyer. I realised I had to do something to give a little balance to proceedings, so I asked Geoff Cardwell to come with me as my 'lawyer' decoy. Geoff would need to look like he was advising, but in fact was just preventing me sitting in a room all day on my own.
As long as you don't expect me to do anything I am happy to have a day out in Leeds, was his reply.
So off we set to our agreed date in Leeds to meet the mediator at her chambers, a well known QC who was acceptable to both the bank and me. RBS arrived mob-handed with three lawyers from the London firm and three representatives from the bank. The QC met with us separately and then we had our preliminary meeting where we each made a statement and all agreed to call each other by first names and be as chummy as we could muster. At a second meeting with me only, the mediator said that she thought I would lose any case I took against the bank as they had a strong legal position, however badly they had behaved. I said I did not agree and felt the combination of events was strong and put to her my reasons for that view. She was not persuaded and at our next meeting she told me that that bank would accept £200,000 and that was their final offer, otherwise the court would have to decide it. I said no. She then took a rather unusual step in mediations of advising me to pay it and repeating the advice that I would lose. When I said no again and that I would rather lose the site than give in, she said she thought we ought to abandon the mediation even though it was not quite lunchtime and we were booked in all day.

During the mutual meeting I had done my usual scan of the opposition team to calculate where the power lay and also for anything that might be relevant or an advantage later. Part of the bank's team was a man called Sandy Clarke who not only appeared to be in charge but seemed a reasonable man. As the mediator was throwing in the towel, I requested that she ask Sandy if he would meet me alone. She frowned and asked why. I said I thought it was worth a try and she said it was not and I was wasting my time. I told her it was my time to waste, that I had paid for the day and asked if she was refusing to do as I asked. She huffily flounced out of the room saying she would ask. She returned a few minutes later saying Sandy had agreed and held open the door for me to go into the meeting room. Sandy joined me and as we both sat down, our mediator also sat. Looking at her I said,

"I'm sorry; I want to talk to Sandy alone"

"WHAT?" she said, "You don't even want me here?"

"Yes that's right" I replied. She scooped up her papers and grunted on her second flounce. I had no real idea what I was going to say, but I thanked him for meeting me and said we were both used to dispute and commercial matters, but I wanted to tell him a story, man to man, without distraction. I gave him a brief history of the site and the garage, including the discovery of the theft, plus what I had to do to keep the site. I then moved on to my complaint against the bank and the promise they had made to me. I never raised my tone above cordial and showed no emotion as we debated the issues for a few minutes and then Sandy said,

"I have listened very carefully to what you have said and I can tell you that this issue has gone to board level at the bank, so I can assure you we are taking it seriously and having enquired about you, we also do not need any persuading of how seriously we should take you. However John, you are a man of business and you know how these things are decided and how they work. It is not personal, but I have a mandate that I cannot go below and that is £200,000". I then said something that was not only spontaneous, but something I had never said before.

"You are right, I am a man of business" I replied "and I do know how things work, but I am also my father's son and he taught me the difference between right and wrong and gave me the strength to fight for what is right. Now you look me in the eye and tell me that what you are doing is right"

There was a pause whilst he looked me in the eye and I struggled successfully to keep my emotions in check, as my statement had been as much a shock to me as to him. The comment had struck home and this very decent man was caught in the embarrassment of truth.

"What are you prepared to pay?" he sighed

Due to a confidentiality clause I can't confirm details, but in five minutes we had settled the matter subject to board approval which he said he would obtain. Our flouncy QC rejoined us and gave me a look as though she thought I had smuggled a gun into the meeting and within an hour Geoff and I were on our way back to Darlington with the matter resolved and full ownership of the site now back with me. As we got into the car and I explained what happened. Geoff looked out of the window and said,
"Well that was my first mediation and what a fantastic job I have done. I should do these more often; I must have a real gift for it" We both howled with laughter as we set off back home.

CHAPTER 28: Multi tasking

During both of my major personal crises in 1992 and 2001 I continued to work and deal with other people's problems, as well as running or assisting to run the various businesses I had started. What I had always been able to do was concentrate on the one case I was looking at or the client I was seeing, without thinking about other cases even if they were urgent. However, in the first few weeks of each crisis I had found it impossible not to have a backdrop of my problems, or the consequences of them, whilst dealing with other matters and that included when I was seeing clients. This meant that when someone was talking to me about their case I was listening to them and taking it in, but against a constant background mumbling of my own problems as though a radio was picking up two stations at the same time. This was alien to me and something I knew I had to overcome. I eventually managed it by forcing myself to focus on the often much greater problems of others and their need for the whole of my attention. I always had a case load of up to 300 active cases and here is a small selection that helped to take me out of my own worries.

A mid afternoon appointment turned out to be with a very pleasant woman in her forties. She was a little nervous, as is often the case and struggled to start her question in response to my standard how can I help you? She was not sure how or indeed if I could help and also unsure what she was asking me to do. I asked her just to tell me what had happened and she said that her husband had been involved in an accident on his motorbike on his way back from playing golf. When she told me he was on a life support machine she broke down into floods of tears and couldn't speak. I gave her a tissue, told her to take her time and tell me what she knew. She composed herself and said that a police officer had called to her house to tell her that her husband had hit a car a short distance from their home. He was in the local hospital, unconscious and in intensive care. The officer went on to say, somewhat tactlessly, that it looked like the accident was her husband's fault and if he survived he may be prosecuted for careless driving. I found out that he was a man in his forties, employed as a train driver and very experienced as a motorcyclist. Although there was no further information available to either of us, I thought it very unlikely that he would be riding his motorbike recklessly, particular at that time of day, so close to home. The important thing was his health regardless of whose fault the accident was and I confirmed we would act on a conditional fee basis (no win/no fee), that she need not worry about costs and that I would deal with the police and any claim from now on.

I went to visit the scene and saw where the man had hit the other vehicle and it was indeed on the wrong side of the road for him. I also noticed that there was a road junction on the left hand side and I felt the most likely explanation was that a vehicle had pulled out in front of my client and he had swerved to avoid it. The police decided to take no action and when I obtained their report, there within the statements was the clear evidence as to what had happened. As my client rode along the route to his house the other vehicle pulled out and turned right, but managed to get to the other side of the road despite not even seeing the motorbike at any point. The point the police seemed to have missed was that a taxi driver behind the first car made exactly the same mistake and also pulled out to turn right. The taxi and the other car were effectively blocking the path of the motorbike, causing a natural inclination for the motorbike to swerve right, resulting in a collision with the first car. The driver of the first car made a statement that he only saw the motorbike when it struck his car and assumed he was speeding on the wrong side of the road. My client was beginning to recover and the hospital discharged him, but he had no recollection of any of the events and indeed never did recall it. The other driver's insurers disputed my theory and we started court proceedings and the gathering of further evidence. I had a conversation with the lawyer appointed to oppose me, in which I said,

"Good luck with your defence. You only have to persuade a judge that a man in his forties decided to ride his motorbike on the wrong side of the road a few hundred yards from his house in the early evening, at such a speed that two drivers pulling out of a junction failed to see him at all. No doubt he fancied trying it after all that safe driving of a train that he does for a living, when hundreds of people rely upon his judgement."

I also added a common line of offering a side bet of £10 between lawyers as to who would win. This was a long running case and I knew a final settlement was quite a way off. I had now become fairly close to this enormously likeable family, who were a delight to support and I was concerned about them. Their house was unsuitable for my client who was going to be left with permanent mobility problems and seemed unlikely to be able to return to work. Well into the litigation I asked the family to find a suitable bungalow and tried to persuade them of the positives of the situation. They finally found the house of their dreams and with quite a bit of arm twisting I got the insurers to pay for it as an interim payment and they duly moved. I called to see them shortly afterwards and it was warming see them so happy with their new home. These cases take years; employment and care experts have to prepare detailed reports and many medical reports are required, but we eventually ended up in our QC's chambers with the insurance legal team in the room next to us and settled the case for a huge sum. They stayed in touch in the years that followed and are still in the bungalow as far as I know.

Some cases, because of the subject matter, are just traumatic from start to finish. Having acted for a lady in a fairly straight forward accident claim and settled it without too much trouble, I noticed she had an appointment to see me and assumed it was a query relating to that. She walked into my office with a girl who she introduced as her sixteen year old daughter. The girl wouldn't look at me and in fact positioned her chair to face her mother and not me. Her mother said she felt very uncomfortable, but during the accident claim she felt I was someone she could talk to and she had something terrible to tell me now. She went on to say that her daughter had been the subject of serious sexual abuse by her husband, the girl's father, beginning when she was around five years old and it was only recently that her daughter had told her about it. They had gone to the police who were very supportive and wanted to bring an action, but the CPS had declined due to insufficient evidence. This had devastated the girl who at this point of the story, had her head bent and was holding her mother's hand with both of hers. The policeman dealing with the matter offered to give me any information I needed and would support any action I felt I could bring.

Everything about what I was hearing rang true. The mother was devastated that she had been unaware of it, but she totally believed her daughter. The girl herself was as damaged as you would expect and as vulnerable as it was possible to be, but had found the courage to tell her mother and the police. In case you're wondering why there was a delay, I asked the question already knowing the likely answer as I had dealt with the evil of paedophilia previously. Paedophiles find a way to not only entrap the child, but leave a threat as insurance. In this case the father had said that if she told anyone, everyone would hate her and he would kill her. The parents were now separated, but the threat still was having an effect. Her mother told me that her daughter was wearing a woollen hat because underneath it she was completely bald, having lost her hair through the worry. I was both moved and furious and could see why the girl could not look at another male authority figure. I spoke to her mother for a time and then turned to the girl and, using her first name, gently said that I could only guess at how she felt and why she should feel uncomfortable, but that we were a powerful firm of lawyers and we would now act for her to protect her and make sure no harm came to her. I spoke for a few minutes, but the phrase that got her to turn and look at me was,

"Do you want me to get him for you?"

She looked at me, nodded and then looked down. I promised I would get him and offered her full protection. I gave her my card and said she could call me whenever she wanted and in particular if she felt frightened.

I contacted a barrister friend of mine, Tom Finch and he like us agreed to act for free or on a conditional fee basis. We made an appointment and went to see the police officer who had dealt with the investigation. He was a specialist paedophile investigator and he took us into a room where he showed us the girl's interview tapes which were compelling. He was certain the girl was telling the truth and there were other matters too delicate to discuss here that pointed to her father's guilt. He confirmed he would give evidence in a civil court. I wrote to the father confirming that we were bringing a civil claim and he should not think that the absence of a criminal prosecution was the end of the matter. He immediately instructed solicitors to defend the claim and they wrote to me to say so. In that letter they said he could not understand why these allegations were being made. After I launched proceedings the lawyer dealing with the case rang me and said that although the father maintained his innocence he was prepared to pay his daughter £5000 to drop the action. I said I thought it unlikely that she would be interested, but I would find out. When daughter and mother came in I explained what had happened, but (and you have to remember this was a great deal of money then for a sixteen year old) she turned it down immediately. I duly wrote and confirmed the position and a couple of weeks later the lawyer rang me again and said he had no particular instructions, but could I name a figure my client would take to settle the matter. Again I spoke to her and her mother, then rang the lawyer where to the best of my recollection I said,

"I can confirm that there is no amount of money that she will take as she is determined to see her father in court and, as frightened as she has been this time she will be fully protected and safe. Your client's day of justice is due and I will have police presence in court so that the criminal investigation will be re opened and a proper penalty applied. Your client's actions are about to catch up with him"

The day in court never materialised as prior to the hearing my client's father hanged himself at his home. I saw client and mother and said they should feel no guilt as in my view an innocent man would not offer money to avoid a court case where such allegations were being made if the allegations were false and similarly, would not commit suicide when the chance was there to clear his name. In any event the pressure was applied by me, not them and I felt no guilt which indeed I did not. What a shame that the many victims of Jimmy Saville did not get the opportunity to make him feel the darkness he imposed upon them. We obtained a judgement against the estate and sometime later a smiling eighteen year old girl came to my office with a full head of hair and a place at college. Her mother was beaming and, as traumatic as things had been and may again be they were working through it. In a final telephone conversation the mother told me that her daughter had three telephone numbers in her diary, her mother's, the police officer from the unit and me. I felt honoured.

Unfortunately there are times when the law is of no help and a lawyer can do little. A lady in her sixties came to see me at our Darlington office. She told me that her daughter had married badly a few years before and the marriage had taken a toll on her daughter's mental health, which had led to a nervous breakdown. Her daughter had divorced the man, but had recently received a letter from a building society which she handed to me. The letter was from the Bradford and Bingley Building Society and was demanding £57,000 as the sum due after repossession of the house her daughter had owned with her former husband. I looked into the matter and discovered that the lady's daughter had signed over the property to her husband when they divorced making no claim on the house or him, but had not realised that she was still named on the mortgage. This meant she was liable for the debt, despite having no interest in the property. When I delivered this bad news to them both the mother told me she was widowed, but her bungalow (former home of mum and dad) was worth £60,000 and she would sell it to pay the debt. I said that bankruptcy for the daughter would be a much easier way and the house would be preserved. They said they would think about it and ring me back.

The following day mum phoned and said she had decided to sell. She was worried that her daughter would have another breakdown if she had to face bankruptcy and that was not a risk she was prepared to take. I asked her to let me try and reason with the building society before she did anything and I wrote to them explaining the unfairness of the situation and the mental health problems at the time. I received a reply within a few days which simply told me that they were entitled to be paid, had failed to trace the husband and that my client was jointly and severally liable for the FULL DEBT. They asked for immediate proposals. I telephoned the author of the letter, as often the need to explain verbally is much harder than writing an unsympathetic cold letter. Not so this time, as the author was colder than his letter and ended by saying it was not their fault and she should have sought advice at the time. I sat for a few moments realising that there was no legal way out and tried to think of something else that might be effective.

After getting permission from my clients I rang a journalist friend of mine, Ernie Brown and asked if he could do me a favour. I told him the story and asked if he would ring Bradford and Bingley's head office for a comment on a story he was investigating of a young woman who was being pursued by them over a debt relating to a house she no longer owned and the only reason they could was because she didn't, due to mental health issues, have her name removed from the mortgage when transferring the property to her husband. Ernie duly obliged and said that the press officer had taken all of the details and would ring him back, which he did within the hour sounding very worried and promising a full investigation and a follow up call tomorrow. The following day the press officer rang Ernie and said there had been a misunderstanding and of course they would not pursue a debt in these circumstances. I asked Ernie to ring them back and request a fax confirmation, including the phrase 'waiving all rights in relation to the debt against (my client's name)'. He agreed and after an anxious few hours wait Ernie rang to say he had a fax in his hand with the precious phrase on it. The debt was gone and the family home saved, but only by the power of the press.

Not all cases were so serious and there were many lighter moments. One I remember was of a Hartlepool client telling me of his desire to get back to work. I suppressed a chuckle when he said,
"You see Mr McArdle the problem with me is that I am what they call a work alcoholic"!

Another new client from Middlesbrough answered my phone call and when I explained I needed some details of his car accident he answered my questions. I then asked if anyone else was in the car and he told me his wife was a front seat passenger and she was injured. I asked for her full name and his reply was,

"Hang on a minute.... Hey, what's your FULL NAME? ....she says it's Mary Louise"!

I often find that men cannot remember their wife's date of birth, but not remembering her name is rare!

One of my favourites was a man from Hartlepool who had been injured at work. I read his medical report to him from Richard Montgomery, a very talented orthopaedic surgeon from the James Cook Hospital in Middlesbrough, and when I had finished I asked him if the report was accurate. Much to my amazement he said,

"I'm not sure if I am supposed to tell you Mr McArdle, but Mr Montgomery is using me as a hamster"

Richard had been a friend of mine for some years and had never mentioned having a giant wheel for patients to run round or asking them to store food in their cheeks, so I was a little confused.

"Did you say Mr Montgomery is using you as a hamster?" I enquired.

"Yes, I am HIS hamster" he said with a smile.

"Do you mean guinea pig?"

"Aye, that's what I mean" he replied to my relief.

So there it was, in the most difficult times of my life I was helping people with their problems....and they were helping me right back.

CHAPTER 29: Retirement

I started this book by saying I can remember the day my career started, but it is more difficult to be precise about when I started to think about retirement. It was always something of an abstract thought to consider the day that I would step down from running the firm, let alone stop working as a lawyer altogether.

I never stopped enjoying being a lawyer, but my attitude to running the businesses was changing. There were a number of factors involved in that change and it was very gradual. When Gillian and I drove Simon down to Warwick University to start his three year stint I had turned fifty and had been running the legal practice for exactly half of my life. When we returned home, for the first time ever, we were on our own. The children had lived with us seven days a week until Nicola went to live with her mother and then Simon left for his halls of residence and, although I loved the time we had together as a family, this was now a time when Gillian and I were free to do more things as a couple.

The Dean at Warwick University made a very good speech to the parents on that first day. He spoke of the mixed emotions of dropping off your children at college and how he and his wife were a little tearful for half of the journey home and for the second half were reminded of that uplifting song 'Free at Last'. I didn't feel that way, but saw that the consolation of my son starting his adult life was more time for us to choose what we would like to do. On reflection I think a large part of my retirement consideration was the cumulative effect of the problems that every manager has in that you find yourself doing and saying the same things over and over again in an attempt to keep the ship afloat and sailing in the right direction. You also often feel that some of the crew are trying to sail in the opposite direction or even digging a hole in the deck to try and sink it. No business survives by staying the same and I had changed all of mine several times to reflect the changes in the industry in which they were operating, and knew I had to continue to do so. If you stand still you are trampled on by those behind you who are moving forward, but generally people are resistant and suspicious of change when you try and introduce it. Add to this the commercial effect of my divorce and the dreadful experience of Mary Blair and, albeit both the subject of recovery, nevertheless they eventually helped to produce the thought that it was maybe time to go.

To begin with I investigated the possibility of amalgamation with a bigger firm. I had raised this with the partners and engaged a company recommended by the bank to help in that search. All was done very confidentially and as the firm was very profitable we had a great deal of interest. We were close to deals with three firms, but in the end we didn't progress any of them. I decided that we should withdraw the business from the market and I sold my shares to two of the existing partners. I gave my partners just over a full year of notice and on the 31st of December 2006 I stood down as managing partner to become a consultant within the firm for a two year period, working two days a week purely as a lawyer. I had in mind working to that agreement and then leaving completely at the age of 55. Part of the reason was that I had an existing caseload and had a commitment to those clients which I wanted to see through to the end if possible. What I had not taken into account was that during that two year period I would take on new cases and feel a similar commitment. All new and returning clients were told that I was now working part time as a consultant and not a partner. I don't recall anyone complaining at all about that and to my surprise I found I was able to come and go from the office without curiosity getting the better of me and delving into how the business was doing.

The two years flew by and when it was up I asked Julie Mathieson (who became managing partner) what she would like me to do as I was quite prepared to leave, but also prepared to stay on fewer days as I was really enjoying the freedom to do other things. We agreed that I would reduce to one day a week and review annually. Again, as it turned out the clients seemed prepared to put up with this and the cases kept coming. I was to continue in this way for a further seven years before finally retiring completely at the end of September 2015.

One of the last cases I took on was a former client from Hartlepool for whom I had acted in a medical negligence case some years earlier. In my career I have never encountered more ferocious defence than from medical practitioners and their insurers. The primary position is either automatic defence or a 'you better prove it' posture, even in the most obvious error. I once sued a hospital who had sent a woman home with a displaced leg fracture after she had fallen from a bicycle, telling her she was just bruised. On her third visit with her husband, who was freshly home from the Merchant Navy and knew a fracture when he saw one, she was given an x-ray that confirmed the displaced fracture which then had to be re broken and set. The hospital sought to defend on the basis that the decision to send her home twice without an x-ray was correct, because x-rays use radiation which can be dangerous.

Anyway, back to my Hartlepool client. She had previously been the subject of a medical error and I had recovered significant damages. I had got to know the client and her husband really well and liked them very much. Her husband had telephoned me again to tell me of a further and devastating unconnected event she had suffered at hospital, but this time she was so badly damaged that she would be confined to a wheelchair and require a life of care. This was the only occasion I had of a client becoming the victim of two completely different medical negligence cases. I was determined to see this through if possible and knowing the difficulty of such cases it was likely to take a long time.

Having been to Hartlepool to see my former client, the life changing event of the second act of negligence was obvious and I was determined to win for them. They faced a long anxious wait whilst we obtained medical evidence and the protocol of such cases played out. I wrote a number of letters to the lawyers dealing with the defence explaining the suffering brought upon this family and it literally did take years for them to admit liability. Once they had done so I was able to help the clients organise the adaption of their home to suit their new needs and, shortly after I retired the case settled for a large life changing amount of money. Throughout this process and knowing I was coming to the end of a long career, I was touched and humbled by how this remarkable couple coped with adversity and sustained a long married life by adapting to their new circumstances without complaint or apparent anger. Their love for each other meant that their priority was to survive and make the best of their lives. They telephoned me to talk about their settlement and the cruise holiday they had organised. What a fantastic example of the human spirit.

It is perhaps a fitting story to finish on. I feel blessed to have had the career that I have enjoyed and to have had the opportunity to practice law in the way that I wanted to. I have learned a huge amount about people and myself, and I continue to do so almost on a daily basis. I have always tried my best when acting for anyone. To those clients that I helped I am really pleased and for those I did not or could not, I am genuinely sorry. I chose to practice adversarial law and have therefore attacked a number of institutions, businesses and individuals on behalf of others. I chose not to act for the big institutions against individuals, not because I thought of myself as some sort of Robin Hood, but because I knew that would not be satisfying for me. Going home at night thinking that I had preserved £30,000 for a big insurance client at the expense of some pensioner would not have made me feel as good as getting that sum for the pensioner from the insurance giant. It is not piety, but self satisfaction.

So let me end where I started with Austin Flynn, my English teacher to whom I owe my career. When I was 25 and had jointly set up the practice, I wrote to him to tell him that all of it was down to him. Five years later on leaving court in Durham City I walked across Elvet Bridge and saw him on the opposite side of the road. I walked across and said,
"Hello Mr Flynn, I bet you don't know who I am"
"Yes I do, it's John McArdle. You look exactly the same!" he replied
"What? Do I look 16 years old or did I look 30 when I was 16?" I asked as we shook hands and laughed. He told me he had been quite ill at the time of my letter, but his wife had given it to him and it lifted his spirits. I told him I didn't expect a reply but I just wanted him to know what an effect he had on my life. Shortly before retiring I tried to find him again and my old school St Leonard's told me they had no record of where he now was. I called to the school a while later to see if the personal touch might help and met the head master in person. He was able to find out that Austin Flynn had sadly died only a few months before my visit to the school.

As a result of his example, the doors to my legal practice were always open to anyone wanting to know about a career in law or indeed in any career we could help them with. Many teenagers sat in with me for an afternoon seeing clients and chatting about how to qualify. Advice on a whole manner of things was available to them, but above all that they should not put hurdles in front of themselves. I gather this process continues at DMA Law. Also because of Austin Flynn there are about 150 jobs still in existence in the businesses that I helped start as well as the countless careers that have started and moved on. I dedicate it all to Austin Flynn who taught me that a single act of kindness and consideration can go a long way. More importantly, he was an example of what a teacher or indeed anyone in authority with the chance to help someone should be, particularly if they are young people who may need to be encouraged to fulfil their potential. As for me, I have always enjoyed being a legal wasp to elephants, particularly big corporate ones.